Rules in School

Kathryn Brady
Mary Beth Forton
Deborah Porter
Chip Wood

The stories in this book are all based on real events in the classroom. However, in order to respect the privacy of students, names and many identifying characteristics of students and situations have been changed.

ISBN: 978-1-892989-10-9

Library of Congress control number 2003103302

Photographs: Peter Wrenn, Marlynn K. Clayton, and Elizabeth Willis

Cover and book design: Woodward Design

NORTHEAST FOUNDATION FOR CHILDREN, INC.
85 Avenue A, Suite 204
P. O. Box 718
Turners Falls, MA 01376-0718
800-360-6332

www.responsiveclassroom.org

09 08   7 6 5

Printed on recycled paper.

We would like to thank the Shinnyo-en Foundation for their generous support of the development of this book.

The mission of the Shinnyo-en Foundation is "to bring forth deeper compassion among humankind, to promote greater harmony, and to nurture future generations toward building more caring communities."

ACKNOWLEDGMENTS

The ideas and teaching strategies presented in this book, first articulated by Northeast Foundation for Children founders Ruth Sidney Charney, Marlynn K. Clayton, Jay Lord, and Robert A. (Chip) Wood, have been tested, refined, and further developed over the past twenty years by many of our colleagues at Northeast Foundation for Children and by hundreds of teachers in a wide variety of classrooms nationwide. The authors wish to express their deepest thanks to all these people for sharing their experiences, for welcoming us into their classrooms and schools, and for always trying to do what's best for children.

It's amazing how much work goes into a book even after the writing is done, especially one like this where there are multiple authors and many people passionately invested in the end result. We wish to thank:

Alice Yang, project manager and editor. Her vision, along with her countless hours of writing, weaving, and pruning, transformed the manuscript from a collection of pieces to a cohesive whole. We appreciate her high standards, her astute editing, her problem-solving abilities, and her kindness through it all.

The readers of the manuscript, for poring over the text in its various stages and offering valuable insights. They helped to give the manuscript clarity and ensure that it accurately reflects current *Responsive Classroom®* practice. Specifically we'd like to thank:

> *Adam Berkin,* for his fresh perspective and his contributions to early discussions about this book while serving on the Editorial Advisory Board.
> *Marlynn K. Clayton,* for her attention to detail and passion for getting things just right.
> *Roxann Kriete,* for always thinking of the big picture and knowing just what to say and do to move the project along.
> *Pam Porter,* for her excitement about the project and for guiding us to create a book that will be truly useful to practicing teachers.

Ruth Sidney Charney, for her vision and lifelong dedication to the premise that teaching discipline is something we all can do. We have all been inspired by her work. We're also grateful for her contribution of classroom anecdotes.

Jay Lord, for securing funding for this project, for providing endless support and encouragement along the way, and for not getting too upset when the timeline needed to be changed.

Leslie and Jeff Woodward, graphic designers, for making the book beautiful, for caring about the all-important details, and for juggling multiple projects with grace and humor.

Janice Gadaire Fleuriel, for copyediting and proofreading the manuscript with speed, skill, and care that went beyond the call of duty.

Mike Fleck, for reading the manuscript with an eye to serving our readers well and for offering valuable observations.

Sharon Dunn, Clement Seldin, and Karen Latka, Editorial Advisory Board members, for providing critical support and feedback during the earliest stages of the project.

Peter Wrenn, photographer, for adding warmth and vitality to the pages of this book with his images of children, teachers, and their work.

The teachers, administrators, and children who welcomed Peter into their classrooms and schools to take photographs. Specifically, we'd like to thank our friends at Reingold Elementary School and B.F. Brown Arts Vision Middle School in Fitchburg, Massachusetts, and Heath Elementary School in Heath, Massachusetts.

Additional Acknowledgments

I would like to thank my husband, Peter, for his continual support and sense of humor. I thank my colleagues in the Fitchburg Public Schools for welcoming me into their classrooms and professional lives. In particular, I am grateful to the staff of B.F. Brown Arts Vision Middle School, especially the *Responsive Classroom* Training Team, and the school's principal, Bernie DiPasquale. —*Kathryn Brady*

I wish to thank my family, Tim, Tess, and Tyler, for their support and encouragement and their willingness to engage in lively, often humorous, conversations about rules. —*Mary Beth Forton*

I would like to thank the staff, parents, and children at Heath Elementary. Especially, I would like to thank our teaching assistants Judy Clark, Jill Kuehl, Lynn Kain, Michelle Howe, Deb Lively, Alice Lemelin, Tom Dean, Sandy Gilbert, Robin Jenkins, and Angela Sonntag for their steadfast commitment and love for the children they teach. —*Deborah Porter*

I would like to thank Sheila Kelly, child psychologist, for all she taught me about discipline. —*Chip Wood*

This book is dedicated to teachers everywhere for believing deeply in the goodness of children, even when the going gets tough.

TABLE OF CONTENTS

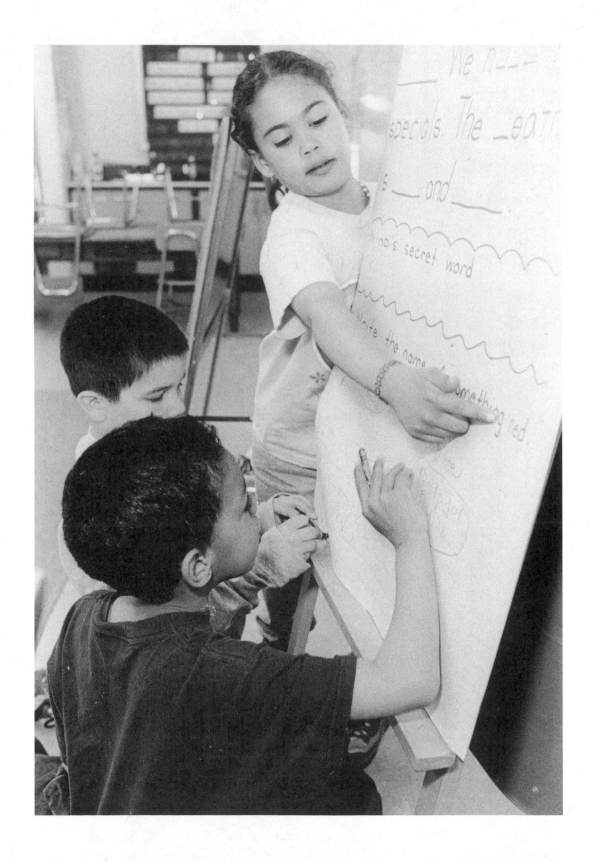

Introduction

WHOSE RULES?

BY MARY BETH FORTON

I *don't care about your stupid rules!*

A comment heard in the principal's office of an elementary school

Rules suck!

Graffiti found in bathroom stalls of
elementary and middle schools

Rules are for fools!

A student comment heard in the hallway of a middle school

"Rules are bad," announced my four-year-old son recently with an indignant "Humph!" when I told him I was working on a book on rules in school. "You want to do something and the teacher just comes along and says you can't!"

This is clearly a four-year-old point of view—*I want what I want and I want it now and anything that gets in my way is bad.* But it's a point of view shared by many students in elementary and middle schools today, where rules are often seen as adversarial, as decrees handed down from the authorities above to keep you from doing what you want.

The teacher is the sole creator and enforcer of these rules, announcing them on the first day of school with little or no discussion of their meaning. This message is clear: Follow these rules or else.

While this approach to rule setting can be effective in establishing a sense of order in a classroom (which we very much need), it does little to help children develop *self*-discipline, ethical thinking, or an understanding of how to be contributing members of a democratic community. At its worst, it invites tension, blind obedience, or a constant battle of wills between adults and children in school.

This book offers a different approach to rules in school. It's an approach to classroom and school-wide discipline that has helped teachers in a wide range of K–8 settings establish calm and safe classrooms and schools while helping children develop self-discipline and a sense of responsibility. It reflects the beliefs that discipline is a subject that can be "taught," just as we teach reading and writing and math, and that children learn best when they're actively engaged and invested in constructing their own understandings.

Whose Rules?

This is not a new approach to discipline. It's been used during the past twenty years by many teachers using the *Responsive Classroom*® approach to teaching (see the page titled "About the *Responsive Classroom*® Approach" at the end of this book). It draws on the thinking of many great educators, theorists, and child psychologists, most notably Rudolf Dreikurs, Alfred Adler, Haim Ginott, Jane Nelsen, William Glasser, and Ruth Sidney Charney.

The primary goals of this approach to discipline are to:

- Establish a calm, orderly, and safe environment for learning.

- Foster an appreciation for the role of rules in school.

- Help children develop self-control and self-discipline.

- Teach children to be responsible, contributing members of a democratic community.

- Promote respectful, kind, and healthy teacher-student and student-student interactions.

Rather than being "handed down from above," rules in these classrooms and schools are created collaboratively with students and teachers during the early weeks of school. Not only are students more motivated to follow rules that they've helped to create, but in the process of creating the rules students learn much about the role of rules in a democratic society.

While there will always be times when students don't like following the rules or choose not to follow them, students in these schools generally view rules in a positive light. They understand that the rules are there to keep them safe and help them achieve their goals in school.

As one third grader so clearly put it, "Rules in school are good because they help keep kids safe and in control so they can learn. But I'm glad at my school there isn't too many rules. Just a few good ones."

In the chapters that follow you'll learn a step-by-step process for creating "a few good rules" with your students and for teaching them to live by these rules day in and day out, both in the classroom and on a school-wide basis. You'll learn practical strategies for modeling and practicing the rules as well as tools and techniques for how to respond when the rules are broken.

The first three chapters provide an overview of the tools and techniques, grades K–8. The following three chapters show these tools and techniques being used at specific grade levels: K–2, 3–5, 6–8. Each of these chapters is written by a teacher at that grade level: Deborah Porter for grades K–2, and Kathryn Brady for grades 3–5 and grades 6–8. The last chapter, written by Chip Wood, offers strategies for working with students, colleagues, administrators, and families to increase consistency around discipline practices outside the classroom.

Below is an overview of the two most common approaches to rules and discipline being used in classrooms and schools today and how they differ from the approach described in this book.

Two Common Approaches to Rules and Discipline

1. An autocratic approach: "Because I said so!"

Some of us are familiar with an autocratic approach to rules from our own years in elementary and junior high school, where the list of rules looked something like this:

No running in the hall.

No hitting.

No pushing.

No cutting in line.

Stay in your seat.

Raise your hand to talk.

No talking back.

Keep your feet flat on the floor.

No gum chewing.

Don't interrupt.

No writing on the desks.

No talking.

Often stated in the negative with a high premium on being quiet and still, the rules were there to keep us in line. They appeared magically on the first day of school and few dared to question them. It wasn't important that we understand the rules. It was just important that we follow them.

If you didn't follow the rules, you knew something bad would happen. The teacher would yell, or you might sit in a corner for ten minutes, or miss recess to write "I will not write on my desk" 100 times, or make the dreaded trip to the principal's office.

Implicit was the notion that without the rules, our natural impulses would take hold and at any moment chaos would erupt: Just imagine thirty children racing around the classroom, screaming at the top of their lungs, gum dropping from their mouths, pushing and fighting with one another.

Whose Rules?

One of the key assumptions behind this approach to discipline is that children are not intrinsically motivated to cooperate or treat others with care and respect. They are by nature unruly and impulsive—largely incapable of self-discipline—and it's the teacher's responsibility to make them behave. Left to their own devices, they'll most likely do the wrong thing.

Many children opt to comply in an autocratic system, but largely out of a fear of what will happen to them if they don't. Others become masterful at putting on a good show for the teacher while completely disregarding the rules when no one's looking. Still others become extremely resistant and defiant or, in the other extreme, so completely dependent on adults to guide their behavior that they find it impossible to make ethical decisions on their own.

The end result may be an orderly classroom, but at what cost? An approach to discipline that's based on fear and punishment keeps children "under control" but it does little to teach them self-control. It achieves compliance but it also yields anxiety, resentment, and anger. While the classroom might appear calm and productive on the outside, students often feel humiliated, afraid, and resentful on the inside, hardly optimal conditions for learning.

2. A permissive approach: "Can you please cooperate now, please?"

On the other end of the spectrum is a permissive approach to rules and discipline where there are no clear limits for behavior. Here rules are negotiable and easily bendable. They may be clearly stated and posted in a prominent place in the room, but everyone knows they won't be enforced consistently.

Teachers consistently ignore misbehaviors or respond to them with repeated gentle reminders and second chances. Students quickly learn that a polite "I didn't really mean to do it" or "Please give me another chance" will almost always release them from responsibility.

Teachers using this approach may believe that the most important thing is for children to like them. They may put a high premium on being "nice" and may worry about stifling or alienating their students by being "too hard" on them. Or they might believe that the best way to influence children's behavior is to ignore undesirable actions while reinforcing desirable ones with generous doses of praise. Or perhaps they've experienced the negative effects of an autocratic approach and don't want to inflict it on others.

Whatever the underlying intention, a permissive approach leads to many problems. Among them, small disturbances routinely escalate into bigger ones, conflicts are unresolved, and rudeness, teasing, and taunting go unchecked, leaving many children feeling physically and psychologically unsafe. If somehow students are "behaving" in such a classroom, they're often doing so to please the teacher and win her/his approval, not because they're intrinsically motivated to do so.

Students in these classrooms can feel just as fearful, tense, and dependent as those in classrooms using an autocratic approach, says Deborah Porter, longtime primary grade teacher. "Instead of being confined by an overly controlling teacher, these students are crippled by the lack of clear boundaries and structure," she says. "We might think that having no limits and no adult guidance makes children feel free, but it actually makes them feel tense and out of control. They're always trying to figure out what's acceptable and what isn't."

Teachers hold so little authority in these classrooms that when they do need to gain control of the classroom, they often resort to pleading, cajoling, or bribing to try to convince students to cooperate. Many grow so thoroughly discouraged by students' behavior and the lack of cooperation that they decide to quit teaching altogether.

A flip-flop approach to rules: "I said 'No.' Well, maybe one more chance. Now, that's it. I mean 'No.'"

There are teachers, many of them in their early years of teaching and without any training in classroom management, who bounce back and forth between the autocratic and permissive extremes. This is perhaps the worst kind of discipline, with the complete lack of predictability and consistency leading to confusion, frustration, and anxiety for students and teachers alike.

I'll never forget my own early years in a classroom, teaching language arts six periods a day to twenty-five to thirty eighth graders. The summer before starting, I spent many hours preparing exciting lessons on literature, creative writing, and journalism. I reflected on my own years in junior high school and reminded myself of all the things I didn't want to be as a teacher. I would not lecture, yell, dominate, or humiliate. I would not put the desks in rows or insist on quiet and solitary work. I would not fill the days with mundane busywork and worksheets.

I didn't spend much time thinking about rules or how I would approach discipline. I figured that by now the students would know what was expected of them. Besides, they'd be so excited by what they were learning there wouldn't be much need to talk about anything as routine and mundane as rules. Not to mention the fact that if there were a need for rules, I didn't have the slightest idea how to address it.

Whose Rules?

I envisioned a vibrant classroom, full of lively debates, plays, poetry readings, and engaging conversations about literature. Students would be self-motivated and industrious. The room would be orderly and calm yet buzzing with the excitement of learning. Students and teachers would treat each other with kindness and respect.

These were great intentions but I didn't have a chance of pulling them off. With little supervision and no roadmaps for creating the social climate I wanted, I bounced back and forth between being too permissive to being too strict, from being too nice to being too mean, from pleading to punishing. I knew full well that what I was doing was ineffective, but I didn't have the strategies or guidance I needed to change it.

The lack of clarity made the classroom tense. Students became increasingly impulsive and testy, always searching for limits that didn't exist or that changed daily. The lively conversations and debates I envisioned became free-for-alls with students interrupting and talking over one another, putting each other down, and laughing at each other's mistakes.

With so few tools to draw on, I watched in horror as I saw myself becoming the teacher I never wanted to be—yelling, lecturing, humiliating, pushing desks back into neat rows, and preparing mounds of busywork just to keep things under control. While I knew there must be a better way, I had so little experience or guidance in how to create a calm, safe, and orderly climate without resorting to punishment or humiliation that I felt demoralized and ready to give up.

Teachers facing greater challenges today

My story is hardly unique. A recent survey of 118 school districts across the country found that the biggest barriers to new teachers' success are poor classroom management skills (eighty-two percent) and disruptive students (fifty-seven percent). (Gordon 1999, 2) Sadly, new teachers are the most ill-prepared to handle the challenge of discipline. Many teacher education programs provide little by way of training in discipline strategies, and too often new teachers receive insufficient collegial support or mentoring about classroom management during their early years in the classroom. Lacking the skills and experience needed to manage twenty-five children in a small space for seven hours a day, many new teachers become discouraged and quit.

But it's not only new teachers who feel this discouragement. Increasingly, experienced teachers are feeling overwhelmed by the growing demands placed on them as more and more students come to school with poorly developed social skills, a lack of impulse control, and little capacity to handle their anger and frustration.

In a recent interview on National Public Radio, retired principal Joanne Busalacchi emphasized that students are increasingly coming to school without the social skills they once had and without the skills they need to learn well. As a result, she said, "Teachers today have a very, very difficult role, much more so than when I began teaching thirty-seven years ago." (Busalacchi 2001)

Discipline in our nation's classrooms and schools is clearly one of the most pressing issues facing educators today. In teachers' workrooms, at PTO meetings, and in national polls, educators and parents consistently identify discipline as one of the most important and challenging jobs teachers have.

In a recent Phi Delta Kappa/Gallup Poll on attitudes toward public schools, discipline was named as the country's top educational concern, as it has been in all but one of the last fourteen surveys by this group. (Gordon 1999, 1) Another national survey found that forty-three percent of public school students felt the behavior of other students interfered with their school performance. (Gordon 1999, 1)

How teachers approach discipline—how they establish rules in their classrooms and schools and live by those rules, day in and day out—can make all the difference between whether children feel safe or threatened in our schools, motivated or discouraged, successful or defeated. It can determine whether a classroom will be orderly or chaotic and whether children will learn or flounder. Ultimately it impacts whether teachers feel fulfilled or frustrated, whether they like their work, and whether they stay in the teaching profession.

Introduction

Discipline in the *Responsive Classroom* Approach

The approach to rules and discipline described in this book is neither autocratic nor permissive. Often referred to as an efficacious, positive, or judicious approach, it aims to help children develop self-control, begin to understand what socially responsible behavior is, and come to value such behavior. It does not rely on punishment or rewards to "get students to behave." Neither does it ignore behavior that is detrimental to the child or to the group. Rather, this approach offers clear expectations for behavior and actively teaches children how to live up to those expectations. Teachers using this approach help children become aware of how their actions can bring positive and negative consequences to themselves and others. When children break rules, the teachers help children recognize and fix the problems their actions may have caused.

Whose Rules?

Teachers using this approach strive to be firm, kind, and consistent in their approach to rules and rule breaking. Their aim is to create calm, safe, and orderly classrooms—one where teachers can teach and children can learn—while preserving the dignity of each child.

This requires a constant balancing of the needs of the group with the needs of the individual, the need for order with the need for movement and activity, the need for teachers to be in control of the classroom with the need for students to be in control of their own lives and learning. It requires taking the time to teach children how to be contributing members of a caring learning community.

Just as teachers don't expect children to come to school knowing how to read or write, teachers using this approach don't make assumptions about the social skills children bring to school. Some children will come to school with highly developed social skills and many years of experience being part of a large group. Others will need to start from the beginning.

School provides an ideal setting for social learning. There are endless opportunities at school for children to learn to control their impulses and to think about the needs and feelings of others. Whether they're learning to wait their turn to talk, ask politely for a marker, welcome a newcomer into a group, or disagree with someone's ideas without attacking them personally, school is rich with opportunities for children to learn to think and act in socially responsible ways.

The time teachers spend on classroom rules is an investment that will be richly repaid. As long-time teacher Ruth Sidney Charney writes in *Teaching Children to Care,* "I've grown to appreciate the task of helping children take better care of themselves, of each other, and of their classrooms. It's not a waste. It's probably the most enduring thing I teach." (Charney 2002, 18)

Three Approaches to Discipline: A Summary

Autocratic

Characteristics

- The teacher alone controls classroom life.
- Behavior standards are high but often not developmentally appropriate.
- Rules are created by the teacher. Children are not allowed to question them.
- The teacher uses punishment and external rewards to get children to obey.

Outcomes

- Students follow rules only when the teacher is watching.
- Students learn submission and little about self-control and assertion.
- Students' relationships with the teacher and with each other are undermined.
- Students may feel anger, fear, humiliation, and a desire for revenge.

Permissive

Characteristics

- The teacher has little control of classroom life.
- Behavior standards are low.
- The teacher uses praise, rewards, cajoling, and empty threats to try to convince students to cooperate.
- The teacher ignores a lot of undesired behavior.

Outcomes

- The classroom is chaotic. Students constantly test limits and show disrespect.
- Students learn self-centeredness and manipulation skills.
- Students' relationships with the teacher and with each other are undermined.
- Students may feel insecure because of the lack of predictability.

Responsive Classroom Approach

Characteristics

- The teacher helps children develop self-control.
- Behavior standards are high and are developmentally appropriate.
- Students help create rules. The teacher helps them practice the rules.
- The teacher uses logical consequences to help students learn from mistakes.

Outcomes

- The classroom is calm and civil. Students show a high degree of responsibility, kindness, and respect.
- Students learn to think and act in socially responsible ways.
- Students' relationships with the teacher and with each other are strengthened.
- Students feel safe in school.

Introduction

Inside the Teacher's Head:
The Importance of Underlying Beliefs

What goes on inside the teacher's head as s/he uses the approach to discipline described in this book is perhaps what distinguishes it most from other approaches. In order to use this approach successfully, teachers must believe in children's intrinsic desire to "do the right thing." They must remember children's need to be engaged in their learning and to feel a sense of belonging and significance.

Instead of believing that children need to be controlled by adults through the use of external motivators such as punishments or rewards, teachers must see themselves as helping children learn to be in control of themselves. That means that when children ignore, forget, or intentionally break the rules, the teacher sees these moments as opportunities for learning and responds in this spirit.

Whose Rules?

For example, picture this fairly typical scene in a fourth grade classroom: It's the beginning of math, and the children have formed small work groups. When the teacher gives a reminder that it's time to settle down, most of the groups begin to focus on their work. One group of four students, however, continues to chat about unrelated topics and makes paper airplanes using their math papers and pencils.

Faced with this situation, a teacher using an autocratic approach to discipline might think, "They can never follow the rules. I should've never let them work together. I knew they couldn't handle this. That's the last time they get to work together!"

A teacher using a permissive approach might think, "Why can't they ever follow directions? Maybe they didn't hear me, or maybe they forgot. I don't want to upset them. Maybe if I ask them nicely."

A teacher using the *Responsive Classroom* approach might think, "The rules were clear and these students aren't following them. Their work isn't getting done. They need to see that sitting together only works if the assignment is getting done."

It's this last way of thinking that is most likely to lead the teacher to effective ways of handling the situation—ways that preserve the dignity of the children and lead children to consider the effects of their actions. It's the way that allows children eventually to become self-disciplined.

Works Cited

Busalacchi, Joanne. 2001. Interview by Susan Stamberg: "Joanne Busalacchi Discusses Her Career As a School Principal." *Morning Edition.* National Public Radio, October 2.

Charney, Ruth Sidney. 2002. *Teaching Children to Care: Classroom Management for Ethical and Academic Growth, K–8.* Greenfield, MA: Northeast Foundation for Children.

Gordon, David T. 1999. "Rising to the Discipline Challenge." *Harvard Education Letter* (September/October): 1–4.

Introduction

Chapter One

CREATING RULES
WITH STUDENTS

BY MARY BETH FORTON

C*hildren are far more invested in following rules that they help to create. It's that simple.*

Gail Zimmerman, second grade teacher

Purposes and Reflections

Walk into any classroom using the *Responsive Classroom* approach to discipline and one of the things you'll notice is a chart of three to five rules such as "Respect each other," "Take care of yourself," and "Take care with classroom property." Rather than listing all the possible dos and don'ts, these rules remind students in a global way of what they should do. Created with the students, these rules set limits and boundaries but do so in a way that fosters group ownership.

Recently I had a good reminder of why the rules in these classrooms are deliberately positive, broad, and few in number. I was at a retreat center that had long lists of rules posted everywhere. Don't leave the door open, don't leave the water running, don't move the furniture, don't make any long distance calls, don't, don't, don't. At first I felt nervous about these rules. *What if I don't remember? What if I break a rule without even knowing it?* Then I felt annoyed. *How can they expect me to remember all of these?* I even felt a bit rebellious. *I'll leave the water running if I feel like it. How would they know anyway?* Finally, there were so many rules posted in so many places that I just stopped paying attention.

Children, too, become overwhelmed or resentful when they are handed long lists of dos and don'ts. Many will decide they have license to do anything that isn't specifically prohibited: think of the all-too-familiar "But teacher, it doesn't say I can't...."

By contrast, rules that are few in number, global in scope, and created with children are likely to be respected. Challenging and guiding students to make good decisions, they become the cornerstone of classroom life.

Goals of creating rules *with* students

The goals of creating rules with students are to:

- Foster a sense of group ownership of the rules
- Establish guidelines and expectations for responsible behavior
- Create a sense of order and safety—both physical and psychological—in the classroom
- Teach children the purpose of rules in a democratic society

Creating Rules with Students

Steps in creating rules with students

Rule creation takes place in the early weeks of school and does require an investment of time. However, teachers find over and over that the payoffs in increased student responsibility and decreased problem behaviors are well worth the effort.

The process involves the following steps:

1. Articulating hopes and dreams

The teacher asks students to share their goals for the school year, often beginning the conversation by sharing her/his own goals for the year. Families are also invited to share their goals for their child.

2. Generating rules

The teacher and children collaborate to generate rules that will allow everyone to achieve their hopes and dreams.

3. Framing the rules in the positive

The teacher works with students to turn the rules into positive statements.

4. Condensing the list down to a few global rules

The teacher and students work together to consolidate their long list of specific rules so they end up with three to five global classroom rules.

Having faith in children's abilities to make sense of the rules

To be successful in creating rules with students, teachers must have faith that children can make sense of the rules and *want* to follow them. In spite of all the alarming news reports about violence and irreverence in schools, it's important to keep in mind that most children, most of the time, want to and do follow the rules, especially rules they view as reasonable and fair.

Not only are children amenable to rules, they crave them. Rules give children a sense of security in an often confusing and unpredictable world. Even in the earliest grades, children can understand that rules are there to help them learn and grow. While they may sometimes resent following rules, especially in moments of anger or frustration, they can understand that rules help make their classroom a good place to be—a place that is safe, kind, and orderly.

William Damon, a developmental psychologist and author of *The Moral Child,* reminds us that "all children are born with a running start to moral development"—"a number of inborn responses predispose them to act in ethical ways." Research over the past fifty years has repeatedly confirmed that children are born with a predisposition to what Damon labels the "four natural virtues: empathy, fairness, respect for others, and self-control." While these early virtues are evident in most infants, Damon asserts, they either develop or stagnate depending on the social influences in a child's life. (Damon 1999)

Along with family, school is one of the most important of such social influences. As teachers, it's our job to help nurture the "four natural virtues." Taking the time to create rules with students and expecting students to live by them is one way of doing that.

Chapter One

When rules make sense: A family story

When I was ten years old, something happened that helped me really understand the purpose of rules.

One day, a day not unlike most in a house filled with five energetic school-age children, my father became fed up with the way we all left trails of books, coats, shoes, papers, food, and toys in our wake. While the rules of the house were clear on this matter, more often than not we chose to ignore them, and no amount of nagging, cajoling, or reprimanding seemed to help. Eventually we would get around to picking things up or they would magically disappear overnight with a little help from our parents. But this day was different. This day my father decided that a new approach was needed. What was missing, he realized, was an appreciation for the rule itself.

He called us down to the living room and soberly announced that as of the next morning there would be no more rules about leaving books, toys, coats, food, etc., around the house. From now on, we could leave things anywhere we wanted and no one was going to pick them up. My two older siblings were a bit skeptical—my father had never done anything like this before—while the younger two jumped for joy. Dancing gleefully about the room, they wanted to know if they could start "throwing stuff all over the place right now" or whether they had to wait until morning.

It was an interesting week. No more nagging when we dropped our books and coats on the floor after coming home from school, no more reminders to clean up one game or art project before taking out another. We giggled as we deliberately abandoned plates of half-eaten snacks on the coffee table and dramatically dropped shoes and sports equipment in the middle of the living room floor. Freedom at last!

After several days the house became a total mess, every room and hallway littered with our things and our trash. The sense of order that we were so accustomed to was suddenly gone and we began to grow uneasy. We continued to play along but now it was with some apprehension. The novelty had worn off and we began to wonder when the game would stop.

Oddly our parents seemed not to notice. They calmly stepped over our debris as if it wasn't there, gently nudged a bag or toy to make their way up the stairs, silently moved a plate of crusty food to make room for their mug. In fact, they never said one word about the growing clutter in the house. Finally, after six days of this, we children couldn't stand it anymore. The chaos was beginning to interfere with our lives, not only making it hard to find things when we needed them but making it hard to feel any sense of order or stability. We begged our parents to end their silence and put the rules back in place.

What followed was the first meaningful discussion I had ever had about rules. *What should the rule be? Why do we need this rule? How should it be enforced?*

For the first time in my life it dawned on me that there was some rhyme and reason behind rules, that they actually served a real purpose and were there to help us, not to control or stifle or irritate us. What a revelation this was! And what a difference it made in my willingness to follow rules, at least the ones that made sense to me.

Creating Rules with Students

Getting Started

It's the first day of school and students walk into your classroom full of anxiety, uncertainty, and a million questions: *What will my new teacher be like? Will she be nice? Will she be in control? What do we do if we need to go the bathroom? Will the other kids be friendly? Do I have to stay at my desk? Will there be a lot of homework? What are the rules here?*

Like master detectives, the children search the classroom, the walls, the books, the teacher's tone of voice, the students' movements, for clues to answer these and other questions. What they want to know is what will reign in this place. Order or chaos? Kindness or cruelty? Calmness or confusion? Respect for materials or reckless abandonment?

By the end of the first few days, many students will have formed conclusions about what kind of year this will be. They'll know whether the teacher feels confident or shaky. They'll know whether the classroom feels friendly or mean. And they'll have a pretty good sense of whether they will be held to high academic and social standards.

Chapter One

We all need this kind of information in new situations. Whether we walk into a new job, a new neighborhood, or a new country, as social beings we need to know the customs and codes of conduct of our new environment. But children especially crave this kind of information, and they need it during the first few days of school.

The first priority: Establish a sense of calm and order

Before ever beginning a discussion of classroom rules, it's essential to create a sense of order, predictability, and trust in the classroom. From day one, teachers need to convey the message that in this classroom, respect, kindness, and learning will prevail. Students need to know in no uncertain terms that the teacher is in control and that the standards for behavior are high. This knowledge gives students a sense of physical and emotional security. It also frees them to participate in rule creation and other classroom activities in a meaningful way.

This point cannot be emphasized enough. Teachers who breeze over establishing order and jump too quickly to creating rules with students often find that the process backfires. When students don't feel safe, they won't invest in rule creation. The conversations become confusing, superficial, even farcical, with students challenging the process every step of the way: *Why are we making the rules? Isn't that your job? I don't care about the stupid rules. Let's make a rule that says we'll have no rules.*

So, how do teachers establish this crucial atmosphere during the early days of school? They explicitly introduce routines—all the basics from how to line up, to what's expected at cleanup, to what to do if you finish your work early. They build a strong feeling of community and trust by taking steps to get to know students and to help students get to know each other. They take time. They go slowly. They do all this before delving into a full-blown curriculum.

The following are suggestions for some essential structures that should be in place before opening a conversation on rules.

(For a detailed discussion of how to create order, security, and community during the early weeks of school, refer to the book *The First Six Weeks of School* by Paula Denton and Roxann Kriete.)

Creating Rules with Students

Establish signals for quiet

Students need to know from day one that the teacher has an effective and calm way—something other than yelling—to get their attention. This is not something that needs to be discussed and should never be negotiated. It is an absolutely essential tool for classroom management that should be established in a matter-of-fact way on the first day of school. The teacher might say, "There'll be lots of times when I or someone else in the classroom needs to get your attention. Here are the signals we'll use for that."

The signals will vary depending on the age of the students, the location (indoors, outdoors, at the meeting area, etc.), and the style of the teacher. Some common examples include:

A visual signal such as the raising of a hand

This is used in whole-group meetings or other situations in which everyone can easily see the teacher or whoever needs the group's attention. The person raises a hand. Children who see this may raise their hands as well to help spread the signal. Everyone in the group responds by becoming quiet and turning to the person who wants to speak. This person waits until everyone is paying full attention before beginning.

An auditory signal such as the ringing of a chime or a handclap

An auditory signal is most often used when children are spread out in the classroom. When the signal is given, everyone freezes and turns to the person who gave it. When finished speaking, the person says something like "You can melt" to signal that people can return to what they were doing.

Primary grade teachers often add the step of children folding their arms on their chest when they hear the signal. This helps younger children keep their hands "frozen" and away from tempting materials while listening to the speaker.

A louder auditory signal for outdoor use, such as blowing a whistle or shouting "Circle up!"

Both of these are effective for getting students' attention when outdoors. In either case, the signal means the students should gather around the teacher for further instructions.

In establishing these signals, it's important to be clear on exactly how they'll be used and why. For example, if the goal is to get everyone's attention and quiet, is it okay if students raise their hands when they see the teacher's hand go up, but then continue to talk with a friend? Is it okay to freeze when the bell rings but not look at the person speaking? Is it okay to continue doodling as long as you're looking at the person speaking? Why not? Children need clarity about these expectations and the reasons behind them. The more consistent, clear, and firm teachers are, the more useful the signals will be.

Many teachers spend time during the first few days of school practicing these signals. Younger students especially enjoy playing games of freezing and melting to the signal of the bell. During these practice sessions the teacher makes her/his expectations clear. The more specific and concrete, the better. For example: "Make sure both feet are firmly on the floor when you freeze"; "Freeze means freezing your mouth as well as your body"; "Remember to turn your body and eyes to the person who rang the bell"; "Put down anything in your hands when you freeze"; "Everyone stay frozen until the speaker says 'You can melt.'"

A common question regarding the use of a signal for quiet is whether it's necessary for all the students to raise their hands when the teacher raises hers/his. The answer is no. Raised hands do not automatically mean closed mouths or attentive listening. Unthinking obedience should never be the goal of a signal for quiet.

The important question is whether you get the response you want. If the children get quiet when you raise your hand or ring a chime or flick the lights, then the signal is working. If some children want to help by also raising their hands (or copying whatever other hand signal you use), that's great. But it's usually counter-productive to wait until every last child copies your signal before you speak.

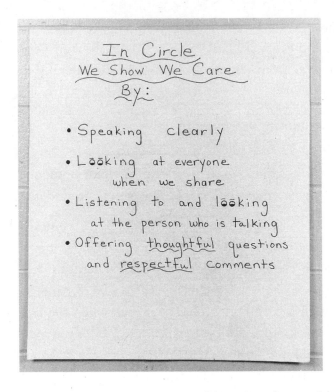

**Creating
Rules with
Students**

*Meeting guidelines in a first grade classroom (left)
and a fourth grade classroom (right)*

Name expectations for group discussions

If students are going to be involved in the rule-creation process, or have group conversations of any substance for that matter, they'll need to learn guidelines for doing this well. Many teachers introduce what they call "meeting guidelines" or "conversation guidelines" during the first week of school.

They might begin, "In our classroom, there'll be many times when we're having large group conversations. This might happen during Morning Meeting or during language arts or science time. It's important that everyone participates in these conversations and that we all feel our ideas are heard. What kind of meeting guidelines do you think we'll need to make that happen?"

Note that while the teacher asks students to construct the specific guidelines, s/he sets clear parameters for this task. Non-negotiable is the idea that the guidelines must support the goals of everyone participating in the conversations and all ideas being heard. With these goals in mind, students will likely construct meeting guidelines that look very similar to what adults would create for their own meetings:

- "Take turns."

- "Raise your hand if you want to say something."

- "Listen and show respect for each other's ideas."

If students frame a guideline in the negative such as "Don't talk when someone is speaking," the teacher asks them to reframe it in the positive: "So if we're not going to talk while others are speaking, what should we be doing?"

Also, if there are essential guidelines that the teacher feels are missing, s/he can add them. For example, a teacher might say, "I know that if I'm talking and people are moving their bodies a lot or waving their hands to get called on, I get distracted. How about adding, 'Keep your body still when someone is talking' and 'Wait until the person is finished talking before raising your hand'?"

Once the list seems complete, the teacher, working alone or with students, can create a final list of four or five guidelines that are then posted in the group meeting area. The teacher can refer students to these guidelines during group conversations, especially during the early weeks of school: "Our guideline says that we should listen when someone is talking" or "Remember we said we'd raise our hands if we want to say something during a meeting."

Chapter One

Begin each day with Morning Meeting

One of the most effective ways of building trust in the classroom is through a special kind of meeting: Morning Meeting, a fifteen- to thirty-minute whole-class gathering at the beginning of each day. This routine is simple, yet powerfully establishes a positive climate for learning, reinforcing academic and social skills, and giving students daily practice in showing respect, empathy, cooperation, and self-control. The meeting consists of four parts:

Greeting

Students greet each other by name. A variety of greetings can be used throughout the year, including ones that involve handshaking, singing, clapping, chanting, and using different languages. The important thing is that every student is acknowledged by name.

Sharing

Two or three students a day share information about an event in their lives. The rest of the class listens. Those who want to can offer empathic comments or ask clarifying questions.

Group activity

All students participate in a brief, lively activity, such as singing, reciting a poem, solving a math puzzle, dancing, miming, or playing a game.

News and announcements

The children read a news and announcements chart that the teacher has written. The chart lets children know of any special events coming up and usually includes a question, riddle, or on-paper activity that reinforces academic skills. Sometimes the class reads the chart aloud as a group. Sometimes they read it silently to themselves. Sometimes they follow along as the teacher reads it.

Creating Rules with Students

The type of greeting and activity, the content of the sharing, and the general flavor of the meeting may differ at different grade levels, at different points during the school year, and from teacher to teacher. But always, Morning Meeting includes these four basic components. The strength of Morning Meeting comes in large part from its predictability. No matter what the morning was like before children set foot in the classroom, once they come into the classroom, they can count on a friendly, respectful gathering, a time when they can get to know others and be known by others, a supportive routine for easing into the day.

Morning Meeting works as a form of proactive discipline because it satisfies children's need for a sense of significance, belonging, and fun. Much social science research has confirmed that in all human beings, behavior is motivated by these three intrinsic needs. Children will always strive to fulfill these needs. If they can't find positive or constructive ways to fulfill them, they'll seek unproductive and even destructive ways. Morning Meeting offers this all-important positive outlet. And it sets the tone for the rest of the day. As Roxann Kriete says, "Morning Meeting is a microcosm of the way we wish our schools to be—communities full of learning, safe and respectful and challenging for all" (Kriete 2002, 3).

For more about Morning Meeting, see *The Morning Meeting Book* by Roxann Kriete with contributions by Lynn Bechtel.

Reflect yourself on the purposes of rules

Why do we need rules in the classroom? For that matter, why do we need rules at all? While it seems a simple question with perhaps obvious answers, it's an essential one for teachers to ask themselves before inviting students into the process of articulating classroom rules.

Many of us have a love/hate relationship with rules. We know that rules are necessary for a well-functioning democracy and we wouldn't want to live in a lawless society, yet we sometimes get annoyed when we're told what to do.

Before discussing rules with students, it's important to examine your own feelings and assumptions about rules. If you're feeling ambivalent about the purpose of rules in the classroom, students will certainly pick up on your feelings. So what do you believe about the value of rules? What purpose do you think they serve? A good exercise is to take ten minutes to write down why you think rules are important in the classroom. Then, compare your list to the one below.

Rules in the classroom:

- Create a sense of order and predictability

- Create a climate of respect and healthy interactions

- Create a climate in which children feel safe enough to take risks

- Serve as guidelines for behavior to help children learn self-control

- Help children develop social awareness and responsibility

- Balance the needs of the group with the needs of individuals

Chapter One

Part of a hopes and dreams display in a first grade classroom

Creating Rules with Students

A third grader's hope and dream illustration.
"I hope to be a better reader and get to level Q in reading."

Begin the rule-creation process with "hopes and dreams"

During the first week of school, teachers using the rule-creation approach described in this book invite students to answer the important question, "What do you hope to learn and do this year in school?" While the question may seem simple, posing it to students and asking them to share their responses can have a profound effect on the classroom. Just think about the messages inherent in the question: What you care about matters at school; your hopes and goals are taken seriously here; you have a say in what you'll learn.

Taking the time to help students articulate their goals for school—or their "hopes and dreams" as they're often called—sets a tone of collaboration and mutual respect. It also fosters reflection and self-knowledge by prompting children to ask themselves questions such as "What's important to me at school? What do I want to get better at? What do I care about?"

Sharing individual goals for the school year creates a meaningful context for creating classroom rules. Once students have articulated their hopes and dreams, the teacher asks, "If these are our hopes and dreams, what rules will we need so we can make all of these hopes and dreams come true?" In this way, rules become logical outgrowths of the students' and teachers' goals, something that will help them achieve their hopes, rather than directives handed down from above.

In order for this process to work, however, teachers must guide students toward thinking about goals that are realistic, learning-oriented, and achievable in school. It's not realistic for a child to "become a famous ballerina" or "become a basketball star" this year, for example. And "having recess all day" or "having lunch all day" is not related to the work of school. Here are essential ways to ensure that children name hopes and dreams that will be truly useful and meaningful:

Set the context by talking about the kinds of work that go on in classrooms

Before asking students what they hope to accomplish, primary grade teachers might give the children a tour of the classroom and talk about some of the things they'll be doing in school this coming year. Teachers of older children might ask students to think back on the previous year and name an accomplishment they felt proud of and something that was difficult for them.

Express your own hopes and dreams for the school year

Many teachers express their own hopes for the students in the coming year before asking students to express theirs. This sets the tone and establishes clear expectations about the kind of hopes and dreams that students will be naming. Although the teacher's language will vary depending on the age of the students, the point is to express a desire for a classroom that is safe, caring, and filled with learning. For example, a second grade teacher might say, "This year I hope our classroom will be a safe and caring place to learn and that everyone will do their best work." A fifth grade teacher might say, "This year I hope that students can be friendly with everyone and learn how to work hard."

Use qualifiers when asking students to name their hopes and dreams

Instead of asking "What do you hope to do this year?" teachers should ask, "What do you hope to learn in our classroom this year?" or "What do you hope you'll be able to work on in our classroom this year?" or "What are some social or academic skills you hope to work on this year in school?"

Limiting the question to the arenas of work, learning, skills, classroom, and school helps make sure students name hopes and dreams that will be attainable.

Below are some examples of how students at various grade levels expressed their hopes and dreams when teachers used the process described above:

"I hope I get to build with the blocks and play a lot."
Kindergarten student

"I hope I get to do lots of hard work."
First grade student

"I hope to learn how to count money."
Second grade student

Creating Rules with Students

"I hope to get better at math."
Third grade student

"I hope I learn to spell better."
Fourth grade student

"I hope I'll make some new friends."
Fifth grade student

"I hope I do a lot of interesting projects."
Sixth grade student

"I hope to improve my grades and enjoy my classes."
Seventh grade student

"I hope to be able to read better and faster and to get over my shyness."
Eighth grade student

Have students share their hopes and dreams

It's important that children share their hopes and dreams with the class because the sharing helps students develop an awareness and appreciation for each other's goals.

How students share their hopes and dreams varies depending on the age of the children and the teacher's style. Students might draw pictures of themselves doing their hope and dream, write in a journal about their hope, or share their hope verbally in a small or large group. Below are some ways that teachers at different grade levels have structured the sharing of hopes and dreams:

Kindergarten to second grade

- Children begin by sharing their many hopes and dreams verbally. The teacher then asks each child to think about his/her *most important* hope for the year and to share this with the group. The teacher records these on a chart.

- Children draw a picture of their most important hope for the year, and the teacher (or the children themselves if they are able) records their words on the picture. These can be displayed immediately as a "Hopes and Dreams" bulletin board or later as part of the display on classroom rules.

- Students draw a picture of themselves achieving their dream and then share this picture with a partner. Children then report what their partner's hope is to the group.

Third to fifth grade

- After an initial conversation about hopes and dreams, students write in journals to express their many goals for the school year. The next day they reread these journal entries and decide on one most important hope for the school year to share with the class.

Chapter One

Part of a hopes and dreams display in a first grade bilingual classroom

- Students make an illustration or collage that expresses their most important hope for the school year. These are shared with the group and then mounted and displayed in the classroom or hallway.

Sixth to eighth grade

- Students write in journals at school or as a homework assignment, reflecting on the previous year of school and articulating their hopes, dreams, and worries for this year. One possible structure for reflecting on the previous year is for students to write about one thing they felt successful at last year, one thing they didn't feel successful at, one thing they loved to do, and one thing they dreaded doing.

Creating Rules with Students

- As a whole class, students brainstorm possible hopes and dreams in different categories: a social hope, an academic hope, an athletic hope, etc. With this to get them thinking, students then write about their own hopes in these categories and choose three or four hopes, each from a different category, to share with the group. The method allows students to express more than one hope for the year, something children this age often like to do.

After hopes and dreams have been named and shared, they are displayed prominently in the room. The teacher can then refer to everyone's hopes and dreams easily as s/he begins the conversation about classroom rules. The display then reinforces the idea that classroom rules grow out of everyone's goals for the year.

Students work on illustrating their hopes and dreams for the school year.

Our Hopes & Dreams for 3rd Grade

Angela hopes to be a better reader.
Nija hopes to learn cursive writing.
Kiana hopes to get better at math.
Jetor hopes to learn the multiplication tables.
Micah hopes to be a better reader.
Justin hopes to get good grades.
Ariela hopes to learn about the continents.
Caroline hopes to become a better speller.
Aldi hopes to learn more about history.
Yaser hopes to meet more teachers and friends.
Najauh hopes to get better at reading.
Adriana hopes to learn more about science.
Erick hopes to learn how to do division.
Daniel hopes to become a better artist.
Ashley hopes to be a better math student.
Julio hopes to learn how to write in cursive.
Omario hopes to learn a lot of new things.
Harrison hopes to make new friends.
Quinn hopes to get better at writing.
Juan hopes to do hard math.
Rene hopes to learn more about computers.
Daphne hopes to read long chapter books.
Mrs. W. hopes that all the students will learn to love books and reading.

Students' hopes and dreams are often displayed as simple lists.

OUR HOPES & DREAMS

Kevin R. - My goal is to pass.
Eddie - to pass the 8th grade and to make new friends
Adam - to pass with at least straight B's.
Alyssa - to pass with good grades
Julie - to do all my homework and do good on tests
Stephanie - pass all of my classes and the MCAS tests
Katie - to stay focused and avoid distractions that keep me from performing to my fullest potential
Destiny - to remain on the Honor Society and to make the cheerleading team
Heather - to do all my homework
Aaron - to pass
Megan - to pass the 8th grade
Karina - to work hard and pass the 8th grade and to reach my destiny
Mrs. Cancellieri - to help my students achieve their full potential and to have fun
Trevor - to pass the eigth GRADE
Frances - to not get in trouble and pass the 8th grade with at least a B average

Bianca - meet new people and get good grades
Shauntay - pass and work hard, pass MCAS, just enjoy being in eight grade
Mi - pass 8th grade, have good grades, pass MCAS, find new friends
Waheed - to do the best that I can do
Marissa - pass the 8th Grade with good grades
Kayla - get good grades
Sheng - pass 8th grade, have good grades, meet new people, get high honors, pass the MCAS test
Alex - pass the 8th grade
Kevin L. - pass the 8th grade
Meng - get the same grades as last year
Celeste - pass the 8th grade by getting good grades and staying out of trouble. And do my best to be a good student.
Choua - to pass and play for the school soccer team
Andrew - go to the high school and get good grades
Ray - to get good grades
C. J. - to have at least a B average + Get homework in on time

**Creating
Rules with
Students**

Hopes and dreams in a music class

By Jennifer Fichtel
Responsive Classroom *consulting teacher*
Fitchburg Public Schools, Massachusetts

Hundreds of drawings of children playing instruments, singing, dancing, and toe tapping adorn the walls, bulletin boards, and closet doors of Donna Dik's music classroom. Beautiful to look at—rich in color, detail, and whimsy—these illustrations represent the hopes and dreams of Donna's students at Reingold Elementary School. In the center of each cluster of drawings is a list of the children's hopes for music class: James hopes to sing a song about fishing; Erik hopes to play the electric guitar; Nou Tsa hopes to sing and dance; Natasha hopes to be in a musical performance.

When Donna began the school year—her first as a music teacher at Reingold Elementary—she was faced with the daunting task of getting to know more than 600 students in grades one through four. She turned to the idea of hopes and dreams. "I couldn't think of a better way to begin to get to know my students and to let them know that I cared about their interests and ideas," says Donna.

During her first meeting with each class, Donna expressed her hopes for music class and asked students to express theirs. She recorded their answers and provided materials for students to draw themselves achieving their hopes. Before long, the classroom was transformed into an art gallery as children from each class added their creations to the display. But that wasn't all that was transformed, according to Donna. "The process, which only took one class period per group, created a sense of shared purpose and set a positive tone that lasted an entire year."

Donna keeps the drawings up all year long, along with the Reingold school-wide constitution. Created with a group of students in the fall, the constitution lists a set of rules that everyone in the school agrees to follow. In addition to using the constitution as a guideline for behavior in music class, Donna frequently draws students' attention to the connection between the school-wide constitution and their hopes and dreams. In this way, she helps them understand how honoring the rules of the community helps all students achieve their hopes and dreams.

"What started as a way for me to get to know the students," says Donna, "has become a wonderful way to build a community of learners."

A display of children's hopes and dreams for music class

Chapter One

Invite families into the process

Many teachers invite families into this process of articulating hopes for the year. There's no question that families are more likely to trust and support this approach to discipline if they understand the thinking behind it. Inviting families to express their own hopes for their child is a good first step to building this important sense of trust. Here are a few possible ways to do this:

- At the first family-teacher conference (preferably before the first day of school), share your hope for the year. Then ask the family to share theirs: "What's your most important hope for your child in school this year?" or "What do you think is most important for your child to learn in school this year?" It's best to send this question to families ahead of time so they can think about it before the conference.

Creating Rules with Students

- Early in the school year, send a letter to families explaining the process of hopes and dreams and inviting them to write back with their goals for their child this year. Some teachers ask families specifically to share an academic goal and a social goal. Others leave the question more open-ended.

- In preparation for the first open house, create a "Hopes and Dreams" display showing all of the students' goals for the year. Students can write a personal letter to their families asking them to share their most important hopes for the child's school year.

Generate a list of preliminary rules

"If these are our hopes and dreams, what rules will we need to help us make them come true?" This is a pivotal question and one that teachers ask soon after students have articulated their hopes for the year. Thinking through this question helps students make the important connection between their personal hopes for the year and the classroom rules.

It also helps them to see that *everyone's* hopes and dreams are important and that the rules are there to help *everyone* succeed. Without these understandings, the rules will hold little meaning.

There are various ways to begin the process of generating rules. Some teachers begin with a whole-group discussion: "If Tai wants to get better at writing and Evalina to learn Spanish and Sheng to learn how to do division, what rules will we need to help them reach these goals? What rules will we need to help all of us reach our goals? Let's start by making a list."

Other teachers, especially those of upper grades, prefer to have students begin by reflecting personally and writing about classroom rules. They might begin: "If these are our goals for the year, what do you think will be the one to three most important rules for our class?" For homework or as an in-class writing assignment, students then name the rules and explain why they think those are the most important ones. To help older students feel freer and more honest with this assignment, teachers can assure students that their responses will be kept confidential. Once the writings are complete, the teacher can assemble a list of proposed rules for discussion, perhaps noting how often each rule appeared in students' writings but without attaching names to the rules.

Help students frame the rules in the positive

Regardless of how a teacher goes about this initial task of generating rules with students, it's likely that many of the rules will be expressed in the negative, a clue, perhaps, to how children generally perceive rules in our society. For example, here's a first attempt at a list of rules from a third grade class:

Do not scare or yell at anyone.

Don't be rude.

Don't lie to the teacher.

Don't fight in line.

No fighting at recess.

Listen to the teacher.

Don't push anyone.

Be nice to other people.

Don't say swear words.

Don't run in the halls.

The task now is to help students reframe the rules in the positive. One way to do this is to stop every time a negative rule is expressed and ask students to try to reframe it in the positive. For example, when a child suggests, "Do not scare or yell at anyone," the teacher can say, "We don't want to scare or yell at anyone here. So if we're not going to scare or yell at anyone, how do you think we should treat or talk to each other?" Some responses from students might include:

"Talk to others in a respectful way."

"Use a friendly voice."

"Stay in control even if you're mad."

Another possibility is to complete the entire list and then change the negative rules into positive ones. The teacher might say, "There are lots of rules here that tell us what *not* to do. I think it's more helpful to have rules that tell us what *to* do. Let's see if we can say those rules in a different way so they will help us know what *to* do."

Thus in the third grade class mentioned above, "Do not scare or yell at anyone" became "Talk to others in a respectful way." "Don't be rude" became "Think about other people's feelings." "Don't lie to the teacher" became "Tell the truth" (here the teacher also helped children realize it's important to be honest not just to the teacher, but to everyone). "Don't fight in line" became "Keep your hands to yourself and be quiet when you're in line," and so forth.

It takes some work to get children to turn their *don'ts* into *dos*. Most children are not accustomed to thinking of rules in positive terms. But it's important work because rather than constantly telling children what they shouldn't do, we want to give children guidelines for positive behavior. By framing the rules in the positive, we shift the emphasis from rules that foster compliance to rules that foster self-control and a sense of responsibility to a group. They are constant reminders of what everyone in the classroom, including the teachers, are striving to become. They represent our community ideals.

Creating Rules with Students

From the long list of positive rules, create a few global ones

Remember the third grader in the introduction who expressed her relief that in her school "there isn't too many rules" but "just a few good ones"? Both teachers and students will feel this same relief when they can consolidate their long list of rules into "a few good ones." Long lists of rules, even when expressed in the positive, are simply too overwhelming to be truly useful.

A long list of specific rules also becomes a prescriptive recipe, encouraging simple compliance. A short list of broad rules, on the other hand, fosters ethical thinking and the practice of self-control by giving children the opportunity to apply general behavior expectations to various situations themselves.

While students might have generated a list of twenty to thirty possible rules in the first round of discussions, the teacher can now help them see that most of these rules will fall into three to five general categories. The categories that teachers typically use are:

- Taking care of ourselves
- Taking care of others

- Taking care of our classroom and materials
- Taking care to do our best work

The teacher might begin the consolidation process by saying, "This is a great list of rules, but there are so many of them. I know that I won't be able to remember all these rules. I wonder if we can put some of them together so that we only have a few rules to remember." Or, for older students, "This is a good list to start with, but I'm noticing that lots of these rules overlap each other. How could we group them so that we have just a few rules for our class?"

For younger students, the teacher might suggest exactly what the three to five sorting categories will be: "Let's see if each of these rules will fit under one of these categories: taking care of yourself, taking care of others, taking care of our classroom, and doing our best work."

In upper grades, the teacher might invite students, perhaps working in pairs, to determine what the three to five sorting categories will be. In all likelihood, the categories they come up with will be very similar to the ones stated above: care for ourselves, care for others, care for materials, and care for our work. But the process of sorting and synthesizing takes the students to a depth of understanding—of the meaning of the rules and of each other—that may not otherwise be possible.

Chapter One

Rules from a first grade classroom.
The families' hopes and dreams surround the children's.

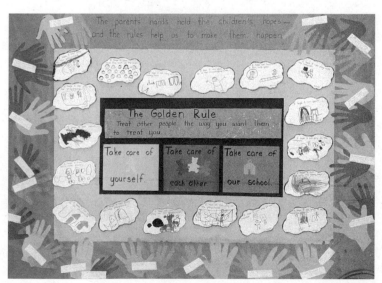

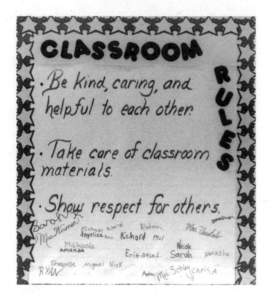

Classroom rules can be displayed in a variety of styles, depending on the children's age and preference.

Creating Rules with Students

When all the rules have been sorted into three to five categories, the class might want to adjust the wording of the categories. It is always illuminating to hear which words students choose to use—their words are a clue to what they really understand the rules to mean. And because their words are a way for students to communicate nuances of understanding to each other, it's appropriate to let students spend some time on wordsmithing. That said, keep in mind that the exact wording of the final rules is less important than the process of getting to them. Try not to let the class, especially if it's a group of passionate debaters, get too hung up on the details of the wording.

Here are a few examples of the final list of rules—global, positive, and few in number—from several classrooms:

From a second grade classroom

- Take care of yourself and keep everybody safe.

- Help and respect other people.

- Be gentle and take care of all the things in our school.

- Try your hardest and do your best work.

From a fourth grade classroom

- Be in control of yourself.

- Be helpful and respectful of others.

- Treat people the way you want to be treated.

- Be a thinking worker.

From an eighth grade classroom

- Cooperate with each other.

- Listen to each other.

- Take care of our classroom and school environment.

- Show respect for others and their materials.

Chapter One

Talk about what the Golden Rule really means

Often children come up with some version of the Golden Rule—"Treat others as you'd like to be treated"—as one of their classroom rules. While this is an accepted tenet that is present in many traditions, it can be confusing for children. Young children, and even many older children, may take this saying literally. A literal understanding works in many situations: "If I want the people at this table to share the markers with me, I have to share the markers with them." But in many situations, it doesn't work: "If I don't mind when people kid me about my clothes, then it's okay for me to kid others about their clothes."

For this reason, many teachers whose students come up with this rule make it a point to talk with them about what the Golden Rule really means. They help students understand that the rule is about the broad idea of treating others with respect and care, just as you'd like to be treated with respect and care. Part of living by the rule, they lead students to see, is learning what respect and care look like, sound like, and feel like to the other person rather than using ourselves as the standard. With this understanding, children will be more able to make sense of the Golden Rule and use it in their everyday school life.

Creating Rules with Students

Celebrate and share the rules

After working so hard to create this final list of rules which will become the cornerstone of classroom life, it's fitting for the class to celebrate these rules and share them with students' families. Here are a few ideas that teachers have used:

Send a letter home to families

In the letter, celebrate the classroom rules and ask for family support. (See the sample letter.)

Have students make a beautiful display of the rules

Perhaps they can write the final rules on a large poster board and surround it with illustrations. In some classes, all students sign the poster to show that they agree to try to live by the rules. Display the poster in a prominent place in the room.

Invite families to the classroom for a rule-signing celebration

Have a poster of the rules ready for students to sign ceremoniously in the presence of their families. Students can prepare a brief presentation for families on how these rules came to be.

So, are classrooms that use this process of rule creation more lax than those using an autocratic approach? This is a common question. The answer is absolutely not. Just because the rules are stated in the positive and students are

Dear Families,

We have been talking a lot during these early weeks of school about our hopes and dreams for this school year. The students and I have articulated many goals for ourselves. Here's a list of our most important ones:

[List the students' and teacher's most important hopes for the year.]

To create a climate where all students can achieve their goals, we have created the following rules for our classroom:

[List the rules that the students and teacher have created.]

You can help us at home. Please keep these lists in a prominent place and review the rules often with your child. We are all working together to create a safe and caring community of learners. I appreciate your support. Please feel free to call me if you have questions about these rules or my approach to classroom discipline.

Sincerely,

involved in creating them doesn't mean that behavior expectations are in any way "fuzzy" or lower than in other classrooms.

On the contrary, behavior expectations are high as teachers strive to be firm, clear, and consistent. Both teachers and students are highly invested in the rules, and both serve as caretakers of them. Children value the rules more when the rules are their own.

Works Cited

Damon, William. 1999. "The Moral Development of the Child." *Scientific American* (August): 56–62.

Denton, Paula, and Roxann Kriete. 2000. *The First Six Weeks of School.* Greenfield, MA: Northeast Foundation for Children.

Kriete, Roxann, with contributions by Lynn Bechtel. 2002. *The Morning Meeting Book.* Greenfield, MA: Northeast Foundation for Children.

Chapter Two

PRACTICING THE RULES:
BRINGING THEM TO LIFE

BY MARY BETH FORTON

*If we want children to get better
at piano, what do we tell them? PRACTICE! If we want them to get better
at reading or math or spelling, what do we tell them? PRACTICE!
But if we want them to get better at developing self-control and responsibility,
then what do we tell them? BE GOOD! The step we too often
miss is PRACTICE! Children need opportunities, under the
caring guidance and support of adults, to practice these essential
skills, over and over again, without criticism or judgment.*

Chip Wood
Seven Principles of The Responsive Classroom

Purposes and Reflections

We all know that just because children can articulate the rules doesn't mean they
will follow them. Far from it. Controlling impulses, expressing feelings in a constructive way, and putting personal needs aside momentarily for the good of the
group are complex, demanding skills—skills that even adults struggle with. I
don't need to think hard to remember the last time I interrupted someone who
was speaking even though I knew it was rude. I often break the speed limit even
though I know it isn't safe or legal. More often than I'd like to admit, I utter
insults or raise my voice even though I know I'm acting out of anger.

If closing the gap between knowing the rules and living the rules is challenging for adults, it can be downright hard for children. Children in elementary and middle schools are just beginning to learn self-control, communication skills, perspective taking, and the myriad other skills needed to live and learn peacefully with others. To be successful they need lots of encouragement, support, and practice. And they need adults who celebrate improvement, rather than demand perfection.

When a teacher or parent constantly points out what a child is doing wrong, rather than focusing on what the child is doing right, the child grows discouraged. Some rebel, some shut down. Eventually, they stop listening. As educator Madeline C. Hunter says, "When someone is humiliated or feeling unworthy, their perception narrows. Our job is to help learners be right, not catch them being wrong."

Practicing the Rules: Bringing Them to Life

However, this does not mean "catching children being good" and using stickers, certificates, and prizes to reward them for their behavior, a common practice in schools today. Instead, it means helping children understand what it means to do the right thing and giving them practice and support in doing it.

These are two very different things. Rewarding children for being good, while seemingly benevolent, can actually undermine a child's intrinsic desire to do the right thing. Using external controls to shape behavior focuses children's attention on what they'll get for doing something good rather than how they'll feel in doing the act itself.

The fact is that most children don't need stickers or pizzas or other rewards for doing the right thing any more than they need scolding or punishment for doing the wrong thing. Children are highly motivated to feel a sense of belonging and competence in the classroom. What they need are kind, firm teachers who can help them learn how to contribute in positive ways. The good feeling they'll get from being able to control their impulses, follow the rules, and contribute positively will be reward enough.

Goals of practicing rules with students

Once the rules are established, it's time to make them real. It's great to start the school year with "We will show respect for other people" as one of the rules, but what does that really mean? During the first few months of school, but most intensively during the early weeks, it's essential to make the three to five global rules real by applying them to different classroom situations.

For example, in preparing children for recess, a teacher might say, "Our rules say that we will take care of each other and keep people safe. What's one thing you'll do to follow this rule when you're on the playground?" The students might respond, "Tag gently," "Help someone if they fall down," and "Let everyone play." Later, when the class comes back in, the teacher and students spend a few minutes reflecting on their outside time: How did we do? Did we follow our rules while playing tag? What was the hardest rule to follow? What could we do better next time?

These short but frequent conversations, along with plenty of practical experiences, help students to make important connections between their ideals and their actions.

The goals of practicing rules with students, then, are to:

- Further students' understanding of the rules

- Translate global rules into concrete actions

- Develop students' skills in following the rules, especially when it's hard

- Establish clear behavior expectations for various settings (reading groups, meeting area, recess, when there's a guest teacher, etc.)

- Encourage ethical thinking and internalization of the rules

- Acknowledge the fact that living by the rules can be hard and support children in correcting and learning from their mistakes

Strategies for practicing the rules

Practicing the rules is not a step-by-step or finite process. It's done continuously throughout the year, as part of planned lessons and in the moment as needed. Learning to follow rules is a gradual process that occurs over time.

There are, however, many specific strategies teachers use to practice the rules with students, especially during the early weeks of school. Many of them are used simultaneously. They include:

Modeling the rules

This technique is used to demonstrate and reinforce appropriate behaviors in situations where there is basically one expected way to do something. Modeling might be used, for example, to teach how to pass materials to someone, what to do while waiting in line, how to carry the scissors, and how to show that you're listening. The teacher or a student demonstrates a specific behavior while others watch and notice what the teacher or child did.

Role playing the rules

This technique is used to suggest a range of possible behaviors in situations where there isn't one single expected way to do something. Role playing might be appropriate for questions such as how to include someone in an activity, how to be a good sport when you're winning or losing a game, and what to do when you disagree with your partner's ideas. The teacher and students discuss the situation, brainstorm possible ways to handle it, then act them out.

Note that this use of role playing is not the same as role playing to resolve a conflict that has occurred. The role playing described in this book is a proactive strategy to help children be prepared with ideas to handle tricky situations that might arise. Reactive role playing, used by children after a conflict or in the midst of a conflict, requires a different set of techniques, partly because of children's heightened level of emotionality. A discussion of reactive role playing is beyond the scope of this book.

Using teacher language to support the rules

Teacher language is a powerful tool for helping students internalize behavior expectations and become self-motivated learners. The teacher uses reinforcing, reminding, and redirecting language to encourage and empower students in their efforts to follow the rules.

Practicing the Rules: Bringing Them to Life

Getting Started

Model routine behaviors

Children are able, even eager, to rise to high standards of behavior, but they need to know exactly what the standards are. It's best not to assume that they know what's expected of them, even in the most routine situations. If we expect students to walk instead of run when moving around the room, put away materials after using them, keep their hands to themselves in the meeting area, share materials, raise their hand to speak, help to put away the sports equipment, or show attention and interest when a classmate is sharing, then we have to be clear and direct about these expectations.

Modeling is a good technique for doing this. Simple and direct, it's best used for non-negotiable behaviors, behaviors that don't require much discussion and that are necessary for the safe, smooth functioning of the classroom. The teacher or a student models the expected behavior while others watch and comment on what they noticed.

Every teacher needs to decide what the non-negotiables will be in her/his classroom, but here's a list of what most teachers consider to be non-negotiable and therefore what should be modeled:

- What to do when you hear the signal for quiet

- How to take out and put away classroom materials

- What to do at cleanup

- How and when to line up

- How to move through the classroom and hallways

- How to use the coatroom

- How to sharpen pencils

- How to signal that you want to talk during a meeting

- What to do when someone else is talking

- How to carry scissors, chairs, paint dishes, water, etc.

- How to use the drinking fountain

- What to do when you come in late

- What to do if you need to use the bathroom

Modeling can be used effectively with children in all elementary and middle school grades. The technique may seem at first most suitable for younger children, for whom many everyday routines are still new. But with some adjustments in language and pacing, it can be invaluable for students in sixth through eighth grades as well.

When middle schoolers toss their homework assignments in a careless heap on the teacher's desk, or loudly make their presence known in the hallways on their way to the bathroom, or slouch down in their chair and roll their eyes when a classmate is talking, they may be acting deliberately. But just as often, they may truly be unaware of their behavior and its effects on others. Whatever the case, modeling conveys the message that in this classroom, everyone is expected to carry out all everyday activities in a caring and respectful way. Modeling shows what caring, respectful actions look like, sound like, and feel like. And it lets students experience themselves doing the expected actions. This experiencing is the beginning of the formation of good habits.

**Practicing
the Rules:
Bringing
Them to Life**

*A group of fourth graders practices sharing materials fairly,
one way to live their classroom rule "Let everyone learn."*

Steps in modeling

While modeling specific behaviors can take time, especially during the first few weeks of school when so many new materials and procedures are being introduced, it is time well spent. Teachers who do this early in the year find they spend less time on discipline problems later.

The technique typically includes the following five steps:

1. *Name the behavior*

The teacher names the expected behavior and connects it to a classroom rule.

2. *Demonstrate the behavior*

The teacher demonstrates the behavior or, if students seem to know something already about how to do the behavior, the teacher might ask a student to demonstrate it.

3. *Ask what students noticed*

The teacher asks students what they noticed about the demonstrator's specific actions, expressions, and tone of voice.

4. *Ask students to demonstrate*

The teacher asks for students (or additional students) to demonstrate the behavior while the class again notices specific actions, expressions, and tone of voice.

5. *Have the whole class practice the behavior*

The teacher observes and uses reinforcing, reminding, and redirecting language to guide children in their practice. (See the section on teacher language later in this chapter for more about these three Rs of language.) The teacher lets the students know that s/he will be noticing how they practice the behavior in their interactions with each other over the next several days and weeks.

Here's how the five steps might look in two examples of modeling:

Example 1—A second grade class: Attentive listening

1. *The teacher names the expected behavior and connects it to a classroom rule.*

"Many times during our school day we'll be listening to each other share ideas. We said that in our class we would show respect for other people. One way to show respect is to listen attentively when someone speaks."

2. *The teacher (or a student) demonstrates the behavior.*

The teacher has arranged ahead of time for Kesha to help with today's modeling. Now he says to the class, "Kesha is going to talk about something that will be happening after school tomorrow. I'll be the listener. Notice what I do." Kesha makes an announcement about a dress rehearsal for a school play. The teacher listens attentively.

Alternatively, if students had seemed somewhat familiar already with respectful listening, the teacher might have asked for their ideas before modeling. "What can I do to show that I'm listening to Kesha respectfully?" He then would have demonstrated using the students' ideas.

If the teacher had chosen to have a student demonstrate the behavior, it would have been important for him to name explicitly the positive behavior to be modeled. "Who would like to show us how to listen respectfully?"

3. *The teacher asks students to notice the demonstrator's specific actions, expressions, and tone of voice.*

"What did you notice about how I listened to Kesha? What did I do to show that I was listening?" Students respond, "You looked at her," "You looked like you were concentrating. You looked serious," "You didn't move around," "You nodded your head," and "You smiled when she told about the dog being on stage."

The teacher then asks students to reflect on the effect of his behavior. "How do you think Kesha felt when I showed I was listening to her?" "It probably felt good to her," "Like you really cared," "Like it mattered what she had to say," students answer.

4. The teacher asks for students (or additional students) to demonstrate the behavior.

"Who else would like to show how to listen in a respectful way?" Randy raises his hand. "OK, this time Randy will be the speaker. He's going to tell about a friend of his who will be visiting tomorrow." Another student, Ariela, volunteers to be the listener. The class watches Ariela as Randy shares. Afterwards, students tell what they noticed.

Many teachers deliberately choose students who have the hardest time following rules to do the modeling at this step. Not only does this offer valuable practice, but it shows these children—and the rest of the class— that they are capable of success. It's important, however, not to choose these children so often that they feel singled out.

5. The whole class practices the behavior.

"Let's all practice attentive listening now," the teacher says. "I'll share something with you and you can all show how you listen."

After the practice, the teacher reflects with the class. "What did we do well? What might we work harder at?"

The practice doesn't end here, however. The teacher lets students know that he expects to see them practicing respectful listening in the days to come. He will be using careful teacher language to guide them in their practice.

Example 2—A seventh grade class: Coming into the room late

1. The teacher names the expected behavior and connects it to a classroom rule.

"We said we would respect everyone and let everyone learn. If you come to class late or if you leave the room for something and then come back,

Practicing the Rules: Bringing Them to Life

one way to be respectful and let everyone learn is to go to your seat quietly and quickly."

2. The teacher (or a student) demonstrates the behavior.

"Let's say I'm a student coming in to class late," the teacher says. She believes that many of these students already know some ways to come in without disrupting others, so she asks for ideas. "What do I need to do to be sure my coming in disrupts the class as little as possible?" The teacher then demonstrates using the students' suggestions.

If the teacher had chosen to have a student demonstrate the behavior, she would have made a point of naming the positive behavior explicitly in asking for a volunteer. "Who thinks they can show us a quiet, caring way to come in if you come to class late?"

3. The teacher asks students to notice the demonstrator's specific actions, expressions, and tone of voice.

"What did you notice about how I came into the room and moved to my seat?" the teacher asks. Students answer, "You opened the door slowly," "You kinda held the door so it wouldn't bang shut," "You didn't, like, wave or yell hi or joke with someone across the room," "Yeah, you just walked straight to your seat without saying anything or making any big movements," and "You looked around to see what everyone was doing and then got your papers out to join in."

"And why do you think this helps the class?" the teacher asks. "Because some people might get distracted easily, and this way maybe they won't get distracted," one student answers. Another adds, "Because it shows you're thinking about them, not just yourself."

4. The teacher asks for students (or additional students) to demonstrate the behavior.

"Now we need one of you to show us how to come in to the room in a respectful way that lets everyone learn." Caren volunteers. Her classmates watch and notice details of what she does.

Next the teacher chooses Rob, a boisterous and often impulsive student, to demonstrate. The teacher's move was deliberate, meant to show Rob and his peers that everyone, including him, can come into class in a quiet, respectful way.

5. The whole class practices the behavior.

"At one point or another in the next few weeks, you'll probably need to leave the room and come back or you might come to class late," the teacher says. "Pay special attention to how you come in and see what you notice about your own actions."

Here the whole-class practice takes place in the days after the modeling. This can be very effective, as long as the teacher lets students know that she will be noticing their actions and the class gathers again to reflect on their practice.

Two weeks after this modeling, this teacher brings students into a circle and says, "It's been a couple of weeks since we talked about and modeled how to come into the room without disrupting class. What are some positive things you noticed about how people did this? Are there things that need more practice?"

Spontaneity and fun in modeling

Modeling doesn't always have to include all of the five steps. Nor does it always have to happen outside of the regular flow of classroom activity. Modeling can be brief and happen spontaneously throughout the day.

For example, Ms. T. rings the bell and tells students that it's time to put away reading materials and line up to go to lunch. She asks, "Who can remind us how to put away our reading materials in a safe and careful way?"

"You should walk."

"Put all the papers back in the folder neatly. Don't just shove them in there."

"Wait for your turn if someone's in front of you. Don't push."

"Great," says Ms. T. "You're remembering our rules about taking care of each other and our materials. Who would like to show us?"

Three children raise their hands. The rest of the students watch from their seats. The three children follow the suggestions given by the students. They put their papers away neatly in the folder, walk to the file cabinet, put their folders away, and line up at the door.

"What did you notice?" asks Ms. T.

"Dwayne had to take all his papers out to get them in neatly."

"Thea waited for Helen to finish 'cause their files were right next to each other."

"They all walked. No one bumped into each other."

"It was *really* quiet."

"Okay, now everyone can put away reading folders and line up for lunch."

Modeling can also be fun. Anything involving acting is inherently fun for children. Students enjoy being the one "on stage" as well as watching others in this role. It's important to recognize and keep hold of the playfulness of this technique. Done in too somber or heavy-handed a way, the technique of modeling will quickly lose its appeal and effectiveness.

The teacher as constant modeler: Children are always watching

When it comes to classroom rules, the adage "Children do as we do, not as we say" couldn't be more true. They learn just as much—if not more—from our spontaneous interactions as they do from our deliberate lessons. That's why it's so important to live by the rules ourselves, in all our interactions with children and adults.

Easier said than done, of course. How many of us have heard ourselves yell at a child, "Do not raise your voice when you talk to me!"? Or speak to a student in a sarcastic or threatening way? Or be dismissive of a parent offering a suggestion for a problem? Just like children, when we're frustrated or angry, tired or stressed, we often lose control of ourselves and forget or ignore the rules. Knowing that we're doing it is often not enough to make us stop.

The point here is not to be perfect. We all know that's impossible. The point is to keep in mind that students are watching at all times, to try to follow the classroom rules whenever possible, and to acknowledge any mistakes we make. A simple "I'm sorry I yelled yesterday. I was feeling angry and I forgot our rule about treating others the way we want to be treated" is all that's needed. This sends the message that the rules are important—even the teacher tries her best to follow them—and that everyone makes mistakes. It says that we're all learners here and we don't have to be ashamed of our mistakes.

Use role playing for more complex situations

Role playing is a technique for teaching appropriate behavior in more complex and demanding social interactions. There are many classroom situations, such as sharing materials, being inclusive, and responding when someone makes a mistake, that require students to think carefully about the case at hand and decide what to do.

Chapter Two

Unlike the modeling scenarios described above, there is not one expected way to do things in these more complex situations. Instead, students must decide from among a wide range of possible behaviors. Role playing is a technique that allows teachers to acknowledge the complexity of these situations and give students practice in making responsible choices.

Choosing and framing role play situations

Role plays are generally done with the whole class but can also be done with small groups or even with an individual child. It's best if the role playing situations spring from the life of the classroom. For example, the teacher may know from prior experience that students are likely to:

- Have difficulty sharing materials

- Laugh at or show intolerance for each other's mistakes

- Become inflamed over accidents such as someone knocking something over, taking something another is still using, or bumping into another

- Exclude certain students

- Interrupt when someone is speaking

The teacher chooses one issue at a time to address through role playing. Before launching into the process, however, s/he reframes the problem into a positive goal. The list of problems above might be reframed in the following ways: "Students have difficulty sharing materials" might become "We need to work on sharing our supplies." "Students laugh at each other's mistakes" might be reframed as "we need to work on being supportive of each other, especially when someone makes a mistake." "Students become inflamed over accidents" might become "We need to work on staying calm when someone does something by accident." And so forth.

During the first few months of school, teachers rely heavily on role playing to teach the behaviors needed to make the classroom a place where everyone feels safe and can do her/his best work. As the year progresses, role playing might be used less frequently.

Steps in a role play

Once the teacher has established the positive goal of the role play, students and teachers work collaboratively to name and act out possible behaviors. While the goal itself is never negotiable—for example, deciding not to be inclusive is not

Practicing the Rules: Bringing Them to Life

an option—how to achieve that goal often is. In a role play, students and teachers work together to come up with several possible solutions to a challenging situation. Here are the steps typically used in a role play:

1. Name the goal

The teacher describes the positive goal, connecting it to the classroom rules.

2. Describe the scenario

The teacher describes the scenario to be role played and helps students perceive how the different people involved might be feeling.

3. Start the action, freeze it at the critical moment, and ask for suggestions

The actors play out the scene. The teacher freezes the action just before the inappropriate behavior, and asks students for possible ways to achieve the goal stated earlier.

4. Act out students' suggestions

The actors replay the scene to this point, then continue, using the suggestions for positive behavior that the class gave. The teacher stops the action at various points to invite students to talk about details they noticed in the actors' behaviors.

5. Role play the same issue using a different scene

If appropriate, new sets of students act out other scenes that involve the same type of problem.

Here's how these steps might look in a role play about being supportive when a classmate makes a mistake:

1. Name the goal

The class is gathered in a circle. Ms. B. says, "We all agreed that we want a classroom where everyone feels safe and included, and that we're going to help each other learn. I'm wondering what you think we might do or say to live up to these rules when someone makes a mistake."

It's important at this point to acknowledge the complexity of feelings and impulses that everyone involved in the situation might have. This means showing compassion and understanding not only for those who feel wronged or hurt, but for those who display the negative behaviors as well.

For example, Ms. B. says, "To start, let's first think about what it feels like to make a mistake. Let's say you're in a reading group or a class meeting or a science lesson, and you make a mistake. How might you feel?"

"Embarrassed."

"Like my face is burning hot."

"It makes me feel like I'm stupid, especially if people laugh."

Ms. B. continues, "So it feels uncomfortable for the person making the mistake. It can also feel uncomfortable for the people watching. Sometimes they show this by laughing or shouting out the right answer or making a mean remark like 'That's so easy.' Has that ever happened to any of you?"

"Yeah, sometimes I laugh when someone makes a mistake because it's surprising what they say, like you're not expecting it."

"Or sometimes it just sounds funny and the person who said it laughs, too."

"If I know the right answer, I feel like saying it."

Ms. B. then says, "So there are lots of reasons why you might do these things when someone makes a mistake, but how do you think the person who made the mistake might feel if people do these things?"

"If it were me I'd feel bad."

"It feels like everyone is ganging up on you."

"You get afraid to say things."

"We're going to act out a situation where someone makes a mistake in our class," Ms. B. says. "We'll figure out together some ways to respond that would be supportive and helpful."

2. Describe the scenario

"Here's the scene," Ms. B. says. "A teacher is about to read a book about Louis Armstrong, a famous jazz musician. But first she asks, 'Does anyone know who Louis Armstrong was?' A boy in the class—we'll call him Sashi— shoots his hand up and is bursting to give the answer. When the teacher calls on him, he says, 'He was one of the first astronauts to go to the moon.'"

Ms. B. continues, "Then another boy—we'll call him Myles—yells out, 'No, that's Neil Armstrong. Louis Armstrong was a great trumpet player!' Then everyone in the class bursts out laughing."

Ms. B. asks the class, "How do you think Sashi would feel in this situation?"

Practicing the Rules: Bringing Them to Life

"Terrible!"

"Embarrassed."

"Really stupid."

Setting the stage for a role play often involves again touching on the possible motivation behind the negative behavior. It's important, however, to do this without judgment and to avoid dwelling on the negative behavior. The dominant focus of the role play should stay on achieving the positive goal stated at the outset. Ms. B. allows a brief exchange about where Myles might be coming from here—maybe he got excited because he doesn't often know the answer or maybe he really likes jazz and wanted people to know that. Then Ms. B. quickly moves on.

3. Start the action, freeze it at the critical moment, and ask students for suggestions

"Let's act this out," Ms. B. says. "I'll be Myles. I need one volunteer to be Sashi and another to be the teacher." Note that in this first round of acting, the teacher takes the role of the main character, the one whose actions are being noted and analyzed. Later, if the class acts out the scene again, a student can take that role.

The acting begins. The "teacher" asks if anyone knows who Louis Armstrong was, and "Sashi" waves his hand madly. When the "teacher" calls on him, he yells out his answer. Just at that moment, Ms. B. says, "Freeze!" It's important to bring the action to the brink of the inappropriate behavior but not cross over into it. There's no need for children to see the hurtful behavior.

With the action poised at this critical juncture, when Myles and the rest of the make-believe class can choose to respond in a positive or negative way, Ms. B. asks students what those characters could do to support Sashi.

"Myles could raise his hand and wait for the teacher to call on him before he says anything," one student suggests.

"And what could he say when the teacher calls on him?" Ms. B. asks.

"He could say, 'I think you might be thinking about Neil Armstrong. Louis Armstrong was a trumpet player.'"

"What kind of voice might he use to say this?" Ms. B. asks.

"He would just say it like, normal. Calm, not yelling or making a face."

"Okay, let's act that out," says Ms. B.

4. Act out students' suggestions

The actors rewind to where Sashi gives his incorrect answer, then act out the scene with Myles saying the line that the students suggested and using a calm demeanor.

Ms. B. again freezes the action and asks the class, "What do you notice about Myles's body language, his hands, and his facial expression?" The students name what they saw.

Ms. B. then asks, "What else could Myles have said in this situation to be supportive of Sashi? What about the rest of the class? What could they do to be supportive?" One student suggests that Myles could wait until later to tell Sashi about his mistake privately. Another says the class should resist laughing even if Sashi himself starts to laugh. These ideas are acted out, with different children trying the roles of Myles, Sashi, and the teacher.

Practicing the Rules: Bringing Them to Life

By stopping the action at key points to invite student commentary, the teacher calls attention to the small but important details that children often miss in everyday interactions. Stopping to notice these, naming several possible ways to keep interactions positive, and seeing these ways acted out all help students develop a repertoire of positive ways to handle similar situations that may crop up in real life.

5. Role play the same issue using a different scene

If time allows and students continue to be attentive, Ms. B. might have students act out a different scene that involves the question of what to do when someone makes a mistake. Examples might be someone misreading a word in a reading group, someone misspelling a word in a spelling group, and someone missing an important catch in a kickball game.

The power of teacher language

I've come to the frightening conclusion that I am the decisive element in the classroom …
As a teacher, I have tremendous power to make a child's life miserable or joyous.
I can be a tool of torture or an instrument of inspiration. I can humiliate or humor,
hurt or heal. In all situations, it is my response that decides whether a crisis
will be escalated or deescalated and a child humanized or dehumanized.

Haim Ginott
Teacher and Child

A teacher's language is one of her/his most powerful teaching tools, and one of the most difficult to master. What we say and how we say it carry tremendous weight in the classroom. Our language can build children up or tear them down. It can foster a deep respect for rules or a deep resentment toward them. It can model respectful and caring social interactions or just the opposite.

Effective language encourages and empowers students to follow the rules, rather than criticizing them for not following them. As child psychologist Rudolf Dreikurs writes, "Each child needs continuous encouragement just as a plant needs water." (Dreikurs with Soltz 1964, 36)

Effective teacher language:

- Is clear, simple, and direct

- Is genuine and respectful

- Gives specific positive feedback rather than general praise

- Focuses on the child's action or behavior rather than generalizing about the child's whole person

- Avoids qualitative or personal judgment

- Shows faith in children's ability to follow the rules

The three Rs of teacher language: Reinforcing, Reminding, Redirecting

In using their language to teach children to live by the rules, many teachers find it useful to think in terms of the "three Rs":

Reinforcing language

Reinforcing language is used to give positive feedback and recognize students' efforts at self-discipline. The teacher names the child's specific actions, avoiding global praise or personal judgment: "I notice…" or "I see…" rather than "Good job!" or "You are so good at… " or "You were such a good boy to…".

Here are some examples of reinforcing language:

"Vinnie, I noticed you offered to help Emelyne clean the table. That's an important way of taking care of our classroom."

"What a smooth cleanup that was. You put away your math work, got your lunches, lined up for music, and talked to each other calmly when you needed someone to move over and let you get by."

"Jenelle, I noticed you were working on using friendly words at the art table this morning. I think your classmates noticed too."

"I see that you are all remembering what to do when you have something to say during meeting."

"What careful and attentive listening I'm seeing. Your questions and comments show that you're really paying attention to the speaker."

"Tyesha, I noticed that you helped Kaylin with her homework this morning. I bet she appreciated it."

Beware of using one child's positive behavior to influence others. For example, it's tempting for teachers to say "I like the way Martina is sitting quietly in her spot" when what they really want is for the other students to imitate Martina. While this often gets children to act as we want them to in the short run, in the long run it can lead to children feeling manipulated and resentful of each other. It can also lead to children turning sour to classroom rules.

Practicing the Rules: Bringing Them to Life

Rather than using Martina this way, a teacher might get better short term and long term results by using the established signal to get all students' attention, then saying "I'll start when you are all sitting quietly in your spot" or "Who can show us what it looks like to sit quietly in our spot?" In the latter case, children have the choice to volunteer or not, which is very different from being pointed to and manipulated into being a model.

(For more on this topic, see "Beyond 'I Like the Way...'" by Hermine Marshall in *Young Children,* January 1995, pages 26-28.)

Reminding language

Reminding language can be effective in two situations. First, it is used to prompt children to think ahead about what they need to do in an upcoming activity or situation. "Who remembers the three things we all need to have on our desks to be ready for dictation?" a teacher might say. This sets the children up for success. It can also be a genuine check-in—the teacher reassures her/himself and the students that they know how to handle the situation.

Second, reminding language is used to steady the course when students are beginning to go off track. For example, just as the noise level in the room begins to rise, the teacher says, "Who remembers what we said about our voices during quiet time?"

In both cases, the teacher gives students an opportunity to tell or show what the appropriate behavior is. The reminder can be in the form of a question ("What are you supposed to be doing right now?") or a directive ("Show me how you should be doing this."). Often, the question or directive is preceded by an observation ("I notice that there are papers all over the floor. What can you do to help here?"). Whatever the case, it emanates from and conveys the teacher's belief in the student's ability to follow the rules, and if given just as students are veering off course, it gives the students a chance in the moment to pull themselves back. The message is "I see that you forgot, but I have complete confidence in your ability to switch gears and do the right thing."

Here are some examples of reminding language:

Before students start on a project that requires them to share markers, the teacher says, "Who can show us how to ask for a marker?" and then "Who can show us how to pass a marker?"

A group of students begins to fidget instead of doing their math work. They look like they're about to start fooling around with each other. The teacher says, "What are you supposed to be doing right now? Show me."

A transition is chaotic and students are wandering aimlessly about the room. The teacher rings the bell and says, "Someone remind us what we're supposed to be doing right now."

Asia is playfully poking Kenneth. Kenneth gets irritated and looks like he's about to lash out at Asia. The teacher steps up and says, "Kenneth, remember what we said about telling people calmly that you don't like what they're doing? What could you say to Asia right now? And Asia, remember what we said we should do when someone asks you to stop?"

LiPing cuts in line. Mona makes an angry face and is about to push him away when the teacher says, "LiPing, what did we say about cutting? Mona, remember how we said we would remind people with calm words if they forgot about not cutting in line?"

Redirecting language

Redirecting language is used when a student's behavior has clearly gone off track and needs to be stopped immediately. Reminders are generally ineffective at this point. In fact, sometimes the teacher has already given a reminder to no avail. Now the teacher must firmly, clearly, and matter-of-factly tell the child to stop the inappropriate behavior and spell out what the child needs to do instead. Unlike in reminding, where the teacher asks the child to name or show this alternative behavior, in redirecting, the teacher names it.

While redirecting language often follows reminding language, it doesn't have to. Often it's appropriate to go straight to redirecting without giving any reminders. What's appropriate depends on the behavior. If a student has clearly forgotten or chosen to ignore a rule and is already acting in an unsafe, hurtful, or uncaring way, then going straight to redirecting language is usually best.

Here are some examples of redirecting language:

Daphne throws the markers across the table instead of handing them to José. The teacher says, "Daphne, in our class we hand markers over. Hand the marker to José now."

Practicing the Rules: Bringing Them to Life

The math group continues to fool around after the teacher reminds them to get to their work. The teacher says, "Go back to your seat and begin your geometry constructions right now."

Gavin taps and pokes his neighbors during a meeting. The teacher says, "Gavin, your hands belong in your lap. Put them there now and tell them to stay put."

Eric won't let anyone else in his group finish talking before jumping in with his own ideas. The teacher says, "Eric, our rule says to let everyone finish speaking. Slow down and wait until each person is done before giving your thoughts."

If the inappropriate behavior continues after a redirection, the teacher might use a logical consequence. For example, if Daphne continues to throw the markers, the teacher might take the markers away from her for the rest of the work period, giving them back only after Daphne and the teacher have come up with a plan for how Daphne will remember to hand the marker to people in the future. Logical consequences will be addressed in detail in the next chapter.

Praise versus encouragement

Most teachers are aware of the praise-versus-encouragement debate that has persisted during the past fifteen years among teachers, researchers, psychologists, and parents. There is mounting evidence that praising students, especially excessively, has negative consequences.

Praise differs from encouragement in that praise is usually general and makes a value judgment about the child ("Good job today" or "You're a good writer").

Three Rs of Teacher Language			
	Reinforcing	**Reminding**	**Redirecting**
When to use	When the teacher notices efforts at self-discipline	1. Before students start an activity or enter into a situation 2. Just as students begin to show inappropriate behavior	When students have clearly gone off course and are definitely showing inappropriate behavior
How to use	Acknowledge positive actions by naming them.	Give students a chance to name or show an appropriate alternative behavior.	Stop the behavior and tell the child what to do instead.
Example	"I see you're all asking relevant questions and making supportive comments."	"Show me how we agreed to share these materials."	"Stop running. The rule says to walk."

Chapter Two

Encouragement, on the other hand, names specific details of the child's behavior and is judgment-neutral ("I noticed you waited patiently for Mari to begin her report" or "You were able to stay in control for our whole meeting today").

While praising students may seem to improve their behavior in the short term, the long-term effects can be problematic. In a recent *New York Times* article on this topic, child-rearing experts cautioned that a steady stream of praise can turn children into praise addicts who lack confidence and who feel manipulated. Over-praised children are less likely to keep up good habits in the long run. They're often less motivated to pursue a creative or academic task because they feel pressured or are afraid they won't live up to expectations. (Belluck 2000)

So does this mean that teachers should stop recognizing children's positive efforts and accomplishments? Absolutely not! Children, like all of us, need to feel recognized for their positive contributions and accomplishments. And they need ongoing information from the teacher about how they're doing with regard to classroom rules. What this caution about praise does mean is that teachers should be mindful of how they give this feedback, exploring the use of techniques other than praise.

While genuine praise such as "Good job" and "Great thinking" may sometimes be appropriate, teachers may want to use this kind of global pat-on-the-back sparingly. If the goal is to help children become self-motivated and feel good inside about their own behavior, teachers might more often give feedback that is specific and that therefore encourages children to evaluate their own work or behavior.

Here are three tips for giving encouraging feedback:

- Comment on the specifics, especially something that you know the child is working hard on: "Carl, I noticed you were looking at Eva the whole time while she was sharing her story today."

- Point out the positive benefits of the behavior: "Carl, you were really concentrating on Eva's sharing today. I bet that made her feel good."

- Ask questions in a way that shows interest, yet allows the child to judge him/herself: "I notice you were paying attention during Eva's sharing today. How do you think that made Eva feel?"

Practicing the Rules: Bringing Them to Life

Focusing on what's behind your words

All this said, it's important to note that getting too rigid about the sometimes subtle distinctions between praise and encouragement can be counterproductive. Rather than focusing hard on whether our words are technically considered praise or encouragement, it's better to focus on the intention behind our words.

Indeed, we can come up with words that are "technically" encouraging but use them in a highly manipulative way. Conversely, it's possible to use language that is "technically" praise but use it in a way that's highly encouraging and supportive of a student. It's the energy behind the words, rather than the words themselves, that really matters. Ultimately the teacher is the one who can truly understand all the subtleties of how language is best used in her/his classroom.

Also, as we all know, it's not simply our words that matter. Our understanding of the child, our relationship with the child, our tone of voice, our facial expressions, and our body language all come into play in determining whether our words are encouraging or damaging.

If we're using language to manipulate or control, or if we're noticing that students are highly dependent on our positive feedback, then something probably needs to change. On the other hand, if we're using language to make meaningful connections with students, to give positive feedback, and to recognize specific accomplishments, then it probably will serve those purposes. While it's worthwhile for teachers to explore their choice of words, it may not be essential to change every expression.

Jane Nelsen, in her book *Positive Discipline,* offers the following questions to keep in mind when considering whether a statement is considered praise or encouragement:

- Am I inspiring self-evaluation or cultivating dependence on others' evaluation?

- Am I being respectful or patronizing?

- Am I seeing the child's point of view or only my own?

- Would I make this comment to a friend?

Teachers often find this last question especially useful. As Nelsen points out, "The comments we make to friends usually fit the criteria for encouragement." (Nelsen 1996, 120, 122)

Ten language tips

Here are ten things to keep in mind when fine tuning your use of teacher language:

1. Be direct

It's easy to say we need to avoid manipulative language. It's much harder to actually do it when we're managing a group of twenty-five students and trying to keep the classroom safe and orderly. To break out of the manipulation mode, be direct when you want children to do something. Instead of "I see Josh has finished cleaning up his table," use the established signal to get everyone's attention, then say, "Time to finish cleaning up and get in line. One minute to go." Even "I see four people ready... I see half of us ready... I see everyone ready" is better than "I see Josh is ready." If you truly want to acknowledge Josh for being so efficient and thorough with the cleanup, make your comment to him directly at another time (for example, "Josh, I noticed you cleaned up quickly and thoroughly after art today").

2. Pay attention to the small things

A teacher's language is generally most effective when the classroom feels calm and orderly. It's at these times that students will be most receptive. When you notice the noise *just beginning* to rise above a productive level, that's the time to ring the bell and remind students to use softer voices. When you notice a group *about* to get off task, that's the time to step in and say, "Remind us what you're supposed to be doing right now." If you wait until the noise level has become raucous or until the group has been off task for ten minutes, your words will have less impact.

3. Keep it simple and clear

Practicing the Rules: Bringing Them to Life

Children are masterful at tuning out adults, especially those that go on and on. Remember the old Charlie Brown movies, in which the adults' words droned on in a long series of blah, blah, blahs? Too many words, whether they're positive or negative, praising or lecturing, simply confuse and overwhelm children. After a certain point, they stop listening.

The most effective teacher language is simple and clear. Say what you mean and say it concisely. If you know that students understand the rules, there's no need to go into a long explanation. Often a single phrase or directive is all that's needed.

Instead of "Class, remember how we talked about how hard it is to hear each other when everyone is calling out at once. It's really important that you raise your hand if you have something to say. All of your ideas are important and I want everyone to be heard," try "Meeting rules" or "Raise your hand to speak."

Instead of "Remember that if we don't take care of our materials we won't have what we need to do projects later in the year. This paper is getting all crunched up and won't be good for certain art projects," try "Our rule says to take good care of our materials. Start this cleanup over."

I remember a cartoon sent to me when my children were very young. An eight-year-old, dressed in a baseball uniform, was standing over a broken lamp in a living room, bat and ball in hand. The mother, leaning over the broken lamp, was saying to the child, "Oh sweetie, maybe we need to discuss carelessness issues and rechanneling our energy in positive ways." The boy, eyes rolling, responded, "Oh man, couldn't she just spank me?"

The point, of course, is not that spanking is good. The point is that simpler and more direct language is needed in this situation. "Baseball is for outside. This needs to be cleaned up now. We'll talk later about how you can fix the lamp."

4. Be firm when needed

Being firm is not the same as being mean. Too often we confuse the two. In an effort to avoid being mean, many of us shy away from being firm. This does a great disservice to students and to us. Students grow uncertain about limits, and we lose our authority to establish them. Students follow the rules when they *feel* like it; we enforce them when it's *easy* to do so. Generally, this creates an atmosphere of confusion and anxiety.

There are many, many times in the daily life of the classroom when firm is exactly what's called for. A simple guideline to keep in mind is "If you mean no, then say no." No hedging, no beating around the bush. "No, you may not use the materials in that closet" rather than "I'd rather you didn't use the materials in that closet, okay?"

5. Don't ask a question when you mean to give a command

When you want children to put their brushes down and look at you, don't say "Could you please put your brushes down and look at me?" Say "Put your brushes down and look at me." This is not the same as being harsh, sarcastic, or disrespectful. The tone of voice is direct and firm. It does not put children down, is not scolding, and does not pass judgment in any way.

6. Expect the best

Adult expectations are a powerful influence in the classroom. Research has shown over and over that children's academic performance is influenced both positively and negatively by teachers' expectations. If a teacher believes a child will succeed, the child has a greater chance of doing so than if the teacher believes the child will fail.

The same holds true for children's behavior. Most children will try to live up to adult expectations. If we expect that children will be respectful and responsible, they will strive to be. If we expect that children will be disrespectful and irresponsible, then that's what they most likely will be.

Language is one key way through which we communicate our expectations to children. Through our language we let children know that we have confidence in their ability to meet high expectations. We tell them, even when things have gone awry, "I believe you can do this. Now show me."

Here are two examples of language that effectively communicates expectations:

- Two children are arguing over who gets to use the hole puncher first. Rather than solving the problem for them or taking away the hole puncher, the teacher says, "I know the two of you can figure out a fair way to solve this problem. I'll give you two minutes. Let me know what you decide."

- Students are waiting in line to go to lunch. There is a lot of poking, pushing, and cutting going on. The teacher rings the bell, but rather than pointing out what's wrong (which all the students already know), she focuses on what the students can do right. She says, "You all know what to do when you're waiting in line. When I ring the bell again I expect you to do it."

7. Invite cooperation

There are many situations in the course of a school day when it's more appropriate to invite children to cooperate rather than demand that they do. Teachers can invite cooperation by creating group challenges, offering choices, or just bringing a playful spirit to the task at hand. Here are some examples of inviting cooperation:

- It's time to clean up. The teacher rings the bell and says, "Here's a challenge. Let's see if we can do a thorough job of cleaning up the entire room in less than two minutes. If you finish your area early, you can help clean another area. The two minutes start now."

- It's writing time and many students are having a hard time focusing on their work. There are lots of side conversations, and several students are wandering about the room. The teacher rings the bell and says, "I see lots of people having a hard time concentrating. This writing work needs to get done. You can choose to focus on it for the next twenty minutes or you can do it this afternoon instead of choice time. Your decision."

- It's meeting time and students are not following meeting rules. There is a lot of fidgeting and interrupting. The teacher says, "I think we've forgotten some of our important meeting rules. I'm going to close my eyes for thirty seconds and when I open them I know you'll be ready to follow our rules again."

8. Be sincere

Students know when we're being fake. While there may be a period of time when our language sounds a bit wooden because of changes we're trying to make, it's important to always maintain our sincerity. Students know when our language is coming from a genuine place and when it's not. We're most effective as teachers when we're being authentic.

9. Pay attention to tone, volume, and body language

Consider the many different ways of saying "Come over here and sit down, Danny." The tone could be neutral, loaded with exasperation, or sound more like a plea than a directive. It could be said in a whisper (for only Danny to hear), in a medium volume, or in an all-out scream.

Most children are keenly aware of the subtle and not-so-subtle alterations in meaning caused by tone and volume. I'll always remember a five-year-old student challenging my use of tone and volume when I lost my temper with her: "You said words meaner and louder to me!" she protested in tears.

While we may not always be able to control the negative tone that slyly slips in or the raised volume that makes a directive sound more like a threat, we can continue to pay attention to our tone and volume and strive to match them to the message we want to send.

The same goes for our body language. Just as students are keenly aware of the tone and volume of our words, they are always paying attention to our body language, especially to that silent but powerful language known as a teacher's "looks." Remember the old chant from elementary school years, "No more pencils, no more books, no more teachers' dirty looks"?

We often need to use our eyes as silent reminders to children to stay on track—that "No, that's not okay" look or "Come on, stay with us" look. But it's important to be aware of how powerful these signals can be. There is often a fine line between the reminding or redirecting look and the "dirty" look. Not long ago my son told me, "One time when you were really really mad, you said 'I hate you and you're the dumbest boy in the world.'" I immediately countered, "I would never have said that to you!" He laughed and said, "No, not with words. You said it with your eyes!"

10. Keep your sense of humor

A teacher might give literally hundreds of reminders and redirections in the course of a normal school day. If you're beginning to feel like a broken record, it might be time to infuse some humor into the situation, as in the following examples:

A math group is off task. The teacher approaches. Rather than giving a reminder or redirection, she says with a smile, "Hmmmm. Tell me what I'm going to say" or "Who thinks they can read my mind and say what I was going to say?" The students quickly respond with their "guesses": "You were going to tell us to get to work" and "Stop fooling around and do your math." It's a playful approach that gets the point across.

A teacher has stepped out of the classroom for a few minutes to speak to the principal, leaving the class in the care of an instructional assistant. When the teacher returns, the classroom is noisy and chaotic. He turns off the light, signaling students to stop what they're doing and look at him. He says, "This couldn't possibly be the same class that I left a few minutes ago. I think we need some magic to get the real class back. I'm going to close my eyes for a minute. When I say 'poof' I want the classroom to magically change back to how it was when I left."

Practicing the Rules: Bringing Them to Life

The process of changing language

Often teachers who want to change their language go through a conscious process. Here are some strategies that can help:

- Listen consciously to your words.
- Tape record yourself in the classroom for a short period of time. Listen to the tape to detect your language patterns.
- Have a colleague observe you for fifteen minutes, recording the words and phrases you use most frequently.
- Focus on changing one phrase at a time.
- Agree with some colleagues to focus on changing the same words or phrases at the same time.

- Enlist students to help you change your language habits. Second/third grade teacher Gail Zimmerman asked students to use phrases such as I notice…," "Show me…," and "Remind us…" with each other and to remind her when she needed to use them. Asking students to help is a way to model being a learner who makes mistakes and works to fix them.

- When you do make a mistake, try fixing it in the moment. You might say something like "Let's erase that. What I wanted to say was…."

- Pause before speaking to give yourself a chance to think.

- Post a list of desirable words and phrases in your classroom for easy reference. Or write them on a card that you can easily carry around and refer to.

- Use more nonverbal signals and cues as a way to get students' attention. This will reduce the amount of "teacher talk," allowing you to focus more fully on the most important language patterns.

Through all of this, remember that change takes time. Be patient with yourself and celebrate the incremental improvements you make along the way.

Chapter Two

Works Cited

Belluck, Pam. 2000. "New Advice for Parents: Saying 'That's Great!' May Not Be." *New York Times* (October 18): A14.

Dreikurs, Rudolf, with Vicki Soltz. 1964. *Children: The Challenge*. Paperback edition. New York: Plume.

Marshall, Hermine. 1995. "Beyond 'I Like the Way…'" *Young Children* (January): 26–28.

Nelsen, Jane. 1996. *Positive Discipline*. Revised edition. New York: Ballantine Books.

Wood, Chip. 1998. *Seven Principles of The Responsive Classroom: A Keynote Address*. (Video) Greenfield, MA: Northeast Foundation for Children.

Chapter Three

WHEN STUDENTS BREAK THE RULES

BY MARY BETH FORTON

G*ood judgment comes from experience, and a lotta that comes from bad judgment.*
Mark Twain

Making mistakes is unavoidable, and the mistake is less important in most cases than what the individual does after he has made the mistake.
Rudolf Dreikurs

Purposes and Reflections

We all know that children learn from their mistakes. Remembering this, how-ever, in the midst of all the demands of daily teaching isn't easy. When Margo refuses to take turns and Dwayne to share the markers, and Nija shoves a classmate and Jeremy interrupts—all while we're trying to teach a reading lesson—it can be difficult to see mistakes as anything but irritating disruptions.

But if children are truly going to learn from their mistakes, and not just make the same ones over and over, they need teachers who can recognize these moments as valuable opportunities for learning. It's in the processing of the mis-take that children learn to move from "bad judgment" to "good judgment."

A teacher's guidance is critical in this journey. Will students learn to hide their mistakes or claim ownership for them? Will they learn to blame others for their mistakes or take responsibility for them? Will they repeat the same mistakes over and over or try another way of behaving next time? The details of how we respond to children's rule breaking can make an enormous difference to the answers to these questions.

Goals in responding to children's rule breaking

Experimenting with rules and testing limits is a normal part of children's development. It's how they construct their understanding of the rules. As we all know, some children are much more persistent in their testing than others, but almost every child has some need to experiment with the rules.

Consciously or not, they'll seek answers to questions such as "Do I *really* have to listen when someone else is speaking?" "Do I *really* have to take care of the materials in this room?" "Do I *really* have to include everyone in the game even if I don't like someone?" "What if I don't?"

In the process of experimenting, students will make lots of mistakes. And just as we do when teaching math and science and reading, we can use students' mistakes as valuable opportunities for learning. Every time a child breaks a rule, there's an opportunity to teach self-control and responsibility.

Of course, there will be many times in the daily life of a classroom when it's simply not possible to seize these teachable moments. If while you're teaching a math group a conflict arises over the science equipment, it's impossible to be in both places at the same time. Or if a child bursts out in anger at a classmate while you're leading Morning Meeting, you can send the child to time-out, but beyond that you cannot abandon your work with the group to attend to the further learning needs of that child in that moment.

Teaching is a constant juggling act. Often we need to put aside the needs of an individual momentarily for the needs of the group, returning to the individual later when we have a moment. While we have a responsibility to the needs of each individual, we also have an important responsibility to the needs of the group. In responding to children's rule breaking, we must constantly be aware of these two sometimes conflicting needs and make sure we have practical strategies in place for balancing them.

The goals in responding to rule breaking, then, are to:

- Help students recognize, fix, and learn from their mistakes.
- Help students internalize the rules so they develop *self*-control.
- Maintain a safe and orderly classroom.

When Students Break the Rules

- Balance the needs of the group with the needs of each individual.

- Help students make reparations and maintain relationships when they hurt each other emotionally.

It's in the spirit of helping children *learn* from their mistakes, rather than *punishing* them or making them *pay* for their mistakes, that the following strategies for responding to rule breaking are offered.

Strategies for responding to rule breaking

Because there are so many reasons why a child might break a rule and so many factors operating in a classroom, teachers need a range of methods for responding to misbehaviors. This chapter presents the following strategies:

Simple cues

The previous chapter talked about using teacher language to remind students about the rules and redirect their behavior when needed. This chapter will look at something similar: quick one-word cues or nonverbal signals that help students get back on track when they're breaking a rule.

Logical consequences

Logical consequences are ways to help fix problems that result from children's words and actions when they break or forget rules. They are used when it takes more than a simple cue to stop a behavior and fix a problem. Logical consequences help children regain self-control, reflect on their mistakes, and make amends for them. Logical consequences should be respectful of the child, relevant to the situation, and reasonable in scale. They should never be punitive.

Used aptly and consistently, logical consequences teach children some basic strategies for what to do when they're feeling out of control or have hurt someone or something. In that sense, the use of logical consequences can be seen as a way of solving problems with children. However, some problems require strategies beyond logical consequences, strategies such as teacher/student problem-solving conferences, conflict resolution techniques, and problem-solving class meetings. While it's beyond the scope of this book to offer detailed coverage of these strategies, Appendix A offers summaries of them with resources for learning more about each one.

Getting Started

Having empathy for rule breakers

If there's one thing teachers must hold in their hearts and minds when faced with children's rule breaking, it's empathy. With empathy for rule breakers, we enable ourselves to stay on the course of helping children recognize and fix their mistakes with dignity. Without it, we can quickly slip down the path of punishing and demeaning children for being "bad."

Children break the rules for the same reasons adults break rules

Even with a deep respect for the rules that they've helped to create, children will break the rules. It's not hard to understand why. Just think about all the reasons you might have for breaking a rule. For example, when you're going fifty in a thirty-mile-per-hour zone, you might be doing it because:

When
Students
Break the
Rules

- You're late for a meeting.
- You didn't know it was a thirty-mile-per-hour zone.
- You don't think it should be a thirty-mile-per-hour zone.
- You don't think you'll get caught.
- You like how it feels to go fast.
- You didn't know you were going that fast.
- You're frustrated that your last meeting went so late and it's "their" fault you have to go so fast now.
- Everyone else is going fifty.

Most likely, you didn't consciously stop and deliberate, "I know this is a dangerous act that could potentially hurt or kill myself and others, but I still think it's worth it because I don't want to be late for my meeting." Like all of us, children will have many moments when impulse wins over reason, desire over logic, feelings over rational thought. They will get curious, they will get carried away, they will forget. As every adult knows, it can take a lifetime to learn how to control our impulses and emotions.

Also keep in mind that children are still in the early stages of learning the rules of the world, no less the rules of the school. They're constantly trying to figure out what the larger world expects of them. Like the well-loved monkey in *Curious George,* they do much of this learning by doing. Through their exploring and experimenting, they come to understand what's acceptable and what isn't during a meeting, on the playground, at the grocery store, during sports practice, at a play, on the bus.

Through breaking the rules they learn about the finer details and purposes of the rules. "But I saw Louise running in the hall," a student protests when stopped for running. "But Billy doesn't mind if I do that, so why should Michael?" when stopped for poking a friend during a lesson. "But everyone was laughing, even Sashi," when the teacher reminds a class of the rule about not laughing when someone makes a mistake.

These are all genuine and important points to explore with children. It is through making mistakes and processing them with a caring adult that students eventually internalize the rules. Rather than simply relying on an adult to tell them what to do, children begin to develop their own understanding of why it's not safe to run in the halls, why it's distracting to a speaker when classmates are poking one another, and why it's hurtful to laugh at someone's mistakes. They gain a deeper understanding of the rules and learn to take responsibility for their actions.

Chapter Three

Begin by assuming the best

There are so many things we don't know about the children and situations that arise in the classroom. For example, when we see Angel ripping up Tony's writing assignment, we don't know what Tony wrote about Angel on that paper. When we see Yazhe jab Ariela, we don't know what Ariela might have done to provoke it. And when Sonya pounds her desk in frustration during writing time, we have no idea what might have happened to prompt such anger before she came to school that morning.

Given the complexity behind children's behaviors, it's best to begin by assuming children's best intentions. This means that the first step in responding effectively to these situations is to suspend our own knee-jerk reactions to them.

Rather than making those quick judgments—*Angel is up to his antics again, Yazhe is so aggressive, Sonya is always trying to avoid work*—we would do better to begin by assuming the best and asking questions to learn more. We might begin with a simple request for facts: "What's going on here?" Or we can make an observation followed by a question: "Looks like you need some help. Do you want to talk about it now or take a few minutes to cool off?"

One question that's probably *not* very helpful to ask children in the moment is why: *Why* did you tear up his paper? *Why* did you jab Ariela? *Why* are you pounding your desk? In the heat of the moment, this question, even if well intentioned, will sound accusatory to children and make them defensive. Often, the children's response will be to quickly blame the other person or to say blankly, "I don't know." And in many cases, they honestly don't.

Questions to ask yourself when a child breaks a rule

There is no such thing as one size fits all when it comes to responding to rule breaking. Different situations call for different responses. When children misbehave, they give us valuable information about how they're feeling and what they need.

Rudolf Dreikurs, child psychologist and author of *Maintaining Sanity in the Classroom,* writes about the need that all people have for a sense of belonging and a sense of importance, or significance (Dreikurs with Pepper and Grunwald 1982). Edward Deci, researcher and author of *Why We Do What We Do,* frames these fundamental human needs as the need for autonomy (the freedom to control oneself), relatedness (being connected to others), and competence (the ability to achieve desired outcomes) (Deci with Flaste 1995). Both Dreikurs and Deci remind us that when people's basic psychological needs are not met, they feel bad about themselves and often act out in negative ways.

Children will look for negative ways to meet their needs if they can't meet them in positive ways. These negative methods, Dreikurs tells us, include seeking negative attention, engaging the teacher and other students in power struggles, seeking revenge, and stopping efforts to do well by feigning inadequacy. Some children will always choose one of these methods; others move through the full range in a desperate attempt to satisfy their needs for belonging and significance. Understanding what's behind a child's misbehavior can help a teacher to choose a response that will help rather than hurt.

Obviously, this is tricky business. It's impossible for a teacher of a large group of children to fully comprehend the complexities behind each child's behavior. However, as much as possible, we need to consider each situation and each child on a case-by-case basis. Here are a few of the questions a teacher might consider in responding to a child's misbehavior:

- What do I know about this child's development, learning style, family, and culture?

- What do I know about this particular situation? Are the expectations clear? Too high? Too low?

When Students Break the Rules

- Is this behavior part of a pattern? Or is it an isolated situation?

- Is the child testing the limits? Is the child engaging me in a power struggle?

- What's been helpful for this child in the past? What hasn't been helpful?

Consider the simplest interventions first: Visual and verbal cues

Often the best thing a teacher can do when a child breaks a rule is to give the child a chance to correct him/herself. Too often we feel the need to correct the situation ourselves immediately—to move the child, to stop the work of the group, to tell the child what to do differently. All of these can deprive children of the chance to recognize their own mistakes and correct them in the moment.

Marianne rolls her eyes at a friend while another student is sharing. Kenya starts to fiddle with the puzzles on the shelf behind her during a lesson. A small group gets off task. Pauline whispers to her neighbor instead of doing her math work. Yaser cuts in line. You know the students know they're messing up. Sometimes all that's needed is a visual or verbal cue to help the children get *themselves* back on track.

The cue can be as simple as saying the child's name or looking into the child's eyes. Essentially you want to communicate, "I know that you can do better than that. Now do it." Here are some common and effective visual and verbal cues:

- Make brief eye contact with the child.

- Say the child's name.

- Nod your head at the child.

- Give a hand signal such as a finger to your lips, a writing gesture, etc.

Notice that none of these require the teacher to stop what s/he's doing or to explain the rule or expectation. They also minimize calling attention to the child. The communication is between the teacher and student involved. The teacher assumes that the student knows what to do but just needs a little nudge to do it.

These simple cues are most effective when they're given before the misbehavior has gone on for too long. Obviously if a child doesn't immediately respond to a visual or verbal cue, then it's time to be more directive. However, giving children this opportunity to recognize their mistake and correct it themselves in the moment helps them to preserve their dignity and develop self-control.

Be careful about giving too many cues

All this said, keep in mind that cues and reminders can have a damaging effect if they're overused. In classrooms where teachers always give a certain number of reminders before taking further action, students quickly figure out that they don't really have to control themselves until the second or third or fourth time around. They become more focused on keeping track of the reminders than keeping track of their behavior.

Recently I was stopped for speeding with my two children in the car. The radar showed that I was going fifteen miles per hour over the speed limit. But rather than giving me a ticket, the officer gave me a warning slip. "You get three warnings a year before getting a ticket," he explained.

My children were incredulous. "That means you get two more times to speed before you get a ticket! Let's go really fast now!" While I explained in my most responsible parental voice that there were many reasons to follow the speed limit besides to avoid getting a ticket, I have to admit that I've been more lax about my speed control ever since. I still have two warnings this year.

Use logical consequences if needed

In nature there are neither rewards nor punishments;
there are only consequences.

Robert Green Ingersoll

Logical consequences are used when neither simple cues nor the reminding and redirecting language discussed in Chapter 2 are effective. Used well, logical consequences help children see the connection between their behavior and the effect it has on others. They help children understand that we are all responsible for the consequences of our actions. At the same time, they protect children because they allow children to fix the problems that their actions caused. As a result, children retain their dignity and are not left in shame. Thus the goal of using logical consequences is never to punish children for their actions, but to teach them to take responsibility for them.

The three Rs of logical consequences

Teachers often ask, "What exactly is the difference between logical consequences and punishment?" The short answer is "everything." What most

When Students Break the Rules

distinguishes logical consequences from punishment is that logical consequences are relevant, realistic, and respectful:

Relevant

The consequence is directly related to the child's action and is effective in repairing the problems the action caused. For example, if a group of children ask to work together on a project and then use the time to talk about their weekend plans, a relevant consequence would be that they lose the opportunity to work together that day.

Realistic

The consequence must be something that is realistic for the child to do and the teacher to follow through on. For example, a logical consequence for a child who writes on a desk is for that child to clean the desk. However, holding the child back from lunch or a special area class in order to clean it would not be reasonable.

Respectful

A logical consequence is communicated with respect for the child. The teacher is firm but caring and focuses on the specific behavior rather than making general judgments about the child's character. For example, if one student pushes another, the teacher might begin, "Pushing is not okay" rather than "Stop being such a bully."

These three Rs make a huge difference to whether a response to rule breaking feels like a logical consequence or a punishment. But there is no question that even with the most skillful use of logical consequences, children will sometimes protest or resist. They may deny any wrongdoing or complain that "you're always picking on me." It can be a painful and difficult process for children to recognize and take responsibility for their mistakes, as it can be for adults.

It's important for teachers to remember that they can't totally control how children feel. Often children feel bad simply for having made a mistake, for having lost their self-control or attracted negative attention. Their protests may be as much a sign of these feelings about themselves as their feelings about the teacher's response. As teachers, our job is to help them restore the situation without further humiliation.

Punishment versus logical consequences: An example

Six-year-old Jacob is zooming around the classroom when suddenly he trips and falls into Michelle's block building. Michelle lets out a scream and the teacher comes over.

Punishment

A teacher using a punishment approach to discipline might say loudly to Jacob in front of the other children, "I've told you over and over not to run in this classroom. Now see what you've done with your carelessness." Feeling irritated, the teacher might continue, "Go sit in that chair and don't move until it's time for lunch."

Logical Consequences

When Students Break the Rules

A teacher who uses logical consequences might also feel irritated, but would take a deep breath and begin by describing the situation to her/himself: "Michelle is upset because Jacob knocked over her building. I need to talk with Jacob first and then we'll figure out how to help Michelle."

Taking Jacob aside, the teacher asks him, "What happened?"

"I just tripped and fell into it accidentally. I didn't mean to knock it over."

"So it was an accident. I did notice that you were running before it happened. Could that have been why you fell?"

"Maybe."

"When kids run in the classroom, accidents often happen. That's why our rule says to be safe. What do you think you could do to help?"

"I don't know."

"Maybe you could help stack up the blocks so Michelle can build again."

Jacob nods and the teacher walks back with him to the block area. Michelle lets Jacob help gather and stack the scattered blocks. She declines his offer to help rebuild her structure.

Here are some key differences between the two approaches:

	Punishment	**Logical Consequences**
Intention	To ensure compliance by using external controls that make the child feel ashamed or bad in other ways	To help children recognize the effects of their actions and develop internal controls
Underlying belief	Children will do better only because they fear punishment and will seek to avoid it	Children want to do better and can do better with reflection and practice
Teacher's approach and tone	Reacts automatically with little thought; voice is angry and punitive	Gathers more information before reacting; voice is calm and matter-of-fact
Nature of the consequence	Not related to the behavior or the damage done; not reasonable for the child to do	Related to the behavior and helps fix the damage done; reasonable for the child to do
Message to the child	The child is the problem	The damage done, not the child, is the problem
Long-term effect on the child	Encourages child to use evasion and deception in the future	Helps child know what to do next time

Three types of logical consequences

There are three basic types of logical consequences: "You break it, you fix it," loss of privilege, and time-out. While there are significant variations in what each looks like at different grade levels, generally all logical consequences fall within one of these categories.

"You break it, you fix it"

This is as simple and clear as it sounds. If children break something or make a mess, whether intentionally or not, the teacher helps them take responsibility for fixing it or cleaning it up. If you jiggle the table and make someone mess up her work, you help her do it over again. If you knock someone down on the playing field, you help him up, ask if he's okay, and go with him to the first aid office if needed.

When Students Break the Rules

Apology of action: A special kind of "you break it, you fix it"

"You break it, you fix it" can be used to mend emotional messes as well as physical messes. For emotional messes, students can use apology of action, in which they do something, beyond saying "I'm sorry," to take responsibility for the hurt that their words or actions have caused.

This strategy comes from the recognition that a simple "I'm sorry" is often not enough to help people truly feel better when they've been wronged. So, when a child wrongs another, the child who was wronged asks for an apology that involves some action beyond a verbal "I'm sorry." Thus when second grader Jules calls Sandra a name, the two children may decide that an appropriate apology of action would be for Jules to make a list of things she likes about Sandra or things that Sandra does well. In an older grade, an appropriate apology of action for lying about someone might be to tell the truth about the person to the class.

One of the greatest benefits of apology of action is that it takes the teacher out of the role of judge and juror in conflicts between children. When a student complains to the teacher that "Adriana said I was a liar" or "Bryan ruined my picture" or "Aldi pushed me on the playground," the teacher can respond by saying, "How about asking for an apology of action?" rather than jumping into the middle of the conflict.

Keep in mind, however, that if apology of action is to work well, teachers need to introduce it to children carefully, give students lots of practice in it, and closely monitor its use throughout the year. How this is done differs according to the children's age (in the following chapters, teachers at different grade levels describe the process they use). But in every grade, teachers find that it's most effective to wait a bit into the school year, to give children a chance to build a sense of community and trust, before introducing this strategy.

Loss of privilege

Most, if not all, things in school can be viewed as a privilege. It's a privilege to participate in Morning Meeting, to use the materials in the room, to be part of a reading group. And with each of these privileges comes important responsibilities. If a child is not using these privileges responsibly, then a logical consequence would be to take away that privilege *temporarily,* perhaps for a class period or a day.

For example, if a student consistently makes snide remarks during Morning Meeting, s/he may be told to sit out of the meeting for a day. If a student habitually comes to reading group unprepared, the student may be told to read alone for a day or two until s/he comes up with a plan for arriving at the group ready to contribute.

The purpose of removing a privilege is not to punish the child, but to help the child understand the connection between privileges and responsibilities. The message is "We want you to be part of our meeting. But being part of the meeting means being supportive of everyone in it. When you make negative remarks, it's hard for others to do their best learning." Or, "When you come unprepared, it makes it hard for everyone in the group to do their best, including you."

Once the child shows s/he is ready to handle the responsibility, it's important to give the privilege back. The goal is for children to show that they can be responsible, not to suffer for being irresponsible. Through words and actions, a teacher demonstrates faith in children's ability to learn responsibility.

Time-out

This is a strategy used to help children learn self-control. A child who is disrupting the work of the group is asked to leave for a minute or two. During this time, the child is expected to regain self-control so s/he can come back to the group and participate in a positive way. In some cases, children can decide themselves to go to the time-out spot because they are losing control and need to leave the scene for a while to regain composure.

In the following chapters, two teachers show in detail how one might introduce and use time-out in different grades. However, because time-out is so often misunderstood, here are some immediate guidelines for using this strategy:

Explain the purpose

Because children may have experienced punitive uses of time-out, it's important that teachers explain clearly that the purpose of time-out in this classroom is to give them a chance to calm down and regain self-control, not to show that they are "bad." It's important to let children know that after they calm down, they will be welcomed back into the group. Letting children know that sometimes they might decide for themselves when they need a time-out can also help remove the stigma surrounding it.

Consider what to call it

Many teachers feel that the term "time-out" carries such negative connotations that they prefer to call this strategy "take a break" or "rest stop." Children, especially in the older grades, may enjoy helping to come up with an appropriate term to use.

Choose a good spot

There should be one or two designated time-out places in the room—perhaps a chair, a cushion, or a beanbag. The spot should be neither isolated nor in the thick of activity. This gives children the separation they need in order to calm down, yet allows them to keep track of what's going on in the classroom so that they can join in the work when they come back. To keep the child safe, the teacher needs to be able to see the time-out area from anywhere in the room.

As students move into middle school, they may no longer require a designated place for time-out. Able to understand that the idea is to cool down, they generally can choose an appropriate place to go for this purpose and appreciate being given this flexibility.

Explicitly teach time-out procedures

This means talking about, modeling, and letting students practice how to do time-out. Older students will need less practice but will like sharing ideas for pulling themselves together, such as looking at a poster, taking deep breaths, writing in a journal, and squeezing a stress ball.

For children of all ages, be sure this teaching covers the following:

- Going to the time-out spot quickly without saying anything, making gestures, or stopping along the way

- Doing whatever it takes to regain self-control as long as it's quiet and doesn't distract the class

- Coming back from time-out quietly and rejoining the work of the group

Remember also to teach the rest of the class what to do when a classmate needs to go to time-out. Talk about, model, and let children practice leaving the classmate alone, going on with the classroom activity as usual, and welcoming the classmate back when s/he returns.

Clarify who decides when the child should return

The ultimate goal is for children to be able to tell when they're in control and ready to return. Often, however, the teacher judges that a particular class isn't ready for the responsibility and retains the decision making. If the teacher lets the children decide, but a child comes back from time-out before having regained control or lingers longer than necessary, the teacher can take over the decision for that child the next time. Whatever the case, it's important to make it clear to children who decides when they can return.

Use time-out just as a child is beginning to lose control

Don't wait until the behavior has escalated and the child has lost face with peers. Using time-out early helps preserve children's relationships and your own feelings of empathy toward students. It can be tough, for example, to feel empathy when a child has become abusive. If a child has progressed to being fully out of control, you need another strategy, perhaps one that involves the principal, a guidance counselor, or other support staff.

Always use a calm, quiet voice to tell a child to go to time-out

Even better, also establish a visual signal to give this direction when possible. This avoids drawing attention to the child.

Never enter into a negotiation in the moment

An important purpose of time-out is to allow the work of the group to go on when a student is acting out. Discussing the situation with the student will only disrupt the group further. Moreover, the student is usually not in a frame of mind at the moment to discuss the situation reasonably. However, in introducing time-out, assure students that they can always talk with you about the situation later.

Use time-out democratically

At one point or another, almost all children in a classroom lose their cool and can use a method to collect themselves. It's important that students see that time-out is used for everyone and not just the same two or three children.

Have a system for time-out in another room

Many teachers set up a "buddy teacher" system for times when a student refuses to go to time-out, continues to be disruptive in time-out, or continues to be disruptive after a time-out. In those cases, the teacher has the child take a time-out in the buddy teacher's room. This prevents the situation from escalating into a power struggle and allows the teacher to go on teaching the class. (See Chapter 7 for more about the use of buddy teachers.)

When Students Break the Rules

Remember that time-out does not work for all children

No matter how carefully you introduce time-out and how skillfully you use it, there will always be some children for whom it doesn't work. If you find yourself sending a child over and over to time-out without seeing any improvement in behavior, or if a child crumbles or becomes extremely distraught at even one use of time-out, more than likely the child needs a different strategy. Seek help from colleagues, parents, and counselors, and consider other problem-solving strategies. (See Appendix A for a summary of three such strategies and resources for learning more about them.)

Introducing logical consequences to students

Why is it sometimes hard to follow the rules?
What are the hardest rules to follow? What makes them hard to follow?
What are the easiest rules to follow?
What's an example of a time you didn't follow the rules?
How do you feel when you're not following the rules?
How do you feel when you are following the rules?

These are some of the questions a teacher might ask students in opening a conversation about logical consequences. In these conversations, it's important to convey the following messages:

- We are all working together on learning to follow the rules.

- Following the rules takes lots of practice.

- Everyone makes mistakes. We all forget or choose not to follow rules from time to time.

- When you forget or choose not to follow a rule, it's my job to help you fix the problems that resulted and help you learn to do better next time.

Carefully define the term "logical consequence" if you use it

In introducing the concept of logical consequences to students, some teachers use the term "logical consequence"; others don't. If teachers do use the term, it's important that they define it as a way to solve problems and learn. This helps take away the punitive ring that the term may have.

**Chapter
Three**

When is taking away recess a logical consequence?

Children need outdoor play much like they need food and sleep. That's why teachers should only take away short periods of recess, if at all.

Taking away recess is a logical consequence only when:

- The misbehavior took place during recess or immediately preceding recess (for example, not getting ready for recess when asked to)

- The consequence does not present a hardship for the teacher (does not require the teacher to give up prep time or miss a team meeting, for example, to stay in the classroom with a child)

Taking away recess is not a logical consequence when:

- It's used repeatedly

- It's used for behavior not connected to recess

- It creates a hardship for the child that will make it more difficult for her/him to succeed

- It creates a hardship for the teacher

For example, a teacher might begin by saying, "We're all working on following our rules. Let's think for a minute about what happens when we follow our rules." The teacher might give some specific examples of rule following (perhaps letting everyone join an activity, working hard with partners even if they're not your best friends, and cleaning the paint brushes carefully after using them), and talk with children about the positive consequences of these actions.

Next, the teacher might say, "In learning to live by our rules, we'll all make mistakes from time to time. Sometimes we might forget a rule, sometimes we might choose not to follow one. What happens when we don't follow a rule—for example, the rules we just talked about?" The teacher now guides children in thinking about the possible problems that might result, including safety risks, hurt feelings, work left undone, and others' inability to do their work.

When Students Break the Rules

"In our classroom," the teacher might continue, "when students don't follow a rule, it'll be my job to help them fix the problems that happen and to learn to follow the rule next time. One way I'll be doing that is by using something called logical consequences." In this way, the teacher casts "logical consequences" in an objective light, removing the connotation of shame and punishment that children may associate with that term.

Give examples of logical consequences

Whether or not teachers use the term "logical consequences" with students, what's important is that they give examples of logical consequences. A teacher might say, for instance, "A student is running in the classroom and accidentally knocks over another student's diorama. If that happens, I might tell that child to help repair the damage to the diorama."

Or the teacher might say, "If we're using the staplers for an art project and someone is using a stapler in an unsafe way, a logical consequence would be for that person to stop using the stapler for the rest of the day. The person could try again the next day, maybe with the teacher watching to help them use it safely."

By giving several such examples, the teacher lets students know ahead of time what sorts of things will happen when they break the rules. Children will feel more comfortable and assured when they have this specific information. They'll know that their teacher expects them to live by the rules, and that if they don't, the teacher will help them to stay safe physically and emotionally and learn to do better next time. Without these examples from teachers, many students will feel anxious and uncertain. Some will constantly test the boundaries in search of clarity. Others will withdraw in fear.

The teacher decides on logical consequences

When introducing logical consequences, a teacher may, for the purpose of helping children understand the intention and characteristics of this way of handling rule breaking, ask students to come up with some consequences that might be appropriate for various hypothetical situations. In real rule-breaking situations, however, the teacher is in charge of deciding on the consequence. (The exception, of course, is in the case of apology of action, where one child requests an action from another child.) Unlike the constructing of rules with students, choosing a logical consequence is not a collaborative process. The strategy is something for teachers to use.

The reason for not asking children to help decide on logical consequences is that most elementary and middle school students have a tremendously difficult time distinguishing between logical consequences and punishments. Asked to decide on a logical consequence, students are likely to quickly take on the role of judge or juror of their peers, doling out harsh punishments and judgments. Deciding on logical consequences for other students is not a position elementary and middle grade students should ever be in. This is best left to the teacher, who has the knowledge and judgment necessary to make these complex decisions.

Chapter Three

The challenge of choosing a logical consequence in the moment

Many teachers struggle with choosing a logical consequence in the moment. They agree with the concepts and want to start using the strategy consistently in the classroom, but they just can't think of an appropriate logical consequence in the moment. Often they ask if there could be a chart that lists certain behaviors and what the logical consequence would be for each behavior.

The reason that such a chart isn't likely to work is because every situation has its own set of unique circumstances. A strategy that's right for one child could be completely wrong for another. Or a consequence that's logical in one situation could be completely illogical in another.

Better than a chart are guidelines for the use of logical consequences. Here are two broad guidelines:

If it doesn't seem obvious, it's probably not logical

The key is to look at each situation and to ask yourself, "What's the problem here? Hurt feelings? A safety issue? Distraction from work? Disturbing others? How can I stop the problematic action? And given what I know about this child and these circumstances, how can I help this child see and fix the problem?"

If the consequence doesn't become obvious after you think about it for a few minutes, then it's quite likely that the situation requires something other than a logical consequence. It's also possible that in that particular situation, no imposed consequence is needed. If a child forgets to get a permission form signed and therefore cannot participate in a field trip or a photo-taking session, not being able to take part is itself a significant enough consequence that it no doubt teaches the child a great deal about taking responsibility. In that case, there's no need for the teacher to impose a further consequence.

Be aware of your feelings of anger and frustration

When Students Break the Rules

There are times when we get so angry and frustrated that we can't think clearly enough to determine a logical consequence. In times like these, when emotions obscure our logic, the best thing is to take time to cool off before deciding on a response.

You might set up a time to talk with the child after lunch, after recess, or at some later point in the day. Keep in mind, however, that this waiting time can be a great source of anxiety for some children. If you think this might be the case for a particular child, keep the cool-off period as short as possible.

Many teachers recognize that during these times of anger and frustration, they themselves need a time-out. They may call on an assistant or a colleague to be with their class for a few minutes while they take a walk down the hall. If this isn't possible, they might change the class activity so that students are working independently. The teacher can then sit quietly at her/his desk for a few minutes.

Try, try again

Responding to rule breaking is challenging, perhaps one of the most challenging aspects of teaching. Even the most experienced teachers make mistakes. But the most experienced teachers will also be the first to say that teachers must allow themselves to make mistakes, just as they allow students to make them. And just as we tell our students—without shaming them—to "try, try again," we must allow ourselves to try again without self-defeating judgments, but with the spirit of learning to do it better next time. As Dreikurs points out, it's not the mistake, but what one does about it, that's important. In time, mistakes *will* give way to successes.

Additional tips for the use of logical consequences

The following tips, compiled by primary teacher Deborah Porter, come from various teachers who have used the approach to discipline described in this book. In Chapter 4, Deborah expands on these tips, showing how they've played out in her K–2 classrooms.

First, stop the behavior

This sounds obvious, but so often teachers skip this step, going immediately to issuing a logical consequence. Children need to hear the words "Stop now" to break the momentum of their running, yelling, teasing, etc., and change course.

Know the child

The same rule-breaking behavior may demand very different logical consequences with different children, since what's motivating each child and what each child understands determine what s/he needs to learn and what problem needs to be fixed. The point is never to apply consequences uniformly, but to understand where each child is coming from and choose a consequence that makes sense for that child.

Have pre-set consequences for certain situations

The "know the child" tip notwithstanding, there are times—particularly when safety is a concern—when a preset response is justified. A teacher might decide that any child who runs in the halls, for example, would, for a period of time, have to be accompanied when leaving the classroom. Each teacher should decide what situations require such non-negotiable, pre-set consequences.

Avoid lecturing

When giving students a logical consequence, the less said the better. Let the consequence do the job. If the consequence is well chosen, it will be

Chapter Three

more powerful than any teacher words. Additional explanations can easily undermine that power and add to any classroom disruption that the child's behavior may have caused.

Rely on colleagues for help

Beyond setting up a buddy teacher system (see Chapter 7 for details), there are informal ways for teachers to get crucial support from each other. If the same behavior problem keeps showing up in your classroom or if a particular child makes you especially angry or frustrated, talk with colleagues about it. Often, good solutions emerge from the collective experience and wisdom of teachers and staff.

When Students Break the Rules

Follow through with the consequence you choose

Children, and often their families, may protest the logical consequences we choose. But as long as the consequences are relevant, realistic, and respectful, it's important that we stand firmly by them. Otherwise, our credibility suffers, as does the children's faith in their ability to meet our high standards.

Have a re-entry check-in or conversation if a child must leave the room

If the logical consequence involves the child leaving the room—to go to a buddy teacher's room or to the principal's office, for example—it's crucial that the teacher have a conversation with the child before bringing the child back into the classroom. The conversation will be about what happened, what needs to be done now, and how to prevent similar situations in the future. Taking the time to do this step shows the child that s/he is still liked and respected, that relationships are intact. And it reassures the teacher that the child is ready to come back to the class.

Works Cited

Dreikurs, Rudolf, Floy C. Pepper, and Bernice Bronia Grunwald. 1982. *Maintaining Sanity in the Classroom: Classroom Management Techniques*. Second edition. Philadelphia: Taylor & Francis, Inc.

Deci, Edward L., with Richard Flaste. 1995. *Why We Do What We Do*. New York: Penguin Books.

Chapter Three

Chapter Four

BY DEBORAH PORTER

I was at the bakery counter in the supermarket one day, when a little girl came skipping up waving a dollar bill.

"My Grandma gave me a dollar to buy donut holes," she proclaimed to the clerk. "How many holes can I get for a dollar?"

The woman behind the counter told her that she could get six.

"Six! That's a lot," the girl replied. Then, without missing a beat, she said, "If I had two dollars I could get twelve of them!"

"Yep," the store clerk replied. "Donut holes are six for sixty-nine cents."

"Oh, but I only have a dollar," the girl said, looking slightly confused.

The clerk explained that sixty-nine cents was less than a dollar and that she would get six holes and some change back.

In her excitement, the girl danced to her grandmother to tell her the good news. Then she danced back to place her order, keeping careful count as she picked out the kind of donut holes she wanted. Then once again to the grandmother to report what she had decided on, and back one last time to pay her dollar.

When the girl finally got both her change and the donut holes, she could hardly contain her excitement. As she departed she exclaimed with great enthusiasm, "You don't need to worry about me returning these donuts. I'm going to love them!"

The Dance of Learning

As I watched this little girl's dance of excitement, I thought about how closely it matched what might have been going on in her mind as she moved back and forth between knowing and confusion, between the joy of making your way in the world and bafflement at how something would actually work out.

Every day in the classroom, I feel as if the children and I do this little dance: I, as I try to understand each child and what it is s/he most needs; and the children, as they learn new concepts, fitting them together with what they already know about the world. The trick of the dance is to hop back and forth between confusion and knowing with light, quick steps so that we are neither flying too fast, trying to absorb too much—nor stuck in place, refusing to evolve in the face of new information.

Grades K–2

Doing this dance of learning requires us to take risks, to be willing to give things a try even though we know there is the possibility of failure. When I think of classroom practices around rules, I think always of supporting children's risk taking. Creating and living the rules well allows children to feel safe about taking risks, and when children feel safe about taking risks, the very quality of their learning goes up.

But how can we find time to teach rules, or any social curriculum, when we're already straining to cover all the academics? I believe it's never a matter of choosing between the academic and the social curriculum. Rather, it's a matter of addressing the social *so that* we can address the academic, and addressing the academic *so that* we can address the social. Children need to know how to take turns, listen, choose respectful words, and use appropriate body language when working together on math problems or doing a group science experiment. They need to know how to read, add and subtract, make charts, and use other academic skills to decide who gets to take the lunch counts this week or how four people can share the paints fairly. If we don't take the time to teach the social curriculum, the academic curriculum is diminished.

Just as it's impossible to separate the social from the academic, it is not easy to speak of rules without considering all the elements of the entire classroom. A commitment to making rules work is embedded in everything that gives rise to positive community life: friendship, collaboration, meaningful work, growth and learning, mental well-being, and physical health and safety. And so we teach rules as part of creating a classroom where every child can learn at his/her best.

In an even larger sense, we are also teaching for the time when we will not be there. The authority of our position rests on this reach beyond the time when students are in our classrooms and our schools. We must therefore use techniques that give children the power to think and act ethically for themselves. Just as we teach children to read so that they might be able to participate in a literate world when they are grown, so too, we must teach children to care for themselves and others so that they might later participate in a democratic society.

Before School Starts

August: My hopes and dreams begin to take shape

The rule-creation process described in this book begins with children articulating their hopes and dreams for the year. But like the children, I, too, need to begin my year by formulating my hopes and dreams. Along about mid-August, I start to put my classroom in order, hoping to find the perfect way to arrange it. I begin by designing on paper what I think will accommodate the range of activities we will be doing and the diversity of children that will make up this year's class. Then, after days of pushing furniture around, I usually hit a frustration point when nothing seems to fit together.

Chapter Four

Always, it is only then that I can suddenly see exactly how the room will fit together. It inevitably is not anything like my original plan, but it's a setup that I feel happy with.

This process of setting up the room always gets me thinking about the previous year, about the challenges and the failures as well as the wonderful successes. As I stack the wooden blocks, my hands remember the fancy buildings that stood here just a few months before. As I arrange the meeting area, my mind dwells on Owen and his struggle to play games without getting mad. As I put books out on display, I read again the colorful books we made: *Old Mother Witch* and *The Big Heath Snow*. As I put the cubbies out to be labeled, I wonder about the children that will make up my class this year.

Each year the physical task of arranging the room finally allows my mind to refocus on the day-to-day life of the classroom, on the children, and on the work we do together. This is when I at last let go of the year before, whether it feels finished or not, and begin to get excited about the year ahead. As I put the final touches on the room, I dream of what the year might look like. I see children working in all the areas of the room, writing stories, painting pictures, and building grand structures or complicated machines. I see them reading books, playing games, and solving problems together. The room is filled with a busy hum, with friendly exchanges and earnest collaboration. This is when my own hopes and dreams begin to take shape.

**My biggest hope: "I would like us to
do fewer things but do them well."**

As I write this, I am in my twenty-eighth year of teaching. I have seen so many changes in these twenty-eight years, both in my own teaching and in the realm of public education itself. I've lived through various educational movements, each with its pluses and minuses, each requiring accommodation and training, each adding to the complexity of our educational institutions.

Grades K–2

Amid all the demands that society places on teachers' work, beginning each year with my own hopes and dreams has become an important way for me to maintain my own clarity and conviction about my work. One year, my hope was to be able to include a severely disabled child as a full, integral member of the classroom. Another year it was to work more with other teachers. Yet another year it was to focus on literacy routines that would give children the skills they needed while helping them develop their own interests and ideas. This year, my biggest hope is that the children and I will do fewer things but do them well.

I teach in a building that is beautifully designed. One of its special features is that it feels bigger on the inside than it looks from the outside. I would like our work to be like our building, making us bigger on the inside. I want to avoid filling the day with just the demands and details of someone else's agenda. I want to have our own sacred class time where children have the leisure to explore, share, discuss, and work together.

I know from experience that this will require me to organize and integrate the curriculum in a way that weaves the much needed skill work into interesting and engaging content areas. I'll plan on carving out one hour each day that the children and I can count on as "our" work time. As schedules are made, I will keep this time clear so that it is possible for us to do in-depth projects.

As the children begin to express their own hopes and dreams, I will be excited to let them know that I, too, have a hope for the year: that the class will be able to do projects together. And as we begin to make the rules, not only will I already have a vision in my mind of what I'll have to do to allow for these projects, but we as a class will think together about what all of us will need to do to allow for them.

**The first family conference:
Families share their hopes and dreams for the year**

Once the room is set up and before school starts, it is time to invite the children and their parents in for a tour. Each family comes for a thirty- to forty-minute visit. These visits are also an opportunity for me to find out parents' hopes for their children in the coming year. Before the visits, I send out a query to help parents formulate their hopes, and they bring the completed sheet with them to the visit. (See sample query.) If parents find filling out the written form intimidating or simply haven't had a chance to fill it out, we do it together during the visit. The information on the sheet helps to focus our conversation on what is most important to parents.

In the early grades, parent goals are often the simple, age-old ones: for kindergartners, to enjoy school and make friends; for first graders, to learn to read; and for second graders, to use their skills to learn about a broader world.

Often parents come with their hopes *and* fears, and leave after the conversation with the sense of possibility that each new school year brings. Of course it is not always that easy to melt away parent concerns, and so I see these conferences as just a beginning, a way to create an important common ground for our shared work ahead.

Chapter Four

Parent Query: First Planning Conference

Name of parent(s): _____

Name of student: _____

Please answer the following questions to help us plan your child's program:

1. What do you feel will be most important for your child in school this year?

2. In what ways would you like to see your child grow? Do you have any concerns about your child's social skills or emotional development?

3. In what ways or areas would you like to see your child grow academically?

Helping families share their expertise

When I invite families into a conversation about the coming year, I also ask for their input as the experts on their children. I ask about the child's special interests, friendships, strengths, how the child tends to handle difficult challenges, and the like.

From the very beginning of the year on, I want to hear from parents what they know about their children so that I can better teach the children. Over the years I have found that though I don't always see the children in the same way as the parents do or always agree with the parents' priorities, this first conference is an important beginning to our working together in a constructive way.

The First Days of School

Grades K–2

I always seem to wake up with a start on the first day of school. It's no wonder. This business of dreaming and formulating hopes and dreams helps to clarify what I and children's families most want, but it is, after all, only the beginning and there is still hard work to be done. All the routines and rules have yet to be established. I know that simply having all the children come and sit in a circle can be a challenge.

Establishing routines

It takes a few weeks for young children to understand and adjust to school life, even if they've been in school before. There's so much they need to learn. There are lunch routines, work routines, fire drills, playground routines, meeting routines, bathroom routines. During the early weeks of school, all of these need to be carefully taught and practiced.

I introduce many of the routines before we begin the work of creating rules because the routines allow children to navigate the day with a sense of order, purpose, and ease. These beginning routines create the safety and boundaries the children need in order to do the focused talking and thinking necessary in creating meaningful rules.

I also find that young children need to have at least a rudimentary understanding of what their new classroom and school year will be like before they can have meaningful thoughts about hopes and dreams or the creation of rules. The way I introduce and reinforce the routines gives the children a context to draw upon in thinking about both what might be in store for the year, and what rules might be necessary.

Guidelines for meetings in a K–1 classroom

Chapter Four

I create the routines

Although I involve the children in creating many aspects of the curriculum and the classroom, I create the routines myself. Empowering children is important, but we need to understand our own responsibilities as the adult in charge. In order to empower children effectively, we have to be clear about the areas we are not willing to let go of, and routines that ensure the smooth running of the day for everyone is one such area.

This is not to say that we shouldn't help children understand the reasons behind the routines. The reasons for raising your hand to talk, walking in a line through the halls, or sitting in a circle in meetings are not obvious to young children who are still egocentric in their thinking.

Sometimes I get students thinking about the reason for a routine by asking questions. "Why do you think we need to line up to get our lunch?" or "Why do we sit in a circle at meeting?" Other times I explicitly tell children the reason for a routine. "Everybody's ideas are important. When we take turns talking, we have a chance to hear all ideas."

I have also found that children are enthralled with the idea of being connected to children everywhere. When I teach them about raising their hand to speak, for instance, I talk not only about wanting to hear everyone's idea, but also about children all over the country learning to raise their hand to talk, just as they're doing. Suddenly children become more interested in raising their hand.

Modeling and practicing until routines are automatic

Grades K–2

Because we can't assume that children will know what a routine should look and feel like, modeling is an indispensable step. I might ask, "Who can show me a safe way to line up for lunch?" or "Who can show me a quiet way to walk down the hall?" Everyone who wants to demonstrate gets a turn.

Recently I watched a class of children modeling how they might listen to someone who was sharing. One by one, the children had a chance to show how they would listen. Their faces and their bodies gave the message, "I get it. I can do this. I understand." I could see them almost puff up while the rest of the class watched with rapt attention. It was evident that by simply acting out respectful ways of behaving, the children not only understood what respectful behavior meant, but actually felt respectful.

The next step after modeling routines is to practice them consciously until they become automatic. I say "consciously" because getting a routine down solid is a gradual process that requires us to stop and reflect as a group, deliberately and repeatedly, on how we are doing. We think together about how well we circled up during recess this past week, about whether we're better at stopping and looking at the teacher when we hear the chime signal, about whether there seems to be a new problem in the art cleanup routine. This conscious focusing on our progress helps children remember the importance of routines, identify rough spots, and solve problems together.

Breaking down the routines: Walking through the halls

Early in the process of learning routines, I help the children by giving them more directions and breaking down complex routines into manageable parts.

For instance, during the first week of school, before we walk through the hall I remind the children with words and a gesture that others are working, so they need to "zip up their mouth and tell their feet to walk." I then lead them along in an exaggerated tiptoe to where we are going, frequently stopping to give the thumbs-up signal to let them know they're doing a great job. If the children become noisy, we stop until everyone is quiet again.

The next week, I might only make the "zip up our mouth" gesture before we begin, stopping the line again if children forget to walk quietly.

Once this step is going smoothly, I give children the challenge of walking on their own. At first I go halfway down the hall and tell them to see if they can bring the line all by themselves to where I am standing. I make sure they will be successful by going only as far as I know they can manage. I then give a thumbs-up signal and go a little farther down the hall so that they can do it again. When this is going well, I go all the way down the hall. Eventually I go out of sight.

When students are able to walk quietly in the halls without me, I know I can walk at the end of the line, and the children will know what to do. Of course they will still forget sometimes, but they understand the expectations, so getting back on track will be all the easier.

This gradual letting go of control on my part and placing it the hands of the children is an underlying goal of all my teaching. Ultimately I want the children to be independent learners in a social setting.

The Quiet Place

In addition to establishing basic classroom routines such as getting quiet at the quiet signal, raising a hand to speak during meetings, circling up, and walking in a line down the hall, we need to give children a structure for comforting themselves when they're upset. In my classroom, there is a "Quiet Place" for this purpose. This is in addition to the time-out space, which I'll discuss later in this chapter. Based on ideas in Jane Nelsen's book *Positive Discipline in the Classroom,* the Quiet Place is a cozy place in the room where children can go voluntarily to be alone and help themselves feel better. (Nelsen, Lott, and Glenn 2000)

I introduce the Quiet Place during the first week of school. As with the routines, I introduce it before we begin working on the rules because when children see that their own emotional needs will be considered, they are freer to think about the issue of classroom rules.

I never insist that a child go to the Quiet Place, but I frequently suggest it. The spot is especially useful to kindergartners making the transition from home to school and struggling with separation anxiety during the early weeks of school.

Alison, a young five-year-old, had a particularly hard time saying goodbye to her dad. After going through all the usual routines—blowing a kiss, waving goodbye at the window, drawing a picture for her dad—Alison was still distressed. Though upset, she knew what to do. She grabbed her stuffed animal and made a beeline to the Quiet Place. After ten minutes of cuddling with her stuffy and looking at a book, she joined the group, happily and on her own. Not that Alison wasn't sad the next day when her dad left; but she had a way to help herself feel better rather than relying on me to try to comfort her.

Grades K–2

The "Quiet Place" in Deborah Porter's K–1 classroom

The room itself

Another important ingredient in developing community and self-control is the room itself. I set up the room to invite interaction among classmates, with tables instead of desks to work at. Eventually, the room will be equipped with a wide range of materials that encourage children to experiment and be creative.

But on the first day of school, there are only a few familiar materials out. Then, in the next few weeks, I'll carefully introduce new materials one by one, guiding children to explore the materials actively and share their discoveries with each other.

My goal in starting with a nearly empty room, however, is not just for the sake of introducing materials. It is also because right from the beginning I want to be able to say yes to the children more than I say no. If the room is full of materials that the children want to use but are not yet able to manage, the first few weeks of school will be one long series of *nos:*

"No, you can't knock down your building."

"Don't splatter the paint."

"No, you can't climb that high."

"No, the pattern blocks are not for catapulting."

The refrain will go on and on, punctuating every activity and framing all interactions in the negative. Seeing school as a place of restriction before one is able to see it as a place of possibilities is counter to the active participation that I want to encourage in all children.

Chapter Four

Creating the Rules

Beginning the process: "Why do we come to school?"

It is in a refrain of yes that we begin the conversations that will help us frame the rules for the classroom. I begin by asking the children, "Why do we come to school?" Sometimes the first response is "You don't know?" But after some thought, children begin to articulate what they think:

"To learn things."

"To get better at making friends."

"To learn the things you need to learn to be a grown up."

"To have fun. Fun! Fun! Fun!"

"Yeah, because you learn better when things are fun."

"So if you come to school to learn things, make friends, and have fun, what do you think our schoolwork will be this year?" I ask. Hands wave madly. I write each child's idea on easel chart paper:

"I think we will learn to read."

"I know how to read. I think I will read more books."

"We will make new friends."

"I think we will learn how to write."

"We might write stories or about stuff."

"We will get to know things."

"Yeah, like science things."

Grades K–2

Soon, I see that we have exhausted most ideas and the children are getting antsy, so I stop this preliminary rule session to go on to other things. I don't want to rush such important work. The purpose of this first session is to set the context for children to think about what their hopes and dreams for the year are. I have found that young children are more thoughtful in this process if they understand precisely what we mean by "schoolwork."

Listing our hopes and dreams:
"Of all these things, what are you most hoping to do this year?"

The next day, we come back to our list of different kinds of schoolwork and reread it to see if we want to add anything. I then ask the children, "Of all these things, what are you most hoping you will get to do this year?" I tell the children to think about the question for a minute before they answer. We then go around the circle so everyone has a turn giving an answer. Those who are not ready to give an answer can simply pass for the moment. We will come back to them.

"I hope I get to build lots of different things."

"I hope I get to build giant snap cubes things."

"I hope to do puzzles."

"I hope to play on the computer."

And so forth.

Interestingly, this list of personal hopes tends to be more concrete and simpler than the children's fairly abstract ideas of what "schoolwork" might be. That's okay. It's a reflection of where children this age are in their thinking.

This list of most important hopes is a rough draft that we will come back to several times. I want the children to think carefully about this question, and as is true for all of us, their first idea is not always what they ultimately want to stick with.

Parts of a hopes and dreams display in a first grade classroom

**Chapter
Four**

Grades K–2

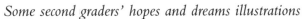

Some second graders' hopes and dreams illustrations

Brainstorming for rules:

"What rules do you think we'll need so that everyone can learn?"

The next day we begin again by rereading the list of everyone's hopes. I then say to the class, "It is important that we all get to do the things we really want to do this year. If we want to get to all our schoolwork and to our own hopes and dreams, what rules do you think we will need? What will make our classroom a safe and friendly place where everyone can learn?"

Again I record everyone's ideas:

"I think we should keep everything nice and beautiful."

"You should work hard and do your best."

"You shouldn't knock anything down."

"Fix up your mistakes."

"Don't be mean."

"You shouldn't hit."

"What about hurting kids in other ways?" I ask.

"Yeah, you shouldn't hurt anyone."

"Treat others the way you want to be treated. That's the … um … What is it?"

"The Golden Rule?" I help out with terminology.

"Yeah, the Golden Rule."

"Stay in your own space."

"Do you mean at meeting?" I ask.

"Yeah, at meeting."

"What about at other times, like if you were at a table drawing?"

"Well yeah, I guess at all times."

Seeing that the children are out of ideas for now, I tell them that this list is also a rough draft and that we will look at it again later to make sure we have everything.

Grouping the rules: Place, self, each other

That night, I look over the list of rules. At the bottom of the list I write "place," "self," and "each other" in three different colors. The next day the class looks at the list again. I have three markers that match the colors of the words at the bottom of the chart.

If an idea for a rule was originally phrased in a negative way, I now ask the children to think about how to phrase it in a positive way.

For example, one of the ideas was "Don't be mean":

"If we aren't going to be mean, what will we do if we are really mad?" I ask. "Nice, you have take care in a nice way."

"Well, what about when you have a problem with someone? Is there a way you should solve the problem?"

"You gotta solve a problem in a nice way."

This turning the negative into a positive is a critical step. So often we assume that if we say what *not* to do, everyone will know what *to* do. But that's not necessarily the case, even for adults. Stating a rule in the positive gives us all a road map to follow as we negotiate the many twists and turns of the day.

After reading through the rules, I tell the children that I notice that all the rules they came up with fit into three different and important categories. I point to the words "place," "self," and "each other" at the bottom of the chart. "Let's see if I'm right."

Grades K–2

We read the ideas on the chart together and decide which category each idea fits into. As we decide, I bracket the idea in the color that matches the category. When we're done, I ask the children if there is a way to say a rule that covers all the ideas in each category. That way, there will be fewer ideas, and that will make them easier to remember, I explain.

Of course, the "place" category is the easiest because there is only one idea in that category. So "Keep everything looking nice and beautiful" is the rule for that category.

We then look at the category about how to treat each other. We decide that if you are treating someone the way you want to be treated, then you would be nice to others and solve problems in a nice way. So that category is easily consolidated. The rule is "Treat others the way you want to be treated."

The last category about how to treat yourself is a little harder. The children look confused about how to consolidate all the ideas in this category into one sentence. I ask them, "If we just said 'Take care of yourself,' would all the ideas fit into that sentence?" They looked doubtful, so I say, "Well, let's try." We then go through each idea to see if it fits the sentence. When everyone is satisfied that all the ideas do, we adopt "Take care of yourself" as a rule.

The final list: The teacher adds a rule

As we read over the final draft of our rules, I tell the class that I have one more rule that I, as the teacher, think it's important to have. I tell them it's a rule that I learned from a student in my class several years ago, a rule I have never forgotten.

"Who in our room should be able to play and learn?" I ask these children. They stare at me as if I had just asked the most obvious question in the world.

"Everyone gets to!" one child exclaims.

"I think so, too!" I declare. "So the rule I want to add is 'Everyone gets to play and learn.' What do you think?"

Several heads nod, and one student remarks, "School wouldn't be fun if you didn't get to play."

"And you gotta learn because if you don't, when you grow up you won't know how to do stuff," adds another.

I add the last rule to our list. We end this meeting by reading over our final rules. From the wiggly bodies and hungry looks, I can tell it's time to stop and have a snack.

"Publishing" the rules

The next step in this process is to "publish" our work. In this case, "publishing" means making a display of the final rules in a prominent place in the room so that we can refer to them throughout the year. This is usually the children's first introduction to the idea of publishing their work, so I emphasize working hard to make the display beautiful.

I make sure the display reflects the children's work. Sometimes I come up with the basic design; sometimes it's a combination of their ideas and mine. But the artwork and the writing are done by the students. And because this is a "publication," I tell students they have to use correct spelling. I help them with the spelling and writing as needed.

It's important to continue linking the hopes and dreams with the rules as we use the rules throughout the year. To help us do this, each student's hope and dream is included as part of the display. This is also the children's last chance to revise their hopes. I sit down with each child to write out her/his statement. If the child is satisfied with the statement, the child signs it, and we add the statement to the display.

Sometimes when I go through this rule-making process, I come away thinking that this task is just too hard for young children. There are years when it feels like I have to pull the ideas for rules out of the children, and often it takes several tries to get a workable list of ideas.

I have to keep reminding myself that this is a first important step in a year-long process of learning to live in a careful and caring way. For most of the

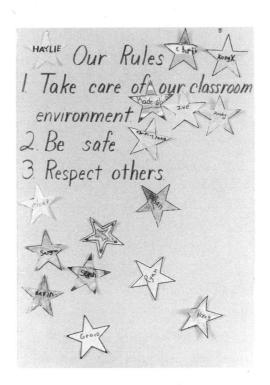

Grades K–2

Above: Rules in a second grade classroom. The stars, bearing the students' names, show that the students agree to the rules.

Below: Rules in a first grade classroom. Surrounding the rules are the children's hopes and dreams.

children I teach, framing rules in the positive and linking them to what we most want to accomplish is a very new way of thinking. It's no wonder this is hard for them. But it's important that I engage them in this hard work.

Living the Rules

Showing that rules really matter:
Going right into logical consequences

The children have articulated their hopes and dreams, they've created the rules, and the rules are now on display. It's a huge accomplishment. Still, there is quite a gap between saying the rules and living them.

To live the rules, we need to believe that they really matter. Going through the process of generating rules helps children believe this, but that's only the beginning. As teachers, we need to exert leadership in ensuring that this initial commitment is sustained even in the bleakest moments of the year.

One way we show children that the rules matter is by enforcing them. Although we still have a lot of proactive work to do, including thinking about, modeling, and role playing how the rules might apply to different situations, I dive at this point right into the idea of logical consequences. By doing so, I'm telling the children, "The rules we made are important, and I am committed to making them work."

Asking questions to hear children's real thoughts

In discussing logical consequences, my goal is to help children see the sense in discipline. I want them to begin to understand that there is a logic and reason to why certain actions lead to certain results—why, for example, playing a game in an unsafe way might mean you can't play the game for a while. Moreover, I want them to see that they can influence outcomes, that outcomes don't "just happen" or come from some mysterious outside source. If they want to keep playing the game, they can ensure that outcome by playing safely. When children see the role that their "self" plays, they are more likely to develop self-control.

The way I talk to children about logical consequences makes a difference to whether they'll reach this understanding. If I talk in lecture mode, allowing minimum discussion and asking questions only to solicit my predetermined right answers, children will simply try to figure out what I think is right and parrot it back to me.

On the other hand, if I ask questions because I really want to know what children think, and I invite children's ideas and reactions, they'll be more likely to think for themselves, listen to each other, and build upon each other's ideas. They'll be actively involved in making meaning, and discipline will make more sense to them.

Focusing first on the positive consequences of following rules

When I first started using the *Responsive Classroom* approach, I began the conversation about logical consequences by talking about what might happen if children did something wrong. I have since learned that just as children need to frame the rules in the positive so they'll know what *to* do, they also need to think about consequences in the positive so they can imagine the *benefit* of following the rules. So now I introduce logical consequences by having the children think about how following the rules might bring good results for them.

Grades K–2

"We just finished making rules," I say. We read over the rules together and I continue, "These rules are important because they will help us all do the things we want to do in school. All year long we will be working on getting good at following them. I know it is not always easy to remember the rules, and we will all need to work on this. You will, I will; in fact everyone in the school will, even the principal." I want to emphasize that the rules are for grownups too, not just the children.

"As the teacher, it is my job to help us follow the rules. Today I want us to think about how that might look," I say. "Let's look at the first rule, the one about taking care of yourself. Can anyone imagine what would happen if you were playing on the climbing structure and really taking care to do it in a safe way?"

"You probably wouldn't get hurt."

"Yeah, and you would have more time to play."

"Do you think you would have more fun?" I ask.

"Definitely."

"If you were playing safely, would you be following the rule about taking care of yourself?"

"Yes!"

"So the consequence of playing safely is that you would have more fun and that you would get to play longer, yeah? Does anyone know what I mean when I say 'consequence'?"

The response to this question depends greatly on the age and sophistication of the group, but whether or not I have to fill in the blanks, the point I want to convey is that a consequence is the result of an action. I am always prepared to give more examples beyond this one about the play structure if children still seem at all doubtful that following our rules indeed brings positive consequences.

What happens when we don't follow the rules?

We then look at the other side of consequences: what happens when we forget the rules or choose not to follow them. This time I ask, "Can anyone imagine what might happen if you forgot to take care of yourself on the monkey bars?"

Immediately there is a chorus of ideas and gruesome possibilities. Young children are well schooled in accidents and love to describe them in gory detail. I try not to dwell too long on this, moving quickly to my point.

"That's right, when you forget to take care of yourself, a consequence could be that you hurt yourself," I say. "Probably if you hurt yourself you would learn to be more careful next time, but that seems like a hard way to learn about taking care of yourself. If I am your teacher, and I see you doing something dangerous but just let you play until you hurt yourself, I wouldn't be a very good teacher, would I? I wouldn't be doing my job."

I then go on to talk about how it might make more sense for me to tell them they can't use the monkey bars for a while. In this way I introduce the idea of a logical consequence and make it easier for everyone to accept the idea. Although getting off the monkey bars might be upsetting, our conversation has helped children see that it's a helpful and fair way to handle the situation. Later, when a monkey bar situation arises, and I know it will, we will have a common understanding to draw upon as we deal with it.

In this conversation, there are several key points that I want to be sure the children understand:

- Everybody breaks the rules sometimes because everyone is human, and humans are not perfect.

- A logical consequence can help you remember the rules and fix things before you get hurt, before you ruin a friendship, or before you do something that can't be fixed.

- A logical consequence is one that makes sense because it relates directly to the situation at hand. (To illustrate the point, I also give examples of consequences that don't make sense.)

- Having logical consequences is part of the important work of school.

Introducing Three Types of Logical Consequences

It's not enough to leave the conversation here. Although we might have to come back to it later when everyone is fresh, the next thing I do is to share with students the three types of logical consequences as described in Chapter 3. These types—time-out, loss of privilege, and "you break it, you fix it"—are easy even for young children to understand.

Time-out

Of the three types, I usually introduce time-out first. I bring a chair labeled "time-out chair" to the meeting area and tell the children that I want to introduce them to a friend of mine.

Grades K–2

Explaining the purpose of time-out

"Now why would I call the time-out chair a friend?" I ask.

"Because it helps you when you do something wrong," reports an experienced six-year-old.

"Right, this chair can help you," I affirm. "We just made some rules that will help us do the things we most hope to do this year. But I know that it is hard to remember to follow the rules all the time. To get better, we all need to work at it. When you forget to follow the rules, it is my job as a teacher to help you remember, and one way I might do that is by telling you to take a time-out."

I pause a bit, then continue. "If you forget to follow our rules, and I tell you to take a time-out, what do you think I would expect you to do?"

Again the experienced six-year-old is ready with the information. "We would have to go and sit in the time-out chair."

I show children the designated spot for the chair. Time-out goes much more smoothly when the children know just where to go. Because we want children to rejoin the group as soon as possible, the time-out spot should be close enough to the activity of the room for children to see what they are missing. This is especially true of young children, who easily forget about things not immediately near them.

"Now, if you were sitting in the time-out chair, what do you think your job would be?" I ask the group.

"To think about what we did."

"Yes, that might help. Why would you think about what you did?"

"So we could do better when we come back?"

"And do you think I would want you to come back to the group? Yes, I would! If our rule is that everyone gets to play and learn, it will be important that everyone is part of the group."

Now I get the children to consider other things they might do in time-out besides thinking about what they did wrong. I say, "Sometimes it helps me to think about someone who loves me when I am trying to get back in control. Would that be alright too?" The children agree that it would.

I prompt the children to name additional ways they personally might help themselves regain self-control. We all have different ways of coaching ourselves back on track. My intention here is to encourage the children to develop, within limits, their own strategies.

Discussing coming back from time-out

After I'm sure the children understand the purpose of time-out, I talk about coming back from it. "Who is the best person to know if you are ready to come back?" I ask.

Most children answer that the teacher is.

"I might be able to make a good guess," I respond, "but who will know for sure?"

The answer I am after is that the children themselves are the best judges of whether they are ready to return. I believe children can make that decision responsibly if they are given the opportunity to learn what being "ready" means. Sharing and thinking about what being calm and in control feels like, looks like, and sounds like will be part of the ongoing reflective work of the year.

The first time a student goes to time-out, I always let him/her decide when to come back. Sometimes children sit for barely a second, but that's okay as long as they come back ready to contribute positively. However, if a child comes back after seconds, only to resume the same antics, I step in. I tell that child to go back to time-out and "I'll decide this time when you can come back."

Over and over throughout the year, my message to the children is that when they choose not to take care, I will. Not taking care is never an option.

Modeling time-out

Now we're ready to model how to use time-out. Again I lead with a question: "If you need a time-out, how do you think you should go?" Several children show their ideas by walking to the chair and sitting down. Whenever we do this

Chapter Four

modeling, it is the children who need time-out the least who are most eager to try out the chair.

I ask another question: "If someone needs to take a time-out, how will we all help that person do what he or she needs to do? What is our job when someone is in time-out?"

"To leave them alone?"

I nod.

"Not talk to them?"

"Not distract them?"

Often these are tentative answers because for many children the idea that they, too, have a job to do when a classmate goes to time-out has never occurred to them.

Grades K–2

We then watch as a few volunteers demonstrate that job. The modeling session ends when everyone who wants to model has had a chance to and the group has seen good ways to walk to, stay in, and return from time-out, as well as good ways to let the person in time-out do her/his job.

Demystifying time-out

I know that all children will need to take a time-out at some point. That's why, as we begin to use the strategy for real, I make sure that any child who is particularly reluctant to use time-out has an opportunity to experience it sooner rather than later. My goal is to demystify time-out as much as possible. Some children may fear time-out because they see it as "getting in trouble." If these children experience time-out and see that they can survive it, they will be more likely to make good use of this self-control strategy throughout the year.

Sometimes demystifying time-out requires working with parents before that first time-out experience, so that all the adults can be on the same side in supporting the child.

Laura was a child who strove for perfection. She took any small correction as a sign of some major failure on her part. It was easy to see that her first time-out would not be easy. After communicating to children's families what the purpose of time-out is and how we use it in our classroom, Laura's parents and I planned how we would react when Laura needed a time-out. We also recognized that the sooner she had her first time-out, the sooner she might relax about it.

Within a few days the opportunity arose at meeting time when Laura leaned over to whisper a comment to her friend in the middle of someone's sharing.

I quietly told her to take a time-out, and she quietly walked to the chair. The only thing betraying her feelings was her bright red face. After a little while she returned to the meeting, and we all went on with the business of the day.

Later, however, when her mother asked about her day, Laura cried, "This is the worst day of my life."

When her mother asked why, the whole story tumbled out with great emotion and declarations of how unfair it all was. Although her mother responded with compassion, she also asked Laura how Evan might have felt when she whispered in the middle of his sharing.

"Bad," Laura responded.

"If I were Evan, I also might have thought you weren't interested," said her mom.

"Oh."

"So what else happened today? Was it all bad?"

"No!" And on Laura went, happily describing other events of the day.

In Laura's case, her own high expectations made her mistakes particularly painful for her. It was probably unavoidable that her first time-out felt so bad. If we had protected her from her mistakes or tiptoed around her, the message would have been that she was better than the other students or that she was not strong enough to take responsibility for her mistakes. Either way, Laura would have felt more inadequate in the long run. What happened instead was that she lived through time-out and realized in the process that it wasn't the end of the world. She also learned that she was more resilient than she had thought. The next time Laura went to time-out, it wasn't nearly as difficult.

What about the negative connotations of time-out?

Many teachers and parents worry about the negative effects of time-out. Won't it make children feel isolated? Singled out? Humiliated?

There's no question that time-out has frequently been misunderstood and misused. It takes care and practice to use the strategy well. However, I don't believe we should abandon a good teaching technique just because it's challenging to use.

If used well, time-out does not have to be punitive or humiliating. It can be used in the most matter-of-fact way as a time to regroup. (See Chapter 3 for guidelines for using time-out effectively.)

Children must know that when things aren't going well, the teacher will step in and take charge. Sometimes this means that a child will need to leave the group momentarily. I make no apologies for this. Teachers who skirt around this responsibility risk losing their authority as the teacher.

As for concerns that time-out might make children feel bad, it's important to keep in mind that these are times when children are losing their self-control and not functioning well in the group. They will sometimes feel bad about this. While I would never want to humiliate them further, I also know I can't and shouldn't try to take away the bad feelings. Often our feelings of regret are the very thing that drives us to change our behavior the next time.

Because my goal is not to make children feel worse, but to help them pull themselves together, I don't wait until a child is fully out of control before I step in. Instead, I use time-out when a child is just beginning to lose it. This is before the child has lost face in the group and before I've lost my patience. It's at this point that time-out is most effective. Like those grooves on the side of the highway, it's a gentle nudge to get us back on track before we barrel off the road.

Grades K–2

What to call time-out

Even though I make no apologies for using time-out, I sometimes avoid using the term "time-out" with children because for many of them, the term has negative connotations. Perhaps they've seen time-out used elsewhere as a threat or as a punishment. It's often just too hard to shake these preconceptions.

For this reason, many teachers call time-out by a different name. Some have their students help choose one. Some names I've heard are "taking a break," "chilling out," and "rest and return."

Whatever name is chosen, it should be a short, simple description of what time-out is, and should not work against the goals of time-out. The term "sit and think," for instance, can easily become "Sit there until you've thought about what you did." It assumes that children need to think about what they did in order to change their behavior. I know that when I've made a mistake or begun to lose control, usually what I need isn't to think about what I did, but to break out of a negative cycle by disengaging for a moment. That's why I like the term "taking a break." I think it's a neutral term that clearly reflects the purpose of time-out.

Loss of privilege

As useful a tool as time-out is, it's only one possible response to rule breaking. When teachers rely too heavily on it, they may overlook other possibilities that might be far more effective in certain situations. Once time-out is in place, I introduce loss of privilege to students.

As with our other work around rules and logical consequences, we begin with a conversation. I use the following format in this discussion:

- Presenting a common situation to children

- Discussing which rule has been broken

- Thinking together about several possible consequences that would make sense

- Modeling or doing controlled role plays of several possibilities

- Reflecting on the modeling or role play

I find that these conversations require me to really pay attention. I want to stretch and broaden children's thinking. But the temperament, age, and sophistication of each year's particular group of children significantly affect the tone and depth of the discussion. What follows is one possible way the discussion could go, but it is never the same from year to year. If needed, I scale back and simplify. In all cases, though, it's important for the children to feel that their comments in these discussions are taken seriously.

A common situation

"Yesterday we talked about time-out," I begin. "Who can remind us of what we talked about?" I want to establish a connection between time-out and the other kinds of logical consequences we're about to discuss.

"If you are bad, you might have to go and sit in the time-out chair for a while," one student says.

"We did talk about times when you might need to sit in the time-out chair, but is it because you are bad or because you need to remember to follow our rules?"

"Because you need to remember."

"I think so, too. You might need help to follow the rules. Everyone will sometimes. But that doesn't mean you are bad." It's important to keep correcting children's misconceptions that making mistakes is "being bad" or that time-out is a punishment.

Then I introduce the new ideas. "There are some other ways that a teacher might help you follow the rules, and we are going to talk about that today." I decide to present a scenario about unsafe play.

"Remember when we talked about forgetting to play safely on the climbing structure? What was it that we said might happen if you forgot to play safely?"

"You might get hurt?"

"Right. I wonder how our rules would be working if people were not playing safely on the climbing structure?"

"Not very good?" says a tentative five-year-old.

"Yeah, the rules are supposed to help you be safe," relates a more confident six.

"Yeah, and if you get hurt you wouldn't have fun," adds another child.

These children have a pretty good handle on the general purpose of rules.

Grades K–2

Which rule has been broken?

Now I push the children to think more specifically. "So let's look at our rules again," I say, then read through the list. "If you were not playing safely on the climbing structure, which rule do you think you would be breaking?"

"Not taking care of yourself?" one student suggests.

"Yeah, because you might hurt yourself," another confirms.

"And that wouldn't be taking care of yourself," yet another student chimes in.

"That makes sense. Does everyone agree that you would be forgetting the rule to take care of yourself?"

Several heads nod. I go on. "What about the other rules? What about treating others the way you want to be treated?"

"Well, I think that you might be breaking that one," a student says, "because you might hurt someone else if you weren't playing safely, and you wouldn't want someone to hurt you."

This prompts animated conversation, in which children share one story after another of siblings and friends knocking them over, falling on them, or kicking them because of careless play. After several tales, I pull the children back to the work at hand.

"It sounds like everyone agrees that if you weren't playing on our structure safely, you would also be breaking the Golden Rule. How about the other two rules, 'Keep everything looking nice and beautiful' and 'Everyone gets to play and learn'?"

There is silence while everyone thinks. Then one kindergartner raises his hand.

"Well, I wouldn't want to play on the structure if it was too wild. So I wouldn't get to play."

"So it sounds like unsafe play would be breaking the 'Everyone gets to play and learn' rule, too."

Because our classroom rules are general guidelines and not prescribed behavior for specific situations, figuring out which rule has been broken in a particular incident is not as easy as it might seem. Does running through the room mean you are not taking care of yourself? Or does it mean not taking care of others? If you bump into something and knock it over, are you not taking care of the space or not taking care of other people?

Questions like these always arise as the children try to make sense of the rules. It's critically important to refer back to the rules when misbehavior occurs so children will keep seeing how rules help keep the classroom safe and friendly. But in the end, which actual rule the children might pick is not as important as the discussion of the rules themselves.

Chapter Four

What are some consequences that would make sense?

The children still seem engaged, so we continue.

"So if someone isn't playing safely on the structure, what do you think should happen?" I ask.

The children are full of ideas:

"Send them to the principal's office."

"Call their parents."

"Make them stay in for recess for the rest of the week."

These initial ideas are always extreme. It's not that children are bloodthirsty for harsh punishment; it's that following rules is something they really care about. My job now is to lead them toward more tempered thinking without discouraging their dedication to rule following.

So, after affirming their ideas, I say, "When I have to choose a consequence to help someone, I think about it this way. See if it makes sense to you." I show a chart of the three kinds of logical consequences and briefly explain the two new ones—loss of privilege and "you break it, you fix it."

"If you forgot to play safely on the structure, would it be a situation where you broke something you needed to fix?" Several heads shake no.

"Would it be a situation where you weren't careful in how you used something?" Heads nod yes.

"Yeah, I think so too. So does that mean loss of privilege is what fits as a consequence?"

The children think again and I am mindful of the time. I don't want to keep these young children sitting too long, but we are at an important place in the discussion. Finally someone nods his head and then others follow.

I ask why loss of privilege would be a good consequence, and someone pipes up, "Well, if you don't use something carefully, you shouldn't get to use it. That's what my mom says."

"Do you think you should never get to use it again?"

"No, just for a little while."

"That makes sense," I say. "So if you forget to play safely on the structure, a teacher might say that you need to get off the structure for, say, the rest of the recess time?"

Grades K–2

"Yeah."

A logical consequence is a way to help solve a problem, not a punishment. But understanding the difference between this way of solving a problem and a punishment does not come automatically for anyone, child or adult. This discussion is only the beginning of helping these children understand. I know we will need to keep sorting and discussing and thinking together as we confront the many varied instances of classroom misbehavior and conflicts during the year ahead. Again, how deeply I go into the thinking behind logical consequences during these discussions throughout the year depends on the age and maturity of the children.

As for today's conversation, I stop it here to give children a break so they can move their bodies and chat amongst themselves.

Modeling or controlled role playing

After coming back from the break, our next step is to get a little taste of what the logical consequence we decided on might look like in the moment. Sometimes I use modeling. But more often I use role playing because usually there are many possible ways for students to act when a logical consequence is applied, and role playing allows for that complexity.

Since this is usually the group's first time doing a role play, I control it by taking one of the parts. As we do more role plays throughout the year, the children will be able to play all the parts. For now, though, I need to be in the action, steering so that all the behaviors acted out stay within a positive and safe range.

"Okay, we decided that if you play unsafely on the structure, a logical consequence would be that you would have to get off the structure," I begin. "Let's see how that might look. Let's pretend I'm playing on the structure and forget what we said about no jumping off the fire pole." I act out starting to jump off the pole.

"A teacher who saw this would say, 'That's not safe. You have to get off the structure,'" I say. "Who would like to play the part of the teacher and say these words?"

Hands wave madly. Everyone wants to be the teacher. I choose one child, and we act out the scene again, this time with the child saying the teacher's line.

After letting several children be the teacher, I move on in the role play. "When the teacher tells me to get off the structure, what do you think I should do?" I ask the class.

"Get off."

"How do you think I might feel about that?"

"Bad."

"Mad."

"Yes, I would probably feel mad and bad," I affirm. "What could I do about those feelings?"

"You could go to the Quiet Place."

"You could see if a friend could play with you."

"You could go play another game."

"If I did these things, would I be following our rules?"

"Yeah," several kids say.

"Would I never get to play on the structure again?" It's important to remind children that a loss of privilege is not forever.

"No," one child responds with a smile.

"Let's see how handling my feelings might look." Again we act out the scene. This time I get off the structure and join a jump-rope game.

Reflecting on the scene

It's important that the role playing doesn't stop there. The final step, reflecting on the role play, is critical. This reflection informs the teacher about what the children understand and can guide the teacher in planning what should come next. More importantly, though, it's often upon reflection that children take a big step forward in understanding the connection between actions and the results they bring.

I open the reflection by simply asking the group, "What did you notice about what just happened?"

"You got off the structure."

"And?"

"Well, you still got to play, just not on the structure," a student responds.

"You knew what to do," another points out.

"How about the teacher, how do you think the teacher felt?" I ask.

"Upset that you weren't following the rules."

"And?"

The children hesitate. Taking this new perspective is hard for them.

Finally one child says, "I think the teacher might feel worried that someone was going to get hurt."

Grades K–2

"She might feel mad that you weren't doing what you were supposed to be doing," another adds.

"Do you think she might also feel impressed that you were able to go off and find something else to do that was safe?" I ask.

Heads nod, with some relief.

"I think if I were the teacher here, I might feel all of these things," I add.

This has been a very substantive conversation. I don't believe children truly understand the idea of logical consequences until they encounter them in action, but our discussions begin the process.

"You break it, you fix it"

Within the next few days, I present a situation for which the third type of logical consequence—"you break it, you fix it"—would be appropriate. I use the same five-step conversation format as before, but because we have already had a good introduction to the idea of logical consequences, this conversation does not have to be quite so involved.

I present the situation where someone knocks over someone else's building by mistake. Again, the class examines together which rule was broken, determining that "treat others the way you want to be treated" was the main one, although several children also point out that maybe the rule "keep everything nice and beautiful" was broken, too.

As before, we look at the chart to figure out what kind of consequence would make sense. Because I know this group of children is capable of fairly sophisticated thinking, I push them to consider why neither time-out nor loss of privilege would work.

"Well, the building wouldn't get fixed," an astute child responds.

"So what do you think should happen?" I ask.

"The person should fix the building," another child proposes.

"What if they don't know how it went?" objects a third.

"That would be a problem," I agree, and turn to the class for ideas for solving this problem.

"Well, you could ask the person that was making the building."

"Maybe you could go tell the person that you knocked it over and see what they want you to do."

"Okay, let's see how this might look." I take the children into role playing. I play the student who built something with pattern blocks. Aisha is the child who accidentally knocks the building over, and Gabe is the teacher.

Aisha smiles self-consciously as she gently knocks my building down.

Gabe says, "Aisha, you should fix that building."

"Oh, okay," responds Aisha. She says to me, "I didn't mean to knock your building over. I'll fix it."

I reply, "Okay, let me show you how it goes."

After we put the building to rights, I ask the children what they noticed.

"The building got fixed!" one exclaims. Then, as we did before, the class talks about how each character might have felt in the scenario.

I then push a little further. "When you make a mistake, do you think you could do a fix-up without the teacher's help?"

"Yeah!" a confident child exclaims. And so we pick new players and act out the scene again, this time without the teacher intervention. When the role play is finished, I ask the class what they noticed. They point out that the children "didn't need a teacher to help" and "the building still got fixed."

"Yesterday we talked about working independently," I say, reminding children of another conversation from the day before. "Do you think Ramon was being independent when he fixed the building without a teacher to remind him?"

Several heads nod, and I leave the discussion there for the moment. We will act out more scenarios in the weeks to come, so that the children will have a lot of practice in "you break it, you fix it." Often I make use of some of those five-minute transition times to do a quick role play.

Apology of action: Fixing hurt feelings

I don't believe any teaching of "you break it, you fix it" is complete without addressing what to do if we "break" someone's feelings. Several weeks into the school year, when children have gotten more familiar with repairing the physical messes they create and have built a level of trust with each other, I introduce the idea of hurt feelings as something we also need to fix.

I begin the conversation by asking the children if anyone had ever hurt their feelings. Of course there is a flurry of tales. Everyone is eager to tell a story, or two, or three, and I try to give everyone a chance to speak.

Then I ask, "When people hurt your feelings, does it usually make everything all right again if they simply say they're sorry?" The children readily say that most often it does not.

"I know that when someone hurts my feelings, I usually feel better if they show me they're sorry by sitting with me, making a picture for me, or helping me with something that I have to do. Do you think something like that would help you feel better if someone hurt your feelings?"

Grades K–2

A chart of possible apologies of action in a first grade classroom. The list gives children some ideas to start with when they need to use this strategy.

Apology of Action

When saying "sorry" is not enough,
        we can:

* Make something for the person
    — a card, a picture, a clay creation, etc.

* Play with them at recess

* Sit with them at lunch

* Play a game together inside

* Bring them a band-aid if they're hurt
    or help them get up if they fell

* Tell them a joke and make them laugh

* Sing a song to them

* Help them learn to read

* Write a story and dedicate it to them

* Help them get something they need —
    like books, paper, markers, etc.

"Yeah," the children answer, nodding.

"So what are some things someone could do to fix hurt feelings?" I ask. Together we generate a list of possibilities:

- Do a choice activity with you.

- Draw a picture for you.

- Play a game with you.

- Read with you.

- Help you do something.

I write the ideas on a sheet of easel chart paper as children name them. I explain that we'll call these things apologies of action because "apology" means letting the person know you're sorry, and "action" means to do something.

**Chapter
Four**

*A chart in a first grade classroom showing
the steps to take in using apology of action*

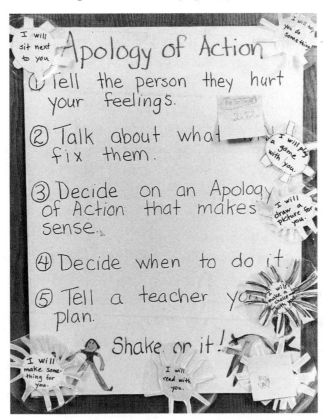

I then bring out a chart I've made ahead of time that lists the steps children should go through if someone hurts someone's feelings. Over the years, I've found that the following sequence works well:

1. The person who feels hurt tells the other child about it. The person might simply say, "You hurt my feelings when you _____."

2. The two children talk about what will fix the hurt feelings. Sometimes the offended child will be happy with just a verbal apology. Sometimes s/he will want an apology of action.

3. If the child wants an apology of action, the two children decide on one that would make sense.

4. The two children decide when the apology of action will be done.

5. The two tell the teacher their plan and shake hands to "seal the deal."

Grades K–2

We go through each step, using a controlled role play to show how each step might go. The steps chart is then posted in a central area in the room. Later I write the apologies of action that the children generated onto small sun-shaped cutouts and attach them to the chart. I also leave sticky notes close by. When two children agree on an apology of action for some incident, the children write their names on a sticky note and attach the note to the appropriate sun cutout as a reminder that the action needs to be done.

I know that after the chart is up, it will still be important to check in frequently with the class to see how apology of action is working. But each year, I'm amazed at how quickly the children learn to use this strategy on their own.

One year, a few days after I introduced apology of action, Gretchen, a kindergartner who loved to be dramatic, came stomping up to me, hands on hips, declaring, "Brendan said my design is dumb!"

"Oh," I responded. "That must have hurt your feelings."

"Yes, it did!" she emphatically replied.

"Didn't we learn about a routine to take care of that?" I asked.

"Oh yeah," she said, and off she went.

I was busy working with a math group and gave little further thought to the incident. At the end of the day, as I was leaving, I glanced over to the apology of action chart and there on the sun cutout for "play a game with you" was a sticky note with both Brendan and Gretchen's names. The next day, before I could even remind them, they were playing a game together, having a great time and showing no sign that any hurtful incident had taken place.

Of course, not every use of apology of action will be this smooth. As with any classroom routine, it takes some care to make this routine work well. Here are some tips:

- Be sure children don't feign hurt feelings as a way to extract an apology of action and get attention. If I suspect this is happening, I intervene and help the child find more appropriate ways to get attention from friends.

- Be clear about when children can do an apology of action. I do not allow them to do it during instruction time or Morning Meeting.

- Have a system for children to keep track of who needs to give whom an apology of action. With all that goes on in the course of a school day, I know I can't rely on my memory. Having the children keep track themselves with sticky notes on the chart or some other system keeps the process going smoothly and encourages independent problem solving.

- Make it clear to children that an apology of action is for truly hurt feelings. Otherwise, children might start wanting it for every little transgression, even ones that didn't make them feel bad.

- Teach children that even if they didn't mean to hurt someone's feelings, it's important to repair the damage if the person says s/he feels hurt. I tell children that sometimes it's okay simply to ask the person, "Are you okay? Is there anything I can do to help?" But if the person wants an apology of action, s/he should get one.

Guidelines for Using Logical Consequences

By teaching routines, generating the rules, and teaching logical consequences this way, I set the stage for creating a caring learning community. But I know that simply setting the stage does not automatically mean the play will go well. In the next few weeks, I can expect a rigorous testing of the limits. Children's eyes will all be on me to see how I handle classroom situations. They'll be looking to see if I really mean all that stuff I said during the early days of school, for they know, rightly, that action speaks louder than words.

Teaching discipline effectively means handling each situation from a position of interest and caring for the child. It requires us to approach momentary struggles not as adversaries of the children, but as their partners. It requires us to greet problems without assigning blame or making excuses, but with a readiness to find solutions together.

This approach to discipline is hard work. Over and over in workshops, at the coffee machine, in staff meetings, I hear teachers talk about their struggles in using logical consequences. I know from my own experience, too, that this is an area that needs constant attention.

The following are some guidelines for implementing logical consequences. They come from teachers who have used this approach to discipline and know the work and vigilance it takes to use it well.

Stop the behavior before you act

Grades K–2

The first step, when a child is acting out, is to tell the child to stop. This sounds obvious; yet so often teachers skip this step and go directly to issuing a logical consequence. The result is that neither the child nor the rest of the class clearly hears the words "Stop now." And "stop now" is what children need to hear in order to break off the hitting, the running, the yelling, so that they can begin to calm down and think about what to do next.

Telling children to stop also gives teachers a chance to think about what consequence would make sense rather than trying to come up with one in the heat of the moment. We don't always need to decide on a logical consequence right then and there. Much better to give ourselves some time, if needed, to collect our thoughts. We can let children know we'll get back to them with a fair and reasonable way to handle the situation. When we act out of frustration, we often decide on an overly harsh consequence that defeats our goal of helping the child develop self-control.

I remember once at Morning Meeting being interrupted for the umpteenth time. Out of utter frustration, I proclaimed that the next person who interrupted would have to stay in for recess. Of course the next person to interrupt was the shiest child in the class who needed all the encouragement she could get to speak up in meeting. Imposing such a consequence on this child only served to silence her further. The fact that the consequence was illogical—because staying in from recess had no relevance to interrupting—made the matter worse.

Analyze the problem

Once you've stopped the behavior, you'll have time to think through what the best action might be. Here are two questions to answer in deciding on an appropriate consequence:

What has to be restored to order?

If a child spills paint, a clean working area is what needs to be restored. Therefore cleaning up the paint ("you break it, you fix it") might be a fitting consequence. If a child refuses to take turns in a game, a respect for the rules of the game is what needs to be restored, and so being removed from the game for a while (loss of privilege) might be appropriate. If a child is moving too fast and furiously through the room, s/he needs to return to a calmer and quieter state. A time-out might be what's needed for the child.

What does the child need to learn?

I recall the time the principal of my school marched one of the class's more impulsive boys back to our room after lunch. The principal announced that the boy had shown atrocious lunchroom manners and, as a consequence, would have to eat alone for the rest of the week. Later, when I asked the principal what he hoped the boy would learn by eating alone, he responded, "To use better manners at lunch." Pointing out that the child may not know what good table manners were, I offered to eat with the boy and give him lessons for the rest of the week. During the course of the lessons I discovered that the boy rarely ate dinner with any adult, which might have explained his behavior. At the end of the week, the child ate passably better—I've learned you can't expect perfect table manners from six-year-olds—and was happy to rejoin his classmates in the cafeteria.

Know the child—understand what's behind the behavior

Using logical consequences consistently is not the same as using them uniformly. The point of using logical consequences is to resolve the problem in a way that makes sense for the child, not to carry out the letter of the law. That means teachers need to read each situation and try to understand where the child is coming from. Consequences very quickly become illogical when we try to apply them uniformly to all situations.

In our school, there is a rule that any student who physically hurts another has to go home for the rest of the day. One year, there was a kindergartner in my class who was having a particularly hard time adjusting to school. Out of the blue one day, he started hitting other children. He had discovered the hitting rule and was using it to get himself sent home.

Needless to say, we did not send him home. Instead, after conferring with his parents, I sat down with the child to ask if the reason he was hitting others was because he wanted to go home. When he said yes, I simply told him we weren't going to send him home, and the hitting stopped. We then worked on other ways to help him adjust to school.

Even if you decide that a consequence is in order, knowing what was behind the child's behavior allows you to handle the incident in the most appropriate way. One year, a six-year-old in my class, excited at getting a fancy new pencil, wrote his name on the back of a bus seat without thinking. Once he saw his mistake, he tried to correct it by using his spit to wash off the seat. The bus driver saw this and gave him a ticket for defacing the bus. Terrified of getting in trouble, the child, rather than owning up to what happened, began to lie about the whole incident.

Grades K–2

When the principal and I finally unraveled the problem, I told the student of a time when I was just learning how to write my name and wrote it all over my mother's bed sheet with a red crayon. I let him know we all make mistakes. The principal then offered to help him wash off the bus seat properly. The child still got the bus ticket, but it was the washing of the seat that helped him fix his mistake in an honest and restorative way.

Have some common "bottom line" consequences ready

Although the goal is to fit the consequence to the situation, there are instances in which a preset response is warranted. Most often these involve issues of immediate safety. When children run through the hall, and know that it is not safe, I respond by taking away the privilege of walking through the halls independently. When children go out of bounds on the playground, they temporarily lose the freedom to play on their own. These are what I call my bottom line consequences, and the children know they can count on these being used without discussion or negotiation.

Avoid lecturing: Have faith that the consequence will do the job

A consequence doesn't need to be accompanied by a lecture to be effective. If in choosing a consequence we follow the three Rs—the consequence is directly related to the child's action, is reasonable, and is respectful of the child—then the consequence itself should do the job. If we lecture or show anger, our good intentions will most likely be undone and our actions will feel like a punishment to the children. The children will focus on defending themselves rather than fixing the mistake. I know that if I feel the urge to lecture or make accusations, it's a good clue that I've waited too long to use a logical consequence and am feeling either ineffective or so angry that I want revenge.

The less said, the better

If children know the rules, often no words need to be spoken at all. I once saw a teacher remind a child to put a toy away. The teacher said, "Toys don't come to meeting. Put it away or I'll keep it until the end of the day." Quickly the child put the toy in his pocket, but just as quickly he pulled it out again. The teacher responded by simply holding his hand out. The child put the toy in his hand, and the teacher put the toy away. Not a word was said during this second interaction, and the meeting was not interrupted a second time.

Sometimes there's no need to use a consequence

In wanting to hold children to high standards, it's easy sometimes for teachers to become over-eager in using logical consequences. There are situations in which no consequence is needed—either because the incident has already brought an outcome that is enough to teach the child what s/he needs to learn, or because the incident truly was not the fault of the child.

I remember one time when our school had a fire assembly for National Fire Prevention Week. One of the firefighters told all the children that if they thought they needed help, they should call 9-1-1 right away. "We would rather you made a mistake than have an emergency situation and didn't have the help you needed," he said.

After the assembly, I brought my class outside for recess. It was still early morning, and the mist rising off the playing fields looked suspiciously like smoke. One impulsive five-year-old ran straight to the pay phone and dutifully dialed 9-1-1. The operator called the fire department, and before the boy knew what was happening, the ten firefighters who were still on the school grounds came around at a run.

Once we had sorted out the whole incident, the fire chief, the principal, and I agreed that if anyone needed a consequence, it was we. We were the ones who told the child to call 9-1-1 without hesitation. The child merely followed our instructions literally, something that young children tend to do. However, even without our imposing a consequence, the child did not miss the gravity of the situation, and he never made the same mistake again.

Look to a buddy teacher for help

When I first started teaching, it was the norm for teachers to close their class-room door and go it alone. Thankfully, that's changing. Increasingly, teachers are encouraged to help each other, and for good reason. Many schools have a buddy teacher system, in which pairs of teachers agree ahead of time to lend each other a hand in using time-out (see Chapter 7 for more). But having a buddy teacher also opens up informal options for handling problems.

One time, I was getting my class ready to go skating for the first time that year. The children were enormously excited, but for some reason I was in a bleak mood. As I was telling them about what to expect at the rink, I had no patience for their antsiness. I was at the end of my rope. Just then my buddy teacher Bob Strachota walked in. Sizing up the situation, he suggested that I call the rink to confirm our reservations and said he would be happy to wrap up the meeting for me. I gladly gave him my seat and went to call the rink. On the way I got a cup of coffee, relaxed a bit, and then rejoined the class feeling much better. In this case it was the teacher who needed a time-out, and I was enormously grateful to Bob for giving me one. If it hadn't been for him, I might've imposed a consequence on the children, which would not have been what they needed.

More recently, I, as a buddy teacher, was able to help a colleague resolve a sticky situation. At lunch this second-third grade teacher was expressing frustration because she wanted to take her class out to study a wooded area near the school that afternoon, but one child had behaved so badly all morning that the teacher felt she couldn't allow the child to go. The choices, she thought, were to send the girl to the principal's office for the rest of the day while the class was out, or cancel the woodland study for the whole class. Both choices seemed too harsh. So I offered to take the child for the rest of the day, which would allow the class to go to the woods.

The girl came into my room with all the work she had been avoiding that morning. Surprisingly, she got right down to work and stayed focused with a minimum of check-ins from me. Meanwhile, the children in my class kept stopping to marvel at her work. This was a child who felt very unsure of herself when it came to schoolwork, and suddenly her work was being greatly admired. As she left the room at the end of the day, she said, "I can hardly wait to show Ms. Carson what I did." Meanwhile, Ms. Carson's class got to have its afternoon in the woods.

Grades K–2

Communicating with families about rules and logical consequences

I find that the more families understand the approach to rules and logical consequences that I use, the more effectively we can work together to help their child. It's important to begin communicating with families early on, then continue throughout the year. Here's a sample letter that I send to families as soon as the class has created its rules:

Dear Folks,

Well, we are off to a great start! The children come in each day with enthusiasm and are busy learning all about their new classroom, their new classmates, and some of the routines in our day. It was great to see so many of you at the open house. The kids did a great job being the tour guides.

One of the important jobs of the first few weeks of school is for the children to make classroom rules together. To make the rules, the children had to first think about what they hoped to do in school, then figure out the kind of rules that would help us all accomplish those hopes. The rules that the children created are:

- **Keep everything looking nice and beautiful.**
- **Treat others the way you want to be treated.**
- **Take care of yourself.**
- **Everyone gets to play and learn.**

These rules are broad guidelines that will take lots of attention and practice throughout the year. We expect mistakes and, as I told the children, it is not the mistake, but how you learn to fix it, that counts. My job, as the teacher, is to help children learn to fix their mistakes as well as to understand the consequences of their actions. If our ultimate goal is for children to become independent, life-long learners, then it is important that they learn how to make good decisions in settling differences and taking care of mistakes in constructive ways.

You can support your child by reading over these rules and talking about them. It's important that your child knows your expectations, too.

Deborah Porter

Chapter Four

Live by what you decide

For logical consequences to be effective, we have to mean what we say and say what we mean. When we set a standard and then fail to follow through on it, our actions say to the children that we don't think they can really meet the standard or that the standard doesn't really matter. In any case, both our credibility and the children's faith in themselves become eroded.

There's no question that it takes courage to stop a kickball game that has become mean-spirited, refuse to go on with a lesson when children aren't listening, or stand up to a parent who is unhappy about a consequence you chose. But as long as they're reasonable, these firm and decisive actions are exactly what children so often need and appreciate in the long run.

Grades K–2

Many years ago a teacher at my school decided to take a group of children caroling. I joined in to help. This was our first trip out into the neighborhood after having moved the school to this new location the previous summer, and even though we would have very little time to practice, we very much wanted to sing our best for our new neighbors. The teacher in charge made it clear to the children that due to these circumstances, choosing to participate in the caroling meant choosing both to sing and act their best without reminders.

With a group of enthusiastic singers, we began our practice. As we started in on "Jingle Bells," one fourth grader began singing at the top of his lungs, "Jingle bells, Batman smells, Robin laid an egg." I quietly went over and sent him back to his classroom, saying he would not be taking part in the caroling. No discussion, no explanation.

That night, I got an irate phone call from the boy's father, who felt I was being far too harsh. I explained that his son knew ahead of time what kind of behavior the situation demanded. Still the father would not be put off. He felt his child deserved another chance. Finally I agreed to talk to his son the next day.

When the boy and I met, I asked the boy if he knew what he had done wrong. He said he did. I then asked if he remembered what Ms. Doris had said would happen if any child couldn't do what was expected. He knew this as well. I then wondered aloud if he was disappointed in himself for not behaving in a way that would allow him to go caroling, and he nodded silently.

Continuing, I asked if he thought it would be fair if I let him go anyway since he was feeling so bad. Surprisingly, he said no. I agreed that I couldn't let him go. "But does that mean you can't sing with the school ever again?" I asked. He smiled and shook his head. I told him that in a week, a student would be leaving the school and we would be singing the traditional goodbye song to her. "I'll be leading that singing. I would love to have you help me and in that way show all the kids what a good job singing you can do," I said. He agreed to the plan and went back to his classroom.

That night I got another call from the boy's dad. "I don't know what you said to him, and I still think he should be able to go caroling. But he seemed happy about the solution, so I guess it's fine," he said.

Keep a sense of humor

Developing self-control is serious work, and we all need a little comic relief sometimes. Amidst all the talk of rules and logical consequences, I am not above being silly or unpredictable on occasion. At cleanup time, for instance, I might put on Groucho Marx glasses and tell the children I am the "Cleanup Inspector" and will be inspecting how well they've done their jobs. I make a big show of walking around the room, examining each space, asking who is responsible for that area. If the space is clean, I congratulate the children by telling them to pat themselves on the back. If it is not clean, I tell them to do a quick "fix up" and then to pat themselves on the back. I only need to do the Groucho Marx routine a few times before the room is always clean the first time around as children clamor to win the approval of the Inspector.

Another thing I sometimes do is exaggerate being in a hurry to get the class ready to go outside. I tell the children I will give a gold star to anyone who is ready in five minutes. As the children race to beat the clock, I go to those who are ready and, with a great flourish, put a star sticker on each child's forehead. Even though I see problems with rewarding positive behavior with prizes and therefore don't give out stickers as a rule, the children and I all have fun with this occasional event because they understand the humor behind it. And we get out to recess on time to boot.

Pick up the pieces after a logical consequence

The use of logical consequences is a way to help children get back on course, a way to restore order and relationships without punishing children. When this involves a child leaving the room, either for time-out in a buddy teacher's room or to go to the principal's office, it's important that the child still have a chance to come to some resolution with the classroom teacher. That means we must take the time to go get the child, talk about what happened, and agree on what needs to be done differently in the future.

Without this step, the air will be thick with questions and uncertainty when the child returns to the room: The child worries, "Does my teacher still like me? Do the other kids like me?" The teacher wonders, "Is this child really ready to be here? Is the child going to blow up again?" Instead of resolution there is tension all around. On the other hand, if we take the time to do a re-entry check-in or conversation, the whole community can be restored to normal.

Try again if you make a mistake

One thing I like about an approach to teaching which recognizes that everyone makes mistakes is that it allows me to gracefully make them as well. If we thought we had to be perfect teachers, our job would overwhelm and defeat us. Like the children, we will make mistakes, and like the children, we need to be able to go back and try again. Being able to admit to mistakes and then fix them is what brings authenticity to the work I do.

Grades K–2

Sometimes when my patience has worn thin, I find myself issuing drastic threats like "There will be no recess if the room is not cleaned up in five minutes." Immediately, I stop and say to the children, "Erase that. Let me try again. As soon as we are all cleaned up, we will go outside. The quicker we clean, the more time we will have to play outside." Other times I simply apologize for saying or doing something that is not in keeping with our rules.

Hold fast to rules in the bleakest moments of the year

No matter how carefully we lay the groundwork for a positive classroom community, there are times in the year that try our patience and test our good will. For me it is usually the end of February, a time when the beautiful white snows of January turn a slushy brown. Soggy mittens litter the radiator, wet boots make puddles outside the classroom door. Sorting out whose sock, mitten, or boot is whose delays our outside play and postpones our silent reading work, making the rest of the day a rush. An air of irritability hangs about the corners of the room, and I, in my rush to get to everything and my worry over the progress of certain students, am often the main source of it.

These bleak moments of the year are a critical time for preserving the integrity of the rules. After all, if the rules don't help safeguard us when our spirits are low, what good are they? From experience, I know that if I allow myself to ignore the rules when my temper is short, the spirit of our classroom community will nose-dive. I've learned that sometimes I can change the weather of the classroom by simply stopping my own behavior and taking stock of the rules.

One recent February day, as I gathered the children at the rug for our cleanup meeting, I realized how tired I was. It had been a full morning: learning subtraction, writing poems for the first time, taking a few Running Records on the first grade readers. I felt impatient with the children who poked along. I was about to erupt into yet another tirade about how it was time to stop work and come to the meeting when I happened to glance over at the rules. "Take care of yourself," I read. I took a deep breath and rang the bell for quiet. I told the class that I needed a quick rest and that I would take one while they came to the meeting rug. "I just need a minute. When I open my eyes, I expect everyone to be ready for our cleanup meeting."

I went and sat at the meeting area and closed my eyes. Quietly and slowly I counted to sixty, while just as quietly all the children put down what they were doing and came to join me. When I opened my eyes, everyone was assembled and I really did feel refreshed enough to go on in a positive way with the rest of the morning.

Later in the day, after recess, while the mittens and boots piled up yet again, I could look at the mess with renewed energy. Playfully I told the children that we were going to have a contest. They would see if they could get all their things off and put away in five minutes. If they could, they would win the contest; if they couldn't, their stuff would win. I set the timer, saying, "On your mark, get set, go!" As the children raced to beat their own stuff, I reminded myself that February would end. I was relieved that this time I was able to stay in control of myself, and confident that my patience would be tried many more times before the end of the year.

The fact that we take such care in teaching and practicing the rules does not prevent difficult times or short tempers, but it does help us deal with these frustrations with a little grace. I knew that on another day, I might not be able to keep myself in check, that I might make mistakes and, like the children, have to do fix-ups. But as I watched the children assemble on the rug for story, all having won the "contest," I also knew that I was in the best of company and looked forward to the work we had ahead of us.

Rules As a Prelude to Problem Solving

During the first weeks of school, so much of the children's attention is on the teacher. But as they go about the business of figuring us out, testing what we believe in and seeing how we react to different situations, they are also busy making friends, learning about their school, and seeing how they themselves fit into the whole picture. It's hard to put your finger on the exact moment when "the first weeks" of school move into the rest of the year, but it certainly comes with the children's discovery of each other. Suddenly I'm realizing that instead of testing my limits, the children are testing each other and reporting back to me every detail and result they find.

"Teacher, Zachary butt me!" "Teacher, Emily says I can't sit next to her!" "Teacher, Lifang won't let me be the mother. I never get to be the mother!" "Teacher, Alden is using all the wheels and I don't have any!"

If we allow ourselves to become drawn into every dispute and apply first aid to every hurt feeling, our firm and consistent enforcement of rules can easily turn into a search and rescue mission. It's tempting to jump in to settle disputes, defend the underdog, erase hurt feelings. It is our job to care, and certainly these are a few of the ways we do that each day. However, we get ourselves into trouble when we confuse rescue with education.

Grades K–2

Rules and logical consequences must lead to the teaching of problem solving if we are serious about giving children the tools they need to work things out for themselves. After teaching rules and logical consequences, it's critical that I give children a repertoire of problem-solving techniques, from whole-class problem-solving meetings for situations involving all students, to conflict resolution strategies for problems involving two or three students.

In several ways, our work on rules and logical consequences is an essential prelude to such problem solving. First, the logical consequences children learn will become part of their repertoire of problem-solving techniques. For example, if Terrance complains to me that Josiah called him "stupid," I could remind Terrance that we learned about apology of action and ask if he and Josiah might want to give that a try. Terrance and Josiah could then go off to handle the problem themselves, with just a brief check-in or two from me.

Our classroom rules also serve as a guide for our problem solving, regardless of the type of problem or the technique we choose to use to address it. If one of our rules is to treat others as we want to be treated, we now ask ourselves, "How can we solve this problem so that we're living by that rule?" If we've agreed to the rule "Take care of yourself," we will now ask whether the proposed solution to a problem would allow us all to take care of ourselves.

Finally, our work on rules and logical consequences helps create an expectation that problems in our community will be solved, and it leads children to feel confident that they can be the ones to solve them. Of course I'll need to reinforce this expectation continually, and I'll need to keep nurturing children's belief in their abilities, but the foundation we laid in creating rules together and using logical consequences makes this work go so much more smoothly.

At a certain point in the fall, I begin noticing that the children, with my help, are starting to solve their own problems. That's when I know that we are beyond the first weeks of school and into the day-to-day living of the rules.

Work Cited

Nelsen, Jane, Lynn Lott, and H. Stephen Glenn. 2000. *Positive Discipline in the Classroom*. Revised 3rd edition. Roseville, CA: Prima Publishing.

Chapter Four

Chapter Five

GRADES 3-5

BY KATHRYN BRADY

By the time third grade rolls around, most students can rattle off a long list of things that shouldn't be done in school. With three years of classroom experience behind them, they've seen a wide range of approaches to discipline and many examples of students' behavior problems interfering with learning. Most come away from these experiences with a clear understanding of the forbiddens: No fighting, yelling, interrupting, running, pushing, cutting in line, chewing gum, and on and on. These, to them, are the rules in school.

But ask third graders what they *should* do if not fight, yell, interrupt, etc., and most of them will say something vague such as "be good." Ask them what "being good" means, and they're likely to say simply that it means avoiding being bad, or at least avoiding being caught being bad. What's missing is the ability to name behaviors that are specific *and* positive.

The flip side of this, of course, is that the students equate breaking rules with "being bad." Unfortunately, when children this age repeatedly see themselves as being "bad" when they break a rule, they're likely to grow discouraged in their attempt to become "good."

The good news is that students in these grades are capable of changing the way they look at rules with relative ease. Still highly receptive to adult guidance and eager to participate in group conversations, they welcome the idea of co-creating rules that are based on their own and their classmates' goals for the year. They appreciate the modeling, role playing, and discussions that clarify exactly what it looks like, sounds like, and feels like to follow the rules.

Over and over I've watched students in these grades dramatically change how they view rules as a result of the process described in this book. While they will still break the rules or complain about following them from time to time, they develop a deeper understanding of why rules are important. They come to see how the rules help them personally and how the rules help them coexist peacefully and productively with others.

Achieving this positive vision of rules, however, takes time, careful planning, and patience. And it all begins from the first day of school.

Setting the Tone from Day One

Grades 3–5 Third, fourth, and fifth graders walk into school on the first day every bit as excited and nervous as their teachers. Although more savvy than their early elementary counterparts, these students still rely on the adults in charge to set the tone for the school year.

Questions like "Will we have homework this year?" "Do we get recess every day?" "Where should we put our things?" "Will we have lots of tests?" and "What are the rules?" are the test questions for the unspoken thoughts and fears of the students: *Will I be safe here? Will I be able to do the work? Does the teacher like to have fun? Is this classroom 'ours' or just the teacher's? Does the teacher like kids?*

The task of creating a positive learning environment for all of the students rests with the teacher. Students in these grades need to know from day one that this is a classroom where they'll feel safe and respected. They need to know that the teacher is organized and in control. They need to know that there are predictable routines and procedures.

Modeling and practicing basic routines

On the first day of school, I spend time modeling and practicing procedures for basic routines such as lining up, coming to the meeting circle, taking out and putting away materials, going to recess, and using the signal for quiet.

We also take time to establish guidelines for group discussions. I tell students that we'll be meeting together as a whole group a lot this year, and we need to make sure these meetings run smoothly. We then brainstorm together to come up with guidelines that will allow everyone to feel comfortable participating and allow everyone's ideas to be heard. (See the discussion and photos of meeting guidelines in

Chapter I.) It's essential to have these basic routines and meeting guidelines in place before opening the discussion of our hopes and dreams for the year.

Articulating Hopes and Dreams

My own hopes: "How do I want this class to be?"

Before talking with students about their hopes and dreams for the year, I always ask myself how I want the class to be: What's my hope for how we'll treat each other? For how students will approach their learning? For what we'll accomplish this year? It's critical that I answer these questions earnestly, because it's my positive vision that will set the tone for students to articulate their hopes earnestly.

It's also critical that my vision be clear and easy to communicate to students and families: "This year I hope everyone will feel safe about trying things that feel hard," for example. Or "My hope this year is that everyone will enjoy coming to school and working hard." Or "My goal this year is for all students to feel excited about learning and be comfortable working at their own pace." Then, when I ask students about their hopes and dreams, I open the conversation by expressing mine.

Posing the question to students:
"What are your hopes and dreams for the year?"

Then I ask the students, "What are your hopes and dreams for this school year?" or "What would you like to accomplish this school year? For example, do you want to get better at reading, or learn to do harder math problems, or write lots of stories?"

There are a variety of ways for children to share their responses. Often I simply gather the students in a circle and invite them to give their answers. Some students will name three or four hopes right away; others will wait, gathering ideas as they listen to their more vocal classmates. I write down all of the students' ideas on a chart pad.

Next I ask students to choose, from all the hopes they named, their *most important* one. Again, I often simply ask students to think about this question for a few minutes while sitting in the circle. Those ready to share their responses do so, and I record each response on the chart with the child's name next to it. Those who aren't ready to share right away will have an opportunity to do so the next day.

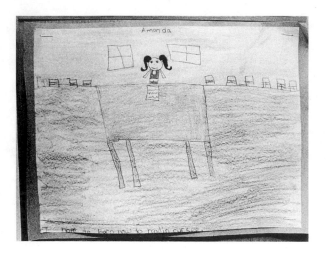

A third grader's illustration of her hope and dream for the school year:
"I hope to learn how to read in cursive."

Grades 3–5

Other times I turn this naming of the most important hope into a writing assignment, to be done during school that day or as a homework assignment that night. The next day, students bring their writing to the circle and share it with the class. Again, I record everyone's response on a chart pad.

Whatever the process, we end up with a chart of each child's most important hope and dream for the year. We post the chart in a prominent place in the room, usually near the meeting area where we'll be able to refer back to it frequently throughout the year.

This public sharing of hopes and dreams conveys the message that everyone's hopes and dreams are important. It sets the stage for the idea, furthermore, that we'll all be helping each other achieve our hopes and dreams, and that we have rules in our classroom for this purpose.

"To make new friends": The importance of social goals

The first time I did hopes and dreams, it was with a class of fourth graders. I didn't know what to expect, but one thing I felt sure about was that students should name goals related to academics. Otherwise, how would we work on the goal within a classroom context?

So when Joshua said that he would like to make some friends, I was tempted to redirect him. But when I stopped to think about it, I realized, "He does need friends." In fact, of all the things Joshua needed to work on at school that year, making friends was probably the most important. Since then I've come to understand that social goals are every bit as worthy as academic ones, and that students are remarkably astute at choosing a goal that's right for them.

Here's a partial list of hopes and dreams from that fourth grade class:

- Ms. B. hopes that students will find learning fun and will want to come to school every day.
- Chris hopes that he will get better at writing.
- Juan hopes that he will get an A in math.
- Marta hopes to read a long chapter book this year during DEAR.
- Katelyn wants to learn fractions and decimals.
- Pha hopes to improve his art skills.
- Shanice hopes to learn to use the Internet.
- Joshua would like to make some new friends.

Chapter Five

From a display of hopes and dreams in a third grade class.
The first illustration says "I hope to do lots of times tables in third grade."

Grades 3–5

What if a student doesn't have a hope or dream?

Occasionally, a student will say s/he can't think of a single hope or dream or won't even want to do the hope and dream activity. Possibly the child has moved a lot and has learned that it can be painful to invest in a classroom s/he will soon be leaving. Or maybe the child has yet to see a hope or dream realized. Ironically, it's perhaps these students who need this process more than anyone.

I try the following to help students who are unable or reluctant to name a hope or dream:

Change the language

With one third grader, I changed the phrase "hopes and dreams" to "hopes, dreams, and wishes." The word "wishes" was more familiar to her and seemed less threatening.

Have the student think about a shorter period

Often, thinking about what we'd like to accomplish in the next month or two is easier than thinking about what we'd like to accomplish in the next year. With one fifth grader, I changed the question to "What's your hope for the month of September?"

Involving families:
"What's one hope you have for your child this year?"

During the first week of school, I send a letter home to families asking two questions: "What do you think was the most important thing your child accomplished last year?" and "What would you like to see your child accomplish this year?" The students will have just done the hope and dream activity, so I also suggest in the letter that families ask their children about the goals the children named, as a way to start a conversation about this topic at home. Here's a sample letter:

Dear Families,

We're off to a great year! One of the first activities in our class this year is thinking about what our most important hopes and dreams for this school year are. I invite you to join this activity by sharing your hopes and dreams for your child. Please take a few minutes to answer these questions:

What do you think was the most important thing your child accomplished last year?

What would you like to see your child accomplish this year?

This week in school I asked the children to name a hope or dream for themselves for this school year. The children wrote down their hope or dream and then illustrated it. You may want to ask your child about the hope or dream that s/he named.

I look forward to talking with you from time to time this year about your goals for your child and his/her progress toward meeting them.

Please send this letter back with your child by September 5.

Thank you.

Sincerely,

Chapter Five

When all the families' hopes and dreams are back, the children and I write them up on a big sheet of paper. We post the paper near the display of the children's hopes and dreams along with the classroom rules. The message to children, then, is that teachers, parents, and students are all working together to help members of this class learn at their best.

I've heard many teachers talk about how rewarding it is to ask families about their hopes and dreams. One teacher said, "I didn't expect the parents to say that they wanted their child to master Egyptian civilizations so they would pass the state standardized test. But I did expect the goals to be achievement oriented."

Grades 3–5

From a fourth grade class's hopes and dreams display

So it was an eye-opener when several parents said they wanted their children to continue to love learning and to remain curious. "I began to think differently about my responsibilities to these children," the teacher said. Like many others, this teacher found that when she involved families in the hopes and dreams process, they were more supportive of her approach to discipline.

Moving from Hopes and Dreams to Rules

When teachers and students speak publicly of their hopes for the year, a sense of group identity emerges, and children begin to feel ownership of the classroom. The next step is to help students see the connection between their hopes and their classroom rules.

"What rules will we need to help all of us reach our goals?"

I always discuss this question as a whole group even if students wrote about their hopes individually, because it's so important for children to hear each other's ideas about what rules are needed.

I might begin by saying, "Now that we've named our hopes and dreams for this year, let's talk about how to make them come true. Classroom rules are one thing that can help. What rule might help you meet your goal or help others meet theirs?"

If this is the first time a particular group of students is doing this activity, I know they'll name a litany of negatively framed statements: "Don't be mean," "Don't yell," "Don't copy other people's work," "Don't interrupt people." This happens simply because children (and adults) are used to thinking of rules as what they shouldn't do. I'm prepared to help students turn their *don'ts* into *dos*:

Chapter Five

"If Juan hopes to get an A in math this year, what can he do to try to make that happen?" I ask.

"I could do all my work," Juan says.

I write Juan's idea on the chart pad. "What could we do to help Juan?"

"We could not bug him when he's working," Chris suggests.

"So if we're *not* going to bug Juan, what *are* we going to do?"

"We could let him work 'til he's done."

I write "Let people finish their work" on the chart. Then I say, "I notice we have several hopes and dreams about learning new skills. What rules might help these people meet their goals?"

Marta, who had told the class she hopes to read a long chapter book this year, says, "I will need to read when it's quiet."

"So what would you like people to do, Marta?" I ask.

"Respect DEAR time and read quietly."

I write "Respect DEAR time" on the chart. "Let's talk about Pha wanting to improve his art skills. What kind of help might Pha need?"

We continue in the same fashion, talking about what would help different students realize their hopes until we've generated a long list of positively stated rules.

I'm always struck by how well this exercise suits children this age. Eight- to ten-year-olds have a developing sense of personal and community responsibility, a keen interest in fairness, and generally like to have explanations and expectations spelled out. A discussion of classroom rules usually proves engaging and fruitful for children this age.

Getting it down to a few global rules

After taking a break, the class goes on to the next step, synthesizing all of the ideas for classroom rules into a few broad ones. There are a number of ways to do this. Many teachers simply ask children to look at the long list of ideas and see if they notice any common themes. I've also seen teachers cut the chart sheet of ideas into strips so there's one rule per strip, then ask the children to place the related strips together.

One method I've used is to group a few of the rules into categories and ask the students to do the same with the rest of the rules. I bring out a chart that I started. It lists just a handful of the many rules we came up with the day before, divided into three columns:

Grades 3–5

Invite others to play. Use nice words.	Take care of basketballs. Take care of art supplies.	Respect DEAR time. Let people finish their work.

Though I haven't labeled the columns, they represent three fundamental categories that classroom rules tend to fall into:

- Treatment of self and others (first column)
- Treatment of personal and communal property (second column)
- Treatment of the learning environment (third column)

The first two categories are familiar and easy for most children to understand. The third is a category not often addressed overtly in upper elementary classrooms, yet it's an issue critical to students' success in school.

Picture a typical scene of students taking a test. One by one, the students finish until only a few children are still working. Often it's these last few children who most need quiet in order to finish. Yet the children who finished early are up, moving about, whispering or talking to others who've finished, and giving no thought to the needs of classmates who are still working. While the early finishers might argue that they aren't specifically bothering those who are still working, they need to be taught to take care of the general atmosphere of the room by being quiet.

The same goes for all other times during school. Children need to be taught why and how they should be quiet during quiet times, participate fairly in activities, use established cleanup routines, respect the quiet signal, and so forth, so that all class members have the kind of environment they need in order to work at their best. In making this an overt category of rules that's equal to the more familiar two, my intention is to draw children's attention to this area of behavior and encourage active discussion about it.

Now, showing children the chart, I invite them to finish the columns and think of appropriate labels for them:

"What do you notice about the rules in the first column?" I ask.

"They talk about how we should be friends."

"Do we have any other rules that could be grouped with them?"

"'Be nice to everybody' could," someone suggests.

I add that rule to the column.

"'Invite others to lunch' fits with those, too," another student says.

I add that idea to the chart as well. The first column now looks like this:

Invite others to play.

Use nice words with others.

Be nice to everybody.

Invite others to lunch.

When the class is satisfied that no other rules fit into this group, I say, "These rules are all very important, but it's hard to remember a long list of rules. It might be easier if we could make one rule that says what all these rules say. How might we say that one rule?"

"How about 'Be friendly with everybody'?" Tayler says.

I write this on the chart pad. "What are some other ideas?"

"Remember that people should get respect?" Cara asks tentatively.

I write that on the chart pad, too. "Other ideas?"

There are one or two other suggestions. The class then looks over the ideas and, taking bits and pieces from each one, decides that "Respect and take care of everybody" would be a good label for column one. This becomes our first classroom rule.

We go through the same process for column two, then column three, until we've come up with three global rules that cover all the specific rules generated the day before. The three are:

- Respect and take care of everybody.
- Use materials carefully.
- Let everybody learn.

Grades 3–5

While this process of synthesizing the rules can feel time-consuming, there's great value in taking children through it. Thinking together about how various rules are related leads the group to a shared understanding of what the rules really mean. Over the course of the year, children will need to make countless decisions big and small as they navigate classroom life. This shared understanding will be critical if the rules are to be truly useful for guiding them in making these decisions in responsible ways.

A final reflection: "Where did these rules come from?"

After the class has arrived at a final list of rules, I ask the children one last question: "Where did these rules come from?" Sometimes children can get so wrapped up in thinking about consolidating the rules and choosing the right

Rules in a third grade classroom (left)
and a fifth grade classroom (right)

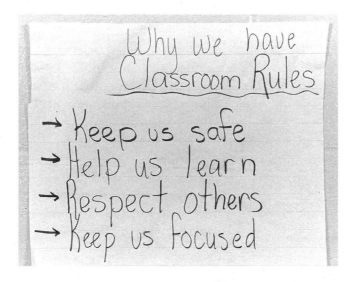

In this fourth grade class, the children made a poster to remind themselves of the reason for having rules.

**Chapter
Five**

words that they forget how the whole process started. This question helps them remember that the rules grew out of their own hopes and dreams. When children keep connecting the rules with some desire of their own, they are more likely to feel that the rules are fair and valuable, and more willing to follow them.

Modeling and Role Playing the Rules

Now that we have our rules, will the students live by them? Some will most of the time; others will less often. Like adults, children, even when they have the best intentions, don't follow the rules all the time. However, all children will be more likely to follow the rules if we teach them how. Two techniques that I've used successfully for this teaching are modeling and role playing.

But first, teachers need to ask themselves a critical question.

"How will I know if students are living the rules?"

This might seem like a silly question at first. "Children are living the rules if no rules are being broken," one might respond. Or, "They're living the rules if they're being good, and they're doing what I ask when I ask."

But the absence of rule breaking and the presence of timely compliance are not measures of living the rules if our goal is to teach children to think for themselves. The purpose of rules is more than to create order and compliance. It's to help us learn about and practice keeping ourselves and each other safe physically and emotionally as we pursue our goals, grow, make mistakes, and try again. To get beyond the idea of compliance, we need to consider what the classroom might specifically look, sound, and feel like if students were living the rules.

Asking children the question

Just like the teacher, students will need to be able to visualize the actions and words that constitute living the rules. A few days after the children create their final classroom rules, I open a conversation:

Grades 3–5

"We've been practicing following our rules for a few days now," I say. "I've noticed each of you putting the rules into action. I think we should look at our rules again one at a time and talk about what each rule might look, sound, and feel like if we were following it. Let's start with 'Respect and take care of everybody.'" I take out a chart where we can record our ideas.

"So if we're respecting and taking care of everybody, what are we doing or saying?" I ask.

Envisioning specific, positive actions and words like this is not something the children are used to doing. They think for almost a minute.

Finally, Joshua says, "When we're at recess, we don't keep kids out of the games." Reverting back to what *not* to do is common. I need to keep pushing children to envision the positives.

"If we're not going to keep kids out of games, what would you like to see happen?"

"When I have to go out to recess late, I want to play basketball instead of watching," Joshua replies.

"What could you do to make that happen?"

"Ask to play with the kids?"

I write "Ask to play or participate" and "Ask for help" under *Sounds like* on the chart. "What might others do to take care of someone who wants to play?"

Pha says, "Let kids join in."

I write "Let others join in" on the chart under *Looks like*. "It sounds like this is an easy thing to figure out on the basketball court," I continue, "but I'm wondering if there might be a time when this is really hard to do."

Marta says, "When we play tetherball, we only play with two kids. What if someone else wants to play?"

"We could take turns playing the winner, but what if we don't want to?" Katelyn joins the discussion.

I write "Take turns" under *Looks like* on the chart, then say, "I hear that there mig   re everybody gets to play. There might no   ght not feel like giving up a turn to let son

Here   on taking another person's perspective   that usually isn't addressed until after a co   g a game," I say. "Imagine that the game   too shy to ask to play and there isn't anot   ld you feel?"

"I wc   ut," some children answer.

"It w   persists. He's clearly identifying that this   lly to do.

"It m   says that we need to respect and take care   g turns might be part of that. I know it's   ou want to keep playing. I think we'll talk

I kno   this group, and I make a mental note that   owledge his efforts whenever he does relin   game.

For n   n. "Now let's flip the situation around. F   d you were standing by the side and asked

"It wc   mething."

"So y

"Yeah

I writ   ng" under *Feels like* on the chart. "Anybod

"It wc   ."

I add   s talk a little about what this rule would loc   classroom or in other places in the buildi

By th   ke, *Sounds like, Feels like* chart for our first rule looks like this.

Respect and take care of everybody		
Looks like (our actions):	**Sounds like (our words, voice, tone):**	**Feels like (how we might feel):**
Let others join in (recess, class, cafeteria). Take turns. Walk quietly in the hallway. Listen when others speak. Raise your hand to speak after others are done speaking.	Ask to play or participate. Ask for help. Ask questions that show we are listening. Use words that encourage. Speak kindly.	I count for something. I belong. I have friends.

Grades 3–5

In the same way, the class talks through what it would look, sound, and feel like to live the other two classroom rules.

Some observers of the "looks like, sounds like, feels like" exercise have wondered whether it merely asks students to restate the specific rules that the teacher asked them to consolidate. But the exercise is more than that. Coming after the students have had a few days to begin putting the rules into action, it helps students reflect on this beginning practice and consolidate what they've experienced so far. Students are now able to be even more specific than before in stating desirable behaviors. They're able to apply the general rules to areas of the classroom and the school that they didn't think of earlier. Further, this second round of conversation helps students see more clearly how the three rules relate to each other and how our words and actions affect how people feel.

Modeling rules: Seeing expected behaviors in action

After we've created clear, positive visions of behaviors that embody following the rules, the students and I move into modeling so that children can see their visions brought to life.

I've seen modeling used effectively to teach everything from how to carry a chair to how to put slides into a microscope. Modeling sessions can be quite simple and yet make an impression on students.

Here's a typical modeling session I did with fourth graders:

"Each morning, we will be coming together in a circle on this rug for our Morning Meeting," I begin. "Some days, we will need to bring our chairs. Does anyone have any ideas about how we might be able to do this quickly and safely?"

Shanice says, "Last year, half of the class would go first one day and then the other half would go first the next day."

"So we can take turns carrying our chairs in small groups to the rug."

"We might be able to go by tables, like how we line up for lunch and recess," Nathan suggests.

"Before we decide on a method, I would like all of you to watch me very carefully as I carry a chair to the rug."

I lift the chair by its back posts, just below the seatback. Holding the chair in front of my midsection with the chair legs several inches above the floor, I walk carefully, looking to either side of the chair as I move. Then I place the chair gently on the outer edge of the rug, putting the front legs down first.

"What did you notice?" I ask after I finish.

"You walked with the chair."

"You didn't carry it over your head."

"So how *did* I carry it?" I ask.

"In front of you, so the legs were up off the floor, too."

"You held the chair by the back part."

I ask the student who made this last remark to come and point to where he saw me carrying the chair. Then more children name other things they saw me do.

"You were looking around at the floor and furniture while you were carrying the chair."

"Why do you think I did that?" I ask.

"I think you were trying to be careful not to bump into stuff."

"That's right. Did anyone notice anything about how I put the chair down?"

"You put the chair near the end of the rug."

"And how did I put the chair down? Was there a loud noise?"

"It was quiet."

Next, I let the students demonstrate this way of carrying a chair safely. One by one, those who want to give it a try come up to do so.

The modeling session ends with my issuing a challenge to the class: to work over the next two weeks on moving the chairs safely *and quickly*. I'll be watching, I say, to see if they can move the chairs faster and faster without sacrificing safety. Our target will be to move all our chairs to the meeting area safely in less than two minutes.

Grades 3–5

Teachers as constant role models

The intercom had interrupted class at least five times already that morning. Then the principal came on again to let us know about a schedule change. The sixth interruption really got to me. The students were looking forward to our science lesson, which would now need to be creatively rescheduled. In my mind, I immediately began planning how I could find another hour of instruction. When I'm frustrated or thinking hard, I show it on my face, but my expression must have looked like a sneer, because one of my fifth graders asked if I was mad at the principal. I explained that I was worried about the work that we would miss. I realized how careful I need to be with my own behavior. The children are always listening and watching.

—Fifth grade teacher

Whether we like it or not, we are always a personal model of rule-following for our students, who seldom miss gossiping, facial expressions, or other signs of disrespect among adults. The fact that students often misread even innocent interactions born of frustration as acts of disrespect just makes it all the more important that we keep watching how our words and body language might be coming across.

Third through fifth graders, in particular, with their emerging sense of justice, will quickly pick up on a two-class system in which adults are somehow held to lower expectations of conduct than students. If the rules we created with students are based on respect for all and by all, then our actions must match this expectation, or we will undermine our own efforts to teach children to live the rules.

Role playing more complex social situations

Throughout the year but especially during the early weeks of school, I also use role playing to teach the rules. Role playing differs from modeling. Rather than teaching students one prescribed way to do something, role playing asks them to make some decisions about how to solve a social problem.

Role playing can be enormously beneficial in teaching children to try to handle their own problems and in helping them develop the verbal and non-verbal interpersonal skills that are so critical to effective problem solving. Note that the kind of role playing I describe here is used before a problem happens. The purpose is to give students a repertoire of positive responses to similar situations that might come up in real life.

For example, one problem that comes up often among elementary students is how to share materials. Especially among nine-year-olds, who sometimes focus to an extreme on issues of fairness, debates about fair sharing can often deteriorate into complete work shutdowns.

One fourth grade teacher uses role playing to cut down on the number of such crises:

"We've been working in pairs for two weeks now," the teacher says to the class. "On Monday, we will begin to work in groups of four during social studies to make some maps." She then asks the class to imagine that there is a disagreement in one group about how to share the materials. One student wants to make a bigger map than the others and needs extra cardboard and papier mache. He thinks that the materials have been divided unfairly.

"Let's do a role play to figure out some ways to handle this problem," the teacher says. She plays the role of Carlos, the student who wants to make the bigger map, and chooses three volunteers from the class to be the other three students. The four actors confer for a moment about their lines, then act out the scene.

After "Carlos" tells the others that they are being unfair, the teacher says, "Freeze!" Turning to the class, she asks, "What's the problem here? What are the students doing or saying that lets you know there's a problem?"

The students name the telling words and expressions: Carlos says the words "This isn't fair." He looks angry. The other students are yelling, too. No one's working anymore.

"What can these students do so that they use our rule 'Let everybody learn'?" the teacher asks.

This launches a lively discussion about what would be fair in this situation and what "fair" means in the first place. Someone suggests that the group may want to talk about how they will use the materials before they divide them up. Some of the students think it is the job of the material managers to help the group decide, but that the roles should rotate through the group. One student points out that other groups may not use all of their materials, so they could share their excess with Carlos.

The four actors now act out the scene again, this time using one or two of the suggestions from the class. Then new sets of students act out the various other suggestions. Between rounds, the teacher asks the class what facial expressions, body language, words, and tone of voice they noticed in the actors. Not only does she want students to see what the various solutions for sharing these materials might look like, but she wants them to be more aware of nuances in the verbal and non-verbal signals people send and how these affect what others understand and feel.

Grades 3–5

The role playing session ends when all the suggested solutions have been acted out. Importantly, there is no ultimate decision on which solution is "best" or "most fair." The point of role playing is not to teach students one right way to solve a problem, but to help students see that problems usually have several possible solutions. The goal is for students to become more flexible in their thinking, more confident that they can solve their own problems, and more aware of how the rules they generated relate to the complex life of the classroom.

Having done this role play, students are now less likely to get stuck in fruitless debate when a real conflict around sharing comes up, and more likely to be able to come up with a solution to try.

Using Language to Support Rules

Careful use of language is obviously crucial in the rule creation, modeling, and role playing conversations during the early weeks of school. But it's also crucial in those quick two- or three-sentence interchanges about children's behavior that take place dozens of times in a school day. In these interchanges, I find it helpful to think of the three Rs of teacher language: reinforcing, reminding, and redirecting.

Reinforcing: Easier to encourage desirable behavior than discourage undesirable behavior

One thing I've learned in working with children is that it's far easier to get them to do what we want than to get them to stop doing what we don't want. In other words, instead of mostly pointing out times when students did something wrong, it's more productive to mostly acknowledge times when they did something right.

Ultimately we want children to notice their own rule-following—this self-noticing leads to an internal willingness to abide by the rules—but letting them know that we noticed is a first step.

"Gregory, I noticed that you welcomed Adam into the basketball game," I might say as Gregory walks past me when the class comes in from recess.

To a small group I might say, "I see that this group figured out a way to share the materials. How did you do it?"

Or, after the class assembles for Morning Meeting, I might remark, "It took only one-and-a-half minutes to set up our chairs for meeting. Everyone did it safely."

I purposely avoid making global judgements such as "Good job!" "You're great!" or "I love that!" when I acknowledge positive behavior. Instead, I name specific behaviors that I saw. Global judgements in essence say to children "I'm happy that you're doing what I want you to do," whereas the naming of specific behaviors says to them "You're doing what's helpful to yourself and others."

Sure, we want children to follow rules for many reasons, and sometimes the reasons include pleasing adults, but the most important reason for following rules is to allow the child or others in the class to achieve a positive goal. If I direct children's focus too often to my pleasure or displeasure by using global praise such as "Good job," I muddy the waters.

Reminding: A quick conversation before problems arise

I use reminding language to do just that: to remind students of the class rules and established procedures before they veer off track.

Sometimes this means a quick review of the rules before students begin an activity. For example, before students launch into an art project that requires the use of some specialty scissors, I say, "Who remembers what we said yesterday about where and how we're to use these specialty scissors?"

"We can use them at our desks or at the art cart," says Pha, the art enthusiast. "We have to be standing still or sitting at our desk."

"Yes. And who can remind us about how these scissors will be stored?"

"We decided to put them away with the sharp points down," Diana says.

I ask Austin, our art cart helper this week, to pass out the scissors. While he's doing that, I turn to the class. "As you're creating the cover for your math notebook, you may want to exchange scissors with a classmate in your group. What's a safe way to pass scissors?"

"We should close the blades and pass them so that we're holding the blades."

This whole conversation, which took little more than a minute, will mean a smoother work session. As the students work, I'll watch them carefully so I can acknowledge the specific positive efforts that I see.

I also use reminding language when I see students about to do something inappropriate. When Danielle begins to put her scissors away with the point facing up, I say, "Danielle, do you remember what we said about how to put the scissors away?"

"Oh yeah, um, put them with the point down?"

"That's right. Do you remember why?"

"So we won't get hurt with the sharp points when we get a pair of scissors?"

"That's it exactly."

Redirecting: Bringing children back to the expected behavior

Grades 3–5

I use redirecting language when a student is clearly doing something that goes against a class rule or an established procedure. I tell the student firmly to stop the behavior and then I tell the student what to do differently.

During the activity using the specialty scissors, I see Malcolm waving the scissors around. "Malcolm, stop," I say. "Put the scissors down." When Malcolm puts the scissors down, I talk with him a bit to see if he needs a review of the procedures for safe and careful use of the scissors. Then I say, "Let's see, what shapes did you cut with your scissors?" to bring the focus back to the project work.

When using redirecting language, it's important that the teacher's voice remains firm but kind. I steadfastly believe that all children are good, even when they've made bad choices. I also know that children don't need to be shamed to change their ways, so there's no reason to make children feel bad about their mistakes. Granted, in the moment of frustration it's easy for teachers to lose their cool, but if we remind ourselves to separate the deed from the doer, we stand a greater chance of treating the child with respect even if we dislike the child's behavior.

Introducing Logical Consequences to Children

The rules have been created. Routines and procedures have been established. I talk with students often about how to take care of each other, the classroom materials, and the learning environment. I acknowledge the students' positive actions. Behavior problems are easily manageable, so students have time for extended learning activities. This is amazing. Should I expect the year to continue without a bump? No.

Children *will* break the rules. They will forget, become unsure, and test limits. I know that my proactive strategies—everything from doing hopes and dreams

---

When a new student joins the class

Integrating new students into the rule-creation and rule-learning process can be tricky, especially in classrooms with high transition rates. But if you've involved students in establishing rules and have devoted time to teaching the rules to students, you'll have built the necessary foundation for easing new students into the group.

When a new student arrives, ask him/her to name a hope for the year just as the other students did. Add the new student's hope to the hopes and dreams display. Explain to the new student that the classroom rules were created to help everybody meet a hope or dream, and ask the new student which of the rules might help make his/her hope a reality. Then ask the rest of the class to explain what each of the classroom rules look like, sound like, and feel like. They may even be able to do some modeling and role playing of the rules for their new classmate.

If you know in advance that a new student will be arriving, hold a discussion with the class beforehand. Talk about how it might feel scary, lonely, or confusing to be a new student and what would make things better.

Chapter Five

to modeling, role playing, and using careful teacher language—have built a strong foundation for a caring learning community. But now I must follow up with effective reactive strategies, most importantly the use of logical consequences to teach children to take responsibility for their actions when they do break the rules.

Empathy for rule breakers: Justifications of a traffic violator

Every year—indeed every month and every week—I find I need to stop and remember that I, too, am a rule breaker. My rationale for speeding, parking in no-parking zones, and committing other traffic violations, for example, comes easily and self-righteously when I'm behind the wheel. Remembering the justifications I give for these violations helps me have empathy for children who break rules. That empathy is what must be in place before I can deal justly and effectively with children's rule breaking.

I know I'm not alone among adults in bending rules and laws when there is "justification" for doing so. Children do the same. Here's a comparison of teachers and third, fourth, and fifth graders talking about their rule breaking:

Grades 3–5

Teachers (talking with one another at lunch about speeding)	Students (explaining their behavior)
"We were running behind to begin with and then the baby threw up on me as we were walking out the door and I needed to change, which put me fifteen minutes behind schedule. I was so late for school that I drove like a crazy woman to get here on time."	On running in the hall: "I had to stay in at recess to finish my work and the team was waiting to play kickball with me, so I wanted to get there as fast as I could."
"The speed limit on Route 495 is sixty-five. I do seventy-five and people still pass me like the wind. So I go seventy-five or even faster. It's dangerous if you don't keep up with the flow of traffic."	On jumping up to slap the top of the door jamb when the class is trying to move the line quickly and smoothly through the doorway: "All the guys on the basketball team do this. It's how we keep fresh for the game."
"The speed limit on 495 is sixty-five miles per hour? I thought it was higher. I drive seventy-five on that road, too. I need to pay closer attention to the posted limits."	On using restricted materials without getting permission: "I thought it was okay to use these paints. I didn't know we couldn't."
"I don't need to worry about getting to school late. I drive the back road, and I can drive as fast as I want because there're never any cops there."	On taking an extra dessert in the cafeteria: "The woman who usually does the desserts wasn't there today, so I thought it would be okay."
"Thirty-five miles per hour is ridiculous for that road anyway. The limit should be at least fifty."	On copying someone else's answer on a test: "It wasn't a fair question anyway! You said there wouldn't be trick questions."

As these examples illustrate, adults and children alike break rules for many reasons. Sometimes we don't know the rule or we forget the rule. Sometimes we have a "good" reason, a mitigating circumstance of some sort, to break a rule. Often we break a rule because we see everyone else doing it. We even break rules because we can, because we know no one will catch us. We may break a rule because we think the rule is unfair or makes no sense. Finally, for some of us, it simply feels good to break a rule.

As a teacher, I remind myself that following the rules can be very hard for children. This doesn't mean, however, that I shouldn't hold children accountable for their actions. In fact, it's in holding them accountable, with empathy for where they're coming from and faith that they can choose a better way, that I can teach them ethical decision making.

Beginning the discussion: "Why do we break rules?"

I introduce the idea of logical consequences to students by gathering them in a circle and exploring why people break rules.

"We've made our rules and we've been practicing them," I begin. "I notice more and more every day how hard people are working to use the rules. But I know that there will still be times when we'll forget the rules or do something in a split moment before we even had a chance to think. What are the hardest rules to follow?"

"It's hard for me to be quiet in the library," Bonita says right away.

"I have a hard time sharing the art materials," Ian confesses.

The children are glad for the chance to tell me which rules are troublesome.

"What makes these two rules hard to follow?"

"There's really neat stuff in the library, like new books and computers. I just want to talk about it," says Bonita.

"And when I get going on an art project," Ian explains, "I don't like people to bother me and ask to take things that I might need later. It's just hard."

The conversation continues as the children share hard rules from home and school. A theme emerges. Often rules are hard to follow, it seems, because the children lack self-control and have a tendency to be self-centered, considering only their personal needs. This is fairly standard for children this age, but it's still helpful for me to hear the specifics in these children's examples. I remind myself to be aware of their self-centered tendencies and to acknowledge their efforts to consider each other's needs.

After a while I turn the talk to instances of deliberate rule breaking even when the rule isn't hard to follow. I share an example of a time I chose to break a rule, then ask children why we do that kind of thing.

"Maybe there's no one watching," Nick says. "Sometimes when there's no one in the hall, you can run and slide on the slippery floor."

"Sometimes when the bell rings at recess and the kids are having fun, they don't want to come in and they stay on the playground, so I stay too," says Laurel.

"So sometimes kids don't follow the rules because they see that other kids aren't following the rules. Is that what you're saying?"

"Yeah, it happened last week on the playground and the teacher was mad," Laurel answers.

The students continue to share instances of deliberate rule breaking. I'm struck by their honesty and enlightened by how familiar they are with the ins and outs of rules.

Grades 3–5

Getting to the positive: "How does it feel when you do follow the rules?"

I decide to dive into a discussion of the feelings that accompany breaking and following rules. I begin with breaking, although ultimately I want to arrive at reflecting on the positive feelings that come with living the rules we've made.

"Think about a rule you chose not to follow one time," I say. "Remember what you were doing? Think about what that felt like." After a pause, I say, "Who would like to share what you felt that time?"

One child says he felt scared that he might get caught. Another offers that she was worried. Then one student said, "Most of the time when I break rules, I get worried. But one time I felt good, like I had power."

"What kind of power did you have?" I ask.

"I cooked my mom a birthday cake, and she was so happy that she didn't get mad that I used the oven," he explains. "But I promised not to do it again."

I continue. "Now think about a time when you *followed* a rule, even when it was hard for you."

"One time these kids were bragging about how they wrote stuff on the bathroom walls, and they were, like, daring each other to do it. I didn't do it though," Marta shares.

"Because you remembered the rule about taking care of our environment?" I ask. Marta nods.

"How did you feel about that?"

I felt proud that I remembered the rule without anyone telling me," says Marta.

"So when you work to follow a rule, you might feel good inside, like you're in charge of yourself," I say. "When students are not in control of themselves or not taking responsibility to follow the rules, it is the job of the teacher to help those students get back to acting responsibly. One way of helping students do this is called logical consequences."

The conversation now turns to the three types of logical consequences and how they can help students fix problems that might happen when they don't follow the rules.

Loss of privilege

"How many of you have ever heard about logical consequences?" I ask. Several students raise their hands.

"Last year, if we didn't treat the books or art cart the right way, we weren't allowed to use them for awhile," Mee shares.

"That sounds like something called 'loss of privilege,'" I say. It doesn't matter to me which of the three types of logical consequences we begin with. Since Mee happened to bring up loss of privilege, I go with that one.

"So if someone misuses one of our classroom materials, they may need to wait awhile before they can use it again. Why do you think they'd need to wait?"

"So they'll learn a lesson," someone says quickly.

"What do you mean by that?"

"So they'll think twice next time before misusing it."

"That's one way of putting it," I say. "But what I want everyone to know is that telling people they have to wait isn't to punish them. It's to give them time to stop and think about the right way to use the material, maybe have the teacher show them the right way again if that's needed, or to make a plan with the teacher for how they can remember the right way from now on."

I pause to let this sink in. Then I continue, "Which one of our rules does this logical consequence seem to apply to?" The children look at the rules chart and hands go up.

"Use materials carefully."

"Yes, this will probably apply most often to that rule. It may also apply to how we work with others and how we act in all places in this school." I describe a situation in which a student loses a special job for a week because she didn't do it responsibly.

When I ask whether anyone can think of other situations in which loss of privilege might make sense, Emily brings up the example of two students fighting over a game. "They could lose playing the game for a while or maybe they could lose playing together," she says.

The class then talks about how the two students could work out rules for playing the game fairly so they wouldn't get mad at each other. If a situation like this happened in this class, I assure the students, the two children would be allowed to go back to playing the game together eventually, once I know they can play the game in a friendly way.

Satisfied that the class understands loss of privilege fairly well, I move on to another type of logical consequence.

"You break it, you fix it"

Grades 3–5

"Another kind of logical consequence is 'you break it, you fix it,'" I say. "This consequence could help with all of our rules. Maybe someone makes a mess in the room or breaks someone else's things. That student may need to fix those situations. Can anyone think of a time in school when they needed to fix something?"

"Last week I spilled some paint on the floor in the art room and I stayed after class to clean it up."

"That's a good example. Does anyone have another example?"

Aubrey tells about a time when a boy accidentally stamped designs all over her half-done origami because he thought it was a piece of scrap paper. The boy got a new sheet of origami paper and folded it up to the point where she had left off, and gave the paper to her so she could continue.

There's one important kind of "you break it, you fix it" that I'll need to teach children, namely the use of apologies of action to "fix" the situation when they've hurt someone's feelings. But I'll wait a few weeks until children trust each other more to discuss that potentially sensitive issue.

For now, we'll go on to the last type of logical consequence. First, the children have a snack and an outdoor break.

Time-out: Talking about it

When the class comes back in, I return to our discussion, focusing on time-out, the third type of logical consequence.

"Time-out is used to help students who are beginning to lose self-control," I say. "One way that a teacher can help a student get control back is to tell that student to leave the area where they are having trouble. That student can then think or just be alone for a while so they can regain control. How many of you have ever heard of this idea?" Most hands go up.

Because some students may have seen time-out used as a punishment or have had other negative experiences with it, I make a point of saying right off the bat exactly what time-out will be in this classroom. "Time-out can mean many different things to different people," I say. "Here's what it means to me. It means someone has made a mistake or broken a rule and will be able to regain control. And, because everyone makes mistakes, everyone could spend time in time-out."

I say this matter-of-factly. Still, there are some astonished looks. The children are not used to the idea that time-out is for everyone. I pause to let that concept sink in.

Then I continue. "Time-out is not a punishment. It's a way that teachers help students learn to be responsible in the class community. And finally, time-out happens quickly. You stay in time-out just as long as it takes for you to get back into control, then you come back."

I've given children a lot to take in. Now I want to hear some from them.

"What do you think are some times when time-out could be helpful?" I ask.

"When we are not listening and just doing what we want to?" one student suggests. Another says, "When we're not letting others get their work done."

"Last year, my teacher put *herself* in the break chair when she got mad at us!" Joshua exclaims.

"It sounds like she was trying to get her self-control back," I respond. I'm glad for this opportunity to reinforce the idea that anyone, even the teacher, might need a time-out sometimes, and it's not a big deal.

Joshua's remark also provided a nice bridge to the question of what to call time-out, which often goes by different names in different classrooms.

"In Joshua's class last year, the time-out place was called the 'break chair' because that's where you went to take a break and get in control again," I say. "What should we call it in this room this year?"

After a brief discussion, the children decide they'd also like to call it the "break chair." I then tell them that "take a break" will be the words I use to let them know that they need to go to the break chair.

I don't always invite children to help decide what to call time-out. Some years I come up with a name myself, and often I simply call it "time-out."

But I try to be alert to clues that the term "time-out" might have particularly negative connotations for that group of students and families. If there are any indications, I choose a different term.

Time-out: Modeling it

We now move to the crucial step of modeling the appropriate way to use time-out. "When you use the break chair, it's important to get back in control as quickly as possible so that you can join the class again," I begin. "I'll model this for you."

Our real break chair will be near the quiet reading area away from the traffic and action, but for the purposes of this modeling I put a make-believe break chair in the middle of the circle where everyone can see it clearly. Chris has agreed ahead of time to be the "teacher" in this modeling while I play the part of the student.

Grades 3–5

"Let's pretend that I start talking while someone is sharing," I tell the class. "Chris will give me the cue to go to the break chair. Everyone else, watch me during the whole time that I go to the break chair and the whole time I'm in it. Ready, Chris?"

Chris nods. I lean over to whisper to a student sitting next to me.

"Ms. Brady, take a break," Chris says in a steady voice.

I rise slowly and, with a soft sigh, walk to the break chair. I sit and stare ahead for about a minute, then move back to my original seat in the circle without a sound.

"What did you notice?" I ask the class.

"You got up and went to the chair when Chris told you to."

"You didn't, like, run, or stomp your feet."

"That's right. What *did* I do?"

"You walked, but I could tell you were a little mad."

"How could you tell?"

"You were making a noise like this." The student mimics my sigh.

"I did make a noise like that. What do you think I was mad about?"

"I don't know. Maybe you were mad at Chris for telling you to take a break or maybe you were mad at yourself."

"If I had to admit it, I'd say I was a little mad at myself because I don't like to miss group time. What did you notice about when I was sitting in the chair?"

The children name several details: I was quiet, not talking to anyone or trying to catch anyone's eye. Just before I came back I looked serious, like I was ready to be back with the group. And, *I* decided when to come back.

I tell the children that when they go to take a break, they will be deciding when they're ready to come back. But if I see them coming back too early, before they've gotten their control back, or spending too much time in the break chair, then I'll tell them when to come back the next time.

Next I ask the children to think about what exactly a person should be doing while in the break chair.

"Figuring out a way not to go to the break chair again!" says Colin. Everyone laughs.

"The way Colin said that sounded funny, but he made a good point. What if I knew I would come back to the circle and sit right next to the friend I was talking to before? I should think about moving to another chair if I knew it would be too tempting for me to talk again. Are there any other ideas about how we might use the break chair to get our controls back?"

Someone suggests stretching and taking deep breaths, an idea that the others seem to like a lot.

Chapter Five

As a final piece of this reflection on time-out, I ask the children to think about how they can be helpful when someone else needs to go to the break chair and regain control.

"We could kinda like ignore them," Chris says.

"How would that help?"

"If I had to go to the break chair, I wouldn't want anyone saying anything to me or looking at me," Chris explains.

"You have a job to do in the break chair, and it sounds like you might need to be left alone so you can do it," I say. "One of our class rules is 'Respect and take care of everybody'. Letting the person in the break chair get their job done as quickly as possible is a way of taking care of them."

I conclude the discussion by reminding the students that everyone might need to use the break chair sometimes during the school year, and that's okay.

Apology of action

A few weeks after this initial conversation about logical consequences, I introduce apology of action, the type of "you break it, you fix it" used for mending hurt feelings.

I ask the children to raise their hand if they ever had their feelings hurt. Every child's hand goes up. I then ask what types of things people do that hurt or "break" one another's feelings. The children have no trouble naming a long list of insults, from name calling to saying bad things behind a person's back.

Grades 3–5

APOLOGY OF ACTION

If someone...	Then the person could...
1. Makes fun of you or your family	1. Write an apology letter that says something nice about you or your family
2. Laughs at you when you make a mistake	2. Write you a note telling you some things you do well
3. Snaps or yells at you	3. Do something nice to make you smile
4. Excludes you from a game or activity	4. Invite you to play a game or do an activity
5. Lies to you, or about you	5. Tell you the truth, or tell the truth to the class
6. Speaks to you in a mean way	6. Say it again in a kind way

A fourth grade class came up with this list
of possible apologies of action.

"What usually happens when students are told that they have hurt someone else's feelings?" I ask.

"They need to say that they're sorry, but they don't always really mean it," one child points out astutely.

"How do you know that?"

"They don't sound like they mean it. Sometimes they say, 'Sorr-rry!'" the child demonstrates in an exaggerated, mocking tone.

"I've noticed that, too." I say. "In our class this year, when we hurt another's feelings, we'll use something called an apology of action. This means that instead of just saying sorry, we'll show that we're sorry by doing something nice for the person we hurt. That's a way of fixing the mistake of hurting someone's feelings."

At this point I write on an easel pad two of the most common ways that children hurt each other's feelings: name calling, and laughing at someone's mistake.

I have the children work with a partner to come up with ideas for how we can show that we're sorry in each case. I name two requirements. The apologies of action must be things that can be done in school, and they can't cost any money.

The children work for several minutes and come up with a variety of ideas, drawing on experiences from home, religious activities, sports teams, and previous classrooms. There is high investment in this short assignment. All the children have had their feelings hurt at one time or another, and all of them seem hungry to have their hurts fixed in "real" ways.

When the children finish and share their ideas, I write the ideas on the easel sheet I started a moment ago, so that a chart develops:

Apology of Action	
Ways we might break people's feelings	**Ways we might fix people's feelings**
Call names	Compliment the person. Write them an "I'm sorry" card. Think of a nice nickname for them.
Laugh at a mistake	Offer to help next time. List five things that the person does well and show the person the list.

Over the course of the year, the class will periodically revisit this chart and add more ways that feelings can get hurt and more ideas for fixing those hurts. When children find themselves needing to give an apology of action, they can look at the chart for ideas.

Now the class turns to the question of how to decide whether someone should get an apology of action. After a discussion, we agree that the student who's been hurt will let me know, and I'll set up a meeting between the two students. The two students will then decide together how to handle the situation. If the hurt child is satisfied with a simple verbal "sorry," that'll be the end of the story. If s/he wants an apology of action, the two children will determine together what action would be appropriate in their case.

The details of where and when to meet, whether the teacher is present, when to carry out the action, how to keep track of whether the action has been taken, and so forth, vary from classroom to classroom. I've used different processes in different years depending on the children's age and ability. Whatever the process, there are three main ideas that I hold tight to and teach children:

If a child says s/he has been hurt, others have to honor that.

We can't say, for example, "I wouldn't be hurt by that, so you shouldn't be either."

Apologies of action help us only if we use them responsibly.

They lose their value if students pretend to be hurt in order to exact a favor, a gift, or attention. As a teacher, I'll need to be alert to such abuses.

Grades 3–5

Children should take charge of solving their own conflicts.

The teacher's role is to help, but not to solve the children's problem for them. I might remind children to consider talking to each other about an apology of action, but I won't do the talking for them. I might check in on their progress in choosing and carrying out an action, but I won't choose for them.

Explaining logical consequences to parents

It's just as important to explain your use of logical consequences to children's families as to the children themselves. Like the children, some families may assume that logical consequences are the same as punishments.

Early in the year, send a letter to families telling them the classroom rules and how they were created. Then briefly describe the three types of logical consequences for rule breaking. To show how logical consequences are different from punishment, you may want to give some examples of their use. Explain that you know children cannot be expected to follow every rule all the time, but that you will be teaching them the importance of the rules. Finally, invite families to ask questions. On the opposite page is a sample letter.

Dear Families,

During these first weeks of school, we've been creating our classroom rules and practicing living by them. These are rules that we all agree will help everyone in our class make his/her hope or dream for the year come true. Our rules are:

- Respect and take care of everybody.

- Use materials carefully.

- Let everybody learn.

We recognize that no one can be expected to follow the rules 100% of the time. When children make mistakes in following the rules, I'll help them solve the problems caused by their mistakes through the use of "logical consequences." Logical consequences are not punishments. They are ways to help children see the effects of their actions, repair the situation, and learn to do better next time.

There are three basic kinds of logical consequences:

Take a break— If a child is losing self-control, s/he goes to a designated spot in the room to cool off. The break is short. The child comes back as soon as s/he has regained control. Children may go voluntarily to "take a break."

Loss of privilege— If a child misuses a material or acts out during an activity, s/he will be told to stop using the material or doing the activity for a short period of time. The privilege will be restored when the child and teacher have talked about how to prevent a similar problem in the future.

"You break it, you fix it"— If a child damages something or hurts another's feelings, s/he will try to fix the damage. In the case of hurting another's feelings, the child might offer an apology of action—writing a card, helping with an activity, making an illustration, or taking some other action beyond verbally saying sorry.

My goal is to help children believe in their ability to create a caring learning environment. Learning to live by the rules they've created is an important step. Please let me know if you have any questions. Thank you.

                                      Sincerely,

Chapter Five

Logical Consequences in Action

Below are examples of applications of the three types of logical consequences, along with some things to notice about each scenario. These examples are not meant to be prescriptive, since applying logical consequences is anything but cut and dried. There are a number of possible ways to handle every situation. The appropriate response depends on the child's age and temperament, the needs of the rest of the group, the teacher's style, the overall school climate, and other factors.

In deciding how to handle a situation, I try to be clear on what happened and what rule was broken. Some things I consider are whether the behavior is typical developmentally for children that age, whether the child understands the expectations, and what exactly I'm trying to achieve in resolving the situation. All these will affect which type of consequence might be most appropriate and how best to talk to the child.

Grades 3–5

In many cases, I find that a strategy other than logical consequences is needed. Perhaps I need to go back and role play something that we didn't role play before. Perhaps another type of problem-solving strategy such as a class meeting or an individual social conference with the student is called for. (See Appendix A for more about these problem-solving strategies.) The key is to consider the nuances of each situation and be flexible.

Time-out: Whispering during someone's sharing

The class is gathered in a circle listening to Sara share about a piece of work. Two children start whispering with one another while Sara is speaking. The teacher asks Sara to stop for a moment. He says to the group, "I've asked Sara to stop because I noticed that she did not have the full attention of the class. Who can say what the job of the audience is when someone is sharing?" A student, neither of the whisperers, says the audience's job is to listen carefully so they can ask meaningful questions and learn from the sharer. After this reminder, Sara continues with her presentation.

Fifteen seconds later, Marla, one of the whisperers, starts talking to her neighbor again. "Marla, take a break," the teacher says in an even voice.

Things to notice:

Time-out was used for a small thing.

The teacher set a high standard for behavior in this classroom, and he held students to it. Whispering may seem like a small matter, but it's disruptive to Sara and the group. The teacher had worked hard to impress upon students that respecting the learning time of all class members means not whispering or holding side conversations during a student's sharing. Now he was showing that he meant what he said.

The teacher gave only one reminder.

After one reminder, he told Marla to go to time-out. This tells students that they need to control themselves right away, rather than waiting until they've used up the teacher's and their classmates' patience. Sending the child to time-out immediately is also less disruptive to the group than giving reminders repeatedly.

The teacher used a calm voice and expression.

His demeanor helps students believe that he doesn't dislike them, only their behavior.

The teacher told, rather than asked, the student to go to time-out.

I often hear teachers say "Can you go to time-out now?" or even "Do you need to go to time-out?" Asking children if they need a logical consequence for rule breaking can be confusing at best and an idle threat at worst. It gives the message that the teacher is not in charge. A classroom would quickly become permissive and chaotic if the students were in charge of deciding on their own logical consequences.

Loss of privilege: Running in the halls

Jeremy, a fleet-of-foot fourth grader, is the class courier for the week. His job is to deliver the attendance sheet and lunch count to the office each day. On Monday morning, before Jeremy sets off on his errand, his teacher reviews with him the expectations for the job. She sees that Jeremy understands he needs to walk quietly and leave students alone when he walks past classroom doors, even if he sees his friends inside. Monday goes swimmingly. Four or five minutes after the teacher sent Jeremy off with the attendance and lunch sheet, the child returns without incident.

On Tuesday, Jeremy again returns in four or five minutes. But in the teachers' lunchroom later, some teachers report that Jeremy waved hello to students as he walked past classroom doors and that he ran through the cafeteria. After lunch, Jeremy's teacher pulls him aside as the class files in from recess.

"Jeremy, some of the other teachers told me you were waving hello to your friends and running in the cafeteria when you were doing your errand this morning," the teacher says.

Surprised, Jeremy immediately becomes defensive. "I was just waving a little, and they waved first, and no one was in the cafeteria … "

Seeing that Jeremy was making excuses, the teacher stops this nonconstructive thread of talk before it gets worse. "The courier is an important job in this class. But since you didn't handle this responsibility the way that we talked about yesterday morning, I'm going to reassign the job to someone else for Wednesday and Thursday."

Jeremy starts to cry, but the teacher continues calmly: "During those two days I would like you to come up with a plan for how you will do this job responsibly on Friday. We'll talk more about this tomorrow morning. If you need to splash water on your face, you have two minutes before we begin writer's workshop."

Grades 3–5

As Jeremy goes off to the bathroom, the teacher reflects that given Jeremy's nature, she might have helped him stay in control if she had given him a reminder today before he left for his errand, just as she had done the day before. She makes a mental note to ask Jeremy whether he thinks a reminder Friday morning would help. It wouldn't have to be a verbal reminder. Maybe a sticker to put on his hand that means "Remember our rules." Or perhaps a secret signal she would give him just as he's leaving that means the same thing.

Soon Jeremy returns, looking calmer, and the class begins the writer's workshop.

Things to notice:

Forgetfulness or impulsiveness was not accepted as an excuse.

While having empathy for Jeremy's struggles with self-control, the teacher nonetheless held him to the same high standards as the rest of the class. Lowering the standards for him would have sent the message—to him and the other students—that he is less than a full, authentic member of the class. Instead of lowering the standards for Jeremy, the teacher gives him another chance to succeed.

The teacher looked for specific strategies to help the child.

Holding a child to high standards does not mean refusing to help the child meet them. In this case, the teacher is ready to give Jeremy whatever help he needs, be it a secret signal, a sticker, or a verbal reminder.

Privilege is restored after a reasonable period of time.

When a privilege is removed for too long, children are more likely to feel they're being punished. They may become angry and stop trusting that their teacher will be fair, or they may feel ashamed and lose faith in their own ability to do the right thing.

When does a consequence become a punishment?

It can be hard sometimes to know whether a consequence has crossed the line into punishment. Even when a consequence is relevant to the mistake and the teacher communicates with the child about it with respect, it can fail the "realistic" test. "For years I thought I was using logical consequences with my students, especially around writing on desks," one teacher says. "I'd have the children come after school or stay in from recess to wash *all* of the desks. Obviously this wasn't reasonable. It's like the kid who's attached to the custodian's hip for weeks for writing on the bathroom wall."

I have a personal self-check that I use to see if my responses to children's misbehavior are reasonable. If I catch myself thinking "I'll make sure you NEVER do this again," I know that I'm being ruled by anger and that I'm headed toward a punishment rather than a logical consequence. At those times I know I need to calm down before deciding on a course of action.

Apology of Action: Refusing to be someone's partner

It's midyear in this fifth grade classroom. At the beginning of the year the children were excluding one another from various activities in mean or rude ways. Since then the teacher has been working hard with the children to address this issue, including through role playing. The class also created an "apology of action" chart listing possible ways the children could show that they were sorry for hurting another's feelings. The classroom now feels much more inclusive and welcoming, and children are more likely to advocate for themselves when they've been hurt. However, as can be expected, there are still occasional instances of exclusion and other mean behavior.

Today, the children are drawing names out of the class tin to form pairs for a class project. Zachary is very dissatisfied with the name he drew.

"I'm not working with you!" he hurls at Stephanie.

Stephanie walks over to the teacher. "Ms. G., Zachary doesn't want to be my partner."

"I heard his comment, Stephanie. Give me a minute to speak with him."

Approaching Zachary, Ms. G. says to him, "When you called Stephanie a name and said you wouldn't be her partner, you hurt her feelings."

"But I want to work with one of the boys," Zachary protests.

"There are many choices that students get to make in this classroom, but when we choose partners from the tin, your partner is assigned to you," the teacher says evenly. "Before you can work together, we need to solve this problem. Any ideas?"

Familiar with the class routine, Zachary says that he should apologize to Stephanie.

Grades 3–5

"Okay, I'm turning this conversation over to you," Ms. G. says, but decides a little rehearsal might help. "Tell me what you'll say to Stephanie."

"I'm going to tell her sorry and see if she accepts."

"What if she doesn't?"

"Then I'll think of something to do to say sorry."

Zachary walks over to Stephanie's desk. The two talk for awhile, then Zachary comes back to tell the teacher that he would invite Stephanie to play kickball the next day as his apology of action. Then he goes back to Stephanie to begin their project. Late the next day, the teacher looks in on the kickball game and sees that it's going well.

Things to notice:

The teacher talked to Zachary privately.

If she had talked to him with Stephanie present, Zachary's attention might have gone to Stephanie, rather than his own behavior. He might have come to believe that Stephanie, rather than his mistake, was the cause of his needing to apologize to her. And, if Stephanie were made to stand there and listen while the teacher confronted Zachary, she might have felt embarrassed, as if she needed an adult to manage her life for her.

Zachary and Stephanie talked to each other without the teacher hovering.

The teacher watched and listened from afar, checking in to make sure the process went okay. This shows the children that their teacher trusts them to solve their own problems. This doesn't mean not helping children prepare for the problem solving, however. As the example of Zachary and Stephanie demonstrates, often a rehearsal is necessary.

"You break it, you fix it": Putting off cleanup

Max and Danielle are using tempera paints for a social studies project in a corner of the room. At the end of the social studies block, the teacher rings the chime, indicating it's time to clean up.

Later, after the class has left for lunch, the teacher notices that the back corner where Max and Danielle were working is a mess. The paints and other materials have been left out and there is some paint on the floor. He's sorry he didn't see this while the students were in the room but addresses the situation immediately when the class returns.

"Max and Danielle," the teacher says, "after you went to lunch, I noticed the mess in the back corner with the paints." The students grimace.

"I told you we should clean up," Max says to Danielle under his breath.

Danielle begins to explain: "We just had a little more to finish when you rang the chime, so we didn't want to stop. We were going to clean it up later."

"Clean it up now," the teacher says. "Math is about to begin. Let me know when you're done so I can check this area." He then gets the class started on their math work.

A few minutes later, Danielle and Max tell the teacher they've finished cleaning up. Looking over the area, he sees they've done a good job. "This area looks great. You obviously know how to clean up, and I know you understand why it's important that you clean up when I give the signal," he says. "I expect you to do it independently from now on." Max and Danielle then join the class in math.

Things to notice:

"We were planning to clean up later" isn't good enough.

If the teacher had let this slide, the message would have been that individual agendas are acceptable. In this case, however, they aren't acceptable because there are important reasons for cleaning up at the designated time.

The teacher's response was not overly harsh.

Because this was the first time Danielle and Max failed to clean up when they were supposed to, the teacher allowed that it was a simple mistake. He decided that having them clean up the area as soon as possible and clearly stating his expectation for the future were enough. He makes a mental note that if the students' behavior becomes a pattern, however, then he might say they can't use the paints until they've shown that they can clean up responsibly. Or he might require them to check in with him after all cleanups for a week, so that he can make sure their areas are tidied up before they start the next activity.

Grades 3–5

The "perfect" child who falls apart when given any consequence

Jason is a sensitive, unusually compliant fourth grader who never seems to show inappropriate behavior. One day during a recess soccer game, Ms. D., the duty teacher, sees Jason spitting as he's running down the field. She tells him that if he needs to spit, he should do it in the bushes, not in the field where the spit might hit others. But in the excitement of the game, he soon forgets what Ms. D. said and spits again in the middle of the field. Ms. D. tells him to take a time-out, and Jason's world caves in. He cries, won't look at Ms. D., and won't speak with her. When the rest of the class files into the building at the end of recess, Jason won't budge.

When Jason's classroom teacher comes to handle the situation, she knows that Jason needs to be reassured that it's okay to make a mistake. She reminds him that time-out is a way to help children remember the rules and reviews with him how to let the teacher know he's ready to leave time-out. She then says, "I know your mistake today has been hard for you, but it doesn't change the way I or anyone else at school feels about you."

Every so often there will be a Jason in our class. But even these students who "never" err will make a mistake at some point. When that happens, it helps to review the purpose and procedure for using logical consequences because it's possible that, never expecting to break a rule, these students didn't fully take in the class discussions about logical consequences. And it's important to let these children know they're still liked. Finally, it's best to return to the day's agenda as quickly as possible so that the routine of school is the focus again.

Reflections on Rules at the End of the Year

Periodically throughout the year, I reflect with students on how we're doing in living by our rules—what we're doing well, what we could do better, and what would help us do better. Then, just before school gets out for the year, we do one final reflection. Which rules helped us meet our goals? Which rule was the hardest to follow? Which rule did we like the most? How and why did these rules help us?

Just like I begin the hopes and dreams process in August by articulating my own hope, in June I think back on the year before asking children to do the same.

The first year I did hopes and dreams, I sat in the room one afternoon two weeks before school got out and reread our hopes and dreams display. I was amazed. Every child had achieved his/her dream, whether it was academic or social. My worries about Joshua, the child who set a social goal for himself, were unfounded. Not only did he make friends, but he achieved significant academic growth as well.

Here's what Joshua himself said at the end of the year: "This year I made two good friends. 'Respect and take care of everybody' is the rule that helped me the most 'cause I also learned how to be a good friend."

His classmate Shanice said, "I think 'Use materials carefully' was my favorite rule because we got to learn a lot of stuff like making a short movie on the computer, and we couldn't have done the movies if people weren't safe with the camera and computers."

And finally, Marta said, "My favorite rule was the same as Joshua's. People are nice to each other in this class, and it is a nice place to be."

Creating a nice place to be. There is perhaps no more important reason to have rules in school.

Chapter Six

GRADES 6-8

BY KATHRYN BRADY

J em was twelve.
He was difficult to live with, inconsistent, moody.
His appetite was appalling, and he told me so many times
to stop pestering him I consulted Atticus: "Reckon' he's got a tapeworm?"
Atticus said no, Jem was growing. I must be patient with him
and disturb him as little as possible.

Scout
To Kill a Mockingbird

Middle school is a tumultuous time for children. Not only are their bodies going through enormous physical changes, but how they think, what they think about, and how they relate to others and the world are all changing as well. Uppermost on the minds of these students are questions such as *Who am I? Why am I here? Where do I belong? What's happening to my body? Is this normal? How do I compare to others? Are we going to be graded on this? Who cares? What about sex? What about cigarettes, drugs, piercing, tattoos? When can I drive? When can I vote? Who says so? Don't my feelings count, too?*

These questions speak clearly of the struggles of young adolescents as they begin to form an identity separate from the adults in their lives and find a path of their own into adulthood. They also reveal a fascinating world of contradictions.

On the one hand, being different from adults seems to be *the* goal of adolescents, and rebelling against authority *the* preferred strategy. On the other hand, some of the top concerns of adolescents show a vulnerability that betrays a desire for meaningful interactions with adults and authority.

When one thinks about the rebellious side of adolescents, it may seem hopeless for middle school teachers to try to engage students in any activity having to do with school rules. Recently I saw a student in a middle school classroom wearing a black T-shirt bearing a quotation from the wrestling group New World Order. In big block letters the shirt said "Rules and bones are meant to be broken."

But the fact that adolescents also hunger for meaning convinces me that middle school is actually an ideal time to address school rules. The key, of course, lies in where the rules come from. Rules created by adults, sanctioned by other adults, then handed down to students will immediately become the target of contempt. But rules that middle schoolers develop themselves with caring and respectful guidance from adults often are genuinely respected, even treasured.

Grades 6–8

The rule-creation process described in this book works well with adolescents because it invites them to use their maturing ability to think abstractly and globally. It also requires students to share and listen to each other's ideas, which taps into adolescents' great interest in the opinions of their peers.

Special Considerations in Creating Rules in Middle School

Two questions frequently come up around using the rules approach described in this book with middle schoolers. One has to do with logistics, the other with adolescents' preoccupation with being "cool."

Logistics

In the typical middle school, where students move through five to seven periods with different teachers in the course of the day, how can teachers structure the rule-creation process so that it's workable and meaningful? There are three possible ways:

Create rules in homeroom or advisory that are used to make school-wide rules

This method can work if there is support from the administration, staff, and teachers for a unified school-wide approach to discipline. Each teacher creates rules with students in homeroom or advisory using the process described in this book. Student representatives from each homeroom/advisory then gather the rules from all the homerooms/advisories and, with adult guidance, consolidate these rules into to three to five all-school rules. These then become the rules that all students are expected to live by, whether they are in classes, at lunch, in the halls, at their lockers, on the sports field, or on school trips.

Create rules in homeroom or advisory that are used to make team rules

Many middle schools use a structure in which teachers form teams. Each student in the school is placed with a team, and has homeroom or advisory and all classes with teachers who are part of that team. In this structure, teachers can create a set of rules with their homeroom/advisory students. Student representatives from each homeroom/advisory then gather the rules from all the homerooms/advisories in the team and consolidate them into three to five rules. These become the rules that all students in the team are expected to live by throughout the day.

Create rules in each period of the day

In schools that have neither a team structure nor a school-wide commitment to a unified discipline policy, teachers can still use the rules approach described in this book. In that scenario, they would go through the rule-creation process with each class, asking students what their hopes and dreams are for that class—for example, "What are your most important hopes for language arts this year?" or "What's your greatest hope and dream in math this year?" From these hopes and dreams, each class would produce a set of rules for that class. In language arts, students would be expected to live by the rules they created in language arts; in math they would be expected to live by the rules they created in math; and so forth.

Some teachers go one step further to post the rules from all their classes, then ask students to notice similarities and differences in wording. Talking about these nuances can bring students to a deeper understanding of what the rules really mean.

Of these three methods, having school-wide or team-wide rules is most preferable because that ensures the greatest continuity of expectations and the least confusion as students move from classroom to classroom. However, even with a separate set of rules in each class period, the message is clear: "In this school, we have high expectations for conduct, and we have faith that you can meet those high expectations."

Adolescent "cool"

During the middle-school years, children become more self-conscious, more consumed with questions about identity, and more defensive. For this reason, it's especially important that teachers in these grades establish a climate of trust in the classroom before asking students to share their hopes and dreams.

One of the most effective ways of building this trust that I've seen is to begin each day, or most days, with a routine called Circle of Power and Respect, or CPR for short. CPR is the middle school version of Morning Meeting. As in Morning Meeting at the elementary school level, in CPR the whole class gathers in a circle to greet each other, share news or other interesting information, do a group activity, and hear announcements about the day ahead.

Grades 6–8

CPR offers middle school students stability during a time in their life dominated by tumultuous change. Seated in a circle, all students are seen and acknowledged. Students learn to greet each other with respect, communicate with power and authority without putting each other down, and listen to each other's stories, triumphs, and fears. As one teacher put it, "In the dog-eat-dog world that many kids live in, CPR offers them another way to be." With CPR

An eighth grade advisory's guidelines for Circle of Power and Respect (CPR), the middle school version of Morning Meeting

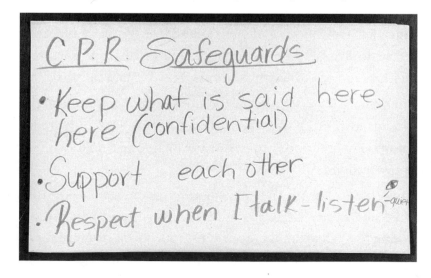

to establish a tone of respect and caring, students are more likely to feel safe sharing their hopes and dreams. (For more about CPR, see *The Morning Meeting Book* by Roxann Kriete with contributions by Lynn Bechtel.)

Another important way of building trust is to establish clear classroom routines early on. This includes agreeing on signals for quiet, procedures for coming into and leaving the room, and rules for meetings. While one might think that by middle school, students would know the expectations for these basic classroom and social interactions, I've found it best not to make any assumptions. Teaching these routines explicitly is critical for students who don't know them, a good review for those who do, and a clear message to all that in this classroom, calm, orderliness, and respect will reign. Students will more likely feel confident that when they speak, they'll have a receptive and respectful audience. They'll therefore be more willing to share authentic hopes and dreams.

Chapter Six

Creating the Rules

Hopes and dreams with middle schoolers

Beginning the rule-creation process by inviting students to think about their hopes and dreams can be very effective with middle schoolers. Students this age tend to be attracted to more in-depth pursuits in areas from science to drama, to debate, to music. They generally like taking on or imagining themselves in adult roles. And they're preoccupied with carving out an identity for themselves. All of these make them very willing on the whole to talk about their goals if they know what they say will be taken seriously.

As with elementary school students, middle school teachers should begin the process by reflecting on their own top goals for the class and sharing them with students. One language arts teacher I work with told her students recently, "I hope all students in this class improve their literacy skills and feel safe taking the risks necessary to learn." She then asked her students to think about their past years in school and some things they'd like to accomplish this year in language arts.

It's important to give students this age plenty of time to think through their hopes and dreams seriously. For example, a teacher might ask students to write in their journals about this topic one day, and then give them a chance to revise their writing the next day. Some teachers choose to make the articulation of hopes and dreams a homework assignment. After sharing her/his own hope for the class this year, the teacher might ask students to answer a series of questions in writing at home:

- One thing I'm proud of having accomplished last year is:
- One thing I would like to have done better last year is:
- One important hope, dream, or goal of mine for this year is:
- One thing I will need from my teacher or my fellow students to help me reach this hope, dream, or goal is:

The next day, students can either share their answers openly or anonymously. If the plan is to have anonymous sharing, it's helpful to tell students ahead of time. Knowing that their names will not be revealed often frees students to be more honest and serious in naming their goals.

Two frequent themes among middle schoolers' hopes and dreams are to achieve academically so that they can have a good future, and to do well socially. Here are some samples of hopes and dreams from middle schoolers:

Grades 6–8

Sixth graders

I hope to get all A's this year.

I hope to learn short division, get good grades, and make lots of friends.

One thing I want to do is learn more about science and learn about batteries.

I hope to get accepted to Vo-Tech by the end of middle school.

My hopes and dreams are to learn short division, pass the sixth grade, and have a lot of good friends.

I hope to do math in my head and get straight A's.

I want to get good grades so I can go to a good college.

I hope to make the basketball team and get good grades so I can go to the Art School next year.

I would like to make a lot of friends, learn more in social studies and science, and to make the garden look pretty.

Eighth graders

I hope to be able to keep up with my studies so that I will pass the eighth grade with good grades and move to the high school next year.

My hope and dream for this class is that I will always be able to work to the best of my ability. I hope that I will get A's or B's and that I will have a positive attitude when I walk into this class.

One of my personal goals is to learn to speak Spanish so that I can speak with my grandmother on my own.

I hope to participate in one of the school plays this year, either helping with the costumes or making the sets.

My hope and dream for this class is to complete my assignments and find a way to make my homework easier so that I can still get good grades in math.

This year I hope to increase my circle of friends. I want to make good decisions around class work and homework so that my grades will improve in all of my subjects.

I hope to be better prepared for the MCAS [state standardized test], so that I will know what is expected of me.

Helping those who resist

Even when teachers take steps to set a climate of authenticity and trust in the classroom, there may be some students who resist investing in the hopes and dreams activities. Maybe school has been a struggle in the past, so that naming a goal feels risky. For these students, I find that asking them to name a goal for the first month or week of school reduces the risk. Keeping students' hopes and dreams anonymous also helps.

Some children, perhaps fearing the judgment or laughter of peers, may try to make a joke of the hopes and dreams process. "My goal is to have no goals" or "My hope and dream is that we have a half day every day," they might say. In *The First Six Weeks of School,* teachers Paula Denton and Roxann Kriete suggest using a "combination of a light touch and serious intent" to handle these situations: "Though you might well wish for school to turn into a video arcade, William, it isn't likely to happen—not this year at least. But I really want school to be a place where all students find enjoyment and get to work at things that really matter to them. I believe there are things that are within the realm of possibility that you could name, things that we could help come true. Do you want to think some more on your own, or would you like me to make some suggestions?" (Denton and Kriete 2000, 77)

When we hold students to the expectation of naming authentic hopes and dreams, and assure them that their words will be taken seriously, students usually drop their defenses and actually welcome the chance to share what matters to them in school.

Grades 6–8

Hopes and dreams for Room 308—

Erica – My hopes and dreams for homeroom and my math class. Is to pass w/good grades and to enjoy homeroom more.

Chelsea – My hopes and dreams are to pass the 8th grade. I also hope that I will get good grades in math and understand the work.

Ibrahim – My hopes and dreams for math are to understand math, and have fun.

Constance – My hopes and dreams for this class is to be everything I can be, and to become to be I want to do good and make good grades.

Mary – My hopes and dreams for this class is to bring all my grades up, and to have a good time learning how to understand more math. To pass in all my homework.

Sarah. My hopes and dreams are to be successful, try my best, have fun, and believe I can do it.

Lynne – My hopes and dreams for this year is to get "NJHS" again this year also to not let anyone distract me in the year

William – My hopes and dreams for this class are to pass and get good grades.

Scott – My hopes and dreams for this class is to get good grades and stay on task the whole year and learn new things in math.

Kiara – My hopes and dreams for math is to understand and get at least a B.

Some eighth graders' hopes and dreams for the school year

Involving families in naming hopes and dreams

In addition to doing the hopes and dreams activity with students, many middle school teachers ask the students' families to name their hopes and dreams for their children. Here's a sample letter that one teacher sends home:

Dear Parents/Guardians,

I have the pleasure of being your son/daughter/loved one's homeroom teacher. Since the beginning of this school year, teachers and students have been sharing hopes and dreams. We would like to know what your hopes and dreams for your son/daughter/loved one are.

Please take a few minutes to share what you want him/her to accomplish during this school year. I have divided the accomplishments into two areas.

1. What academic gains do you wish for her/him?

2. What social goals do you have for her/him?

Thank you for taking this time to share your hopes and dreams. I look forward to working together to help your son/daughter/ loved one reach his/her goals.

Sincerely,

There are great benefits to involving families in this way: It helps establish a sense of community and trust between school and home. Hearing families' goals can be enlightening for the teacher, and reassuring when those goals align well with the teacher's, which is often the case. And asking for families' goals shows the students that their teachers and families are working together to help them.

One word of caution: Middle school children can be embarrassed about having their parents' hopes for them displayed for all to see, so consider students' comfort level before posting the families' hopes and dreams.

Generating the rules:
"What will help you meet your hopes and dreams?"

The next step is to generate some rules by discussing what needs to occur in order for class members to meet their goals. Exactly how to set up this discussion depends in part on how much time the teacher can devote to this activity.

In one school that uses a team teaching approach, seventh grade teacher Ms. Katsuren has gone through the hopes and dreams activity with her advisory students. Now she opens the discussion about rules:

"Yesterday we talked about our hopes and dreams for this year," she begins. "Now let's think about what rules we'll need in school if we're going to make those hopes and dreams happen."

Grades 6–8

Ms. Katsuren asks students to get out some paper and write down two things: first, something that other students and teachers could do to help them meet their goal; and second, something that they themselves can do to try to meet their goal. After they've written their responses, the students pair up to share and clarify their statements.

When all pairs have finished, Ms. Katsuren resumes the discussion. The day before, the students noticed two common themes in their hopes and dreams— academic goals such as getting good grades or learning more about a subject, and social goals such as making new friends. Ms. Katsuren focuses first on the academic. "Those of you who named an academic hope, what ideas did you come up with for how others can help you?" She has a chart ready for recording students' ideas.

"I get easily interrupted. So I need the other kids to quit bugging me so I can get my work done," one student says.

Wanting to steer students toward positively stated rules (what to do) rather than negatively stated ones (what not to do), Ms. Katsuren says, "If we shouldn't bug you, what *should* we do to help you?"

"People could let me learn and ask me if they're interrupting me."

"So does it make sense if I write down 'Let students learn'?" Students nod.

"Now, what can you do to help yourself with your learning?"

The students respond, "I wrote 'Let others know when they're interrupting me'," "Move to a different place to work," "I can just tell myself to keep working." Ms. Katsuren writes these ideas on the chart, which now looks like this:

Hope, dream, or goal	Rules: How others can help	Rules: How we can help ourselves
Academic	Let students learn. Ask if they are interrupting.	Let others know when they are interrupting. Find a better place to work. Tell ourselves to keep working.
Social		
Other		

Continuing in this way, the group generates more ideas for rules in the "Academic" category, then does the same for the "Social" category, and finally for the "Other" category, which includes goals related to sports, music, and other pursuits that don't fall in either the academic or social arenas. By the end of the exercise, the students have a long list of rules that are clearly and positively stated. And, Ms. Katsuren believes, they see more clearly that they have a responsibility to themselves and others in this community.

A few good final rules

During the next two advisories, the group synthesizes the long list of rules into a few broad ones that encompass all the specific ideas. Generally students' rules fall into the categories of respect for self, respect for others, respect for the learning environment, and respect for school materials and property. This class is no different. After noting similarities among their specific ideas and playing with wording, the students come up with the following as their advisory rules:

- Treat everyone with respect.

- Allow everyone to learn at his/her own pace.

- Help to create a safe and caring environment.

- Accept individuals for who they are.

Grades 6–8

All the teachers on Ms. Katsuren's team are committed to this approach to rule creation and have agreed ahead of time to consolidate the individual advisory rules into one final set for the team. This would ensure that expectations are consistent from classroom to classroom. To do this, each advisory elects two students to serve on a committee. Over the next few days, the committee, guided by one of the teachers on the team, sorts through the rules from all the advisories, looking for overlaps, combining similar ideas, and discussing wording that would best capture the spirit behind the original rules. The result is a set of three easy-to-remember rules that encompass all the ideas from the advisories and that can help all students on the team realize their hopes and dreams:

Team 7 Rules

1. Treat everyone with respect.

2. Let each person learn in his/her own way.

3. Keep our community safe and clean.

When the committee members report back, each advisory makes a poster of the team rules and puts it up on a wall near an exhibit of the group's hopes and dreams. Throughout the year, the display will be a reminder to students of the high standards for conduct at school and the purpose behind these standards.

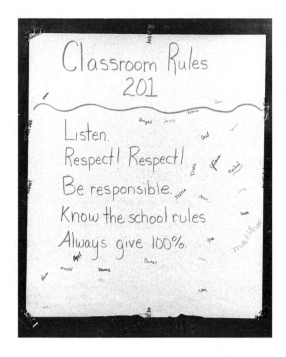

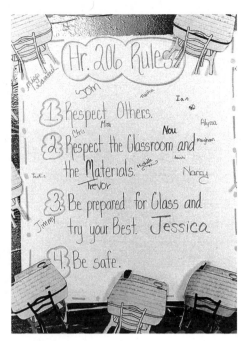

Rules from sixth, seventh, and eighth grade classrooms

Supporting the Rules with Teacher Language

For the rest of the year, but especially over the next few weeks, it's important to talk with students about what their team rules might look like in the everyday life of school. A critical part of the talking is for the teacher to simply acknowledge examples of rule-following that s/he notices among the students.

I saw a simple but effective instance of this recently at a middle school I work in:

It was several weeks into the school year. Alexi, a new student, had just walked into homeroom. The teacher introduced Alexi to the class before Circle of Power and Respect (CPR). Then, without prompting from the teacher, the class chose a CPR greeting which would help Alexi learn names. During the activity portion of the meeting, one student offered to partner up with Alexi so she might be more comfortable.

Grades 6–8

The next day, the teacher tells the group what he noticed. "Yesterday when Alexi came in, I noticed that many of you made an effort to welcome and take care of her. I saw that you chose a greeting that would allow Alexi to learn names. Does anyone have a suggestion for a greeting or activity today that will continue what we started yesterday?" By naming the positive behavior he saw, the teacher reinforces its importance.

"We could do the adjective greeting and then check to see how many we all remember," one student suggests. Students explain the steps to Alexi, and the greeting takes off around the circle.

Notice that the teacher didn't *praise* the students. He didn't say "You were so good yesterday" or "I'm so proud of you" or even "Good job," statements that make a value judgment about the students. Instead, he acknowledged their actions: He named the specific behavior that he noticed and matter-of-factly asked how students might do more of the same.

Many teachers, after trying this kind of language, discover that it makes students more likely to continue to be kind and responsible. Praise isn't necessary. In fact, middle school students seem to dislike praise, even in private. In front of the whole class, praise has the effect of setting them apart as a "teacher's favorite." A simple acknowledgement, on the other hand, serves as a reflection of their competence.

Besides acknowledgement (reinforcing language), Alexi's teacher uses two other language techniques effectively to support rules. The first is reminding language, which he uses before starting an activity, to set students up to succeed. "Who can remind the class about how to handle the microscopes?" He also uses reminders when students begin to act inappropriately so that they have a chance to pull themselves back on track. "Jeremiah, remember what we said about giving everyone a chance to speak."

And when students continue to misbehave, this teacher uses clear redirecting language to tell the student to stop and to change what s/he is doing. When Daniel flings the book carelessly onto the floor after using it, the teacher says, "Daniel, our rule says that we will take care of our materials. That book belongs on the shelf."

In addition to supporting the rules with language, middle school teachers can also model and role play the rules with students. With appropriate adjustments in the language used and the scenes modeled and role played, these strategies can be as effective in middle school as in elementary school. See Chapter 2 for information about modeling and role playing.

Teaching Logical Consequences

Having students formulate hopes and dreams, working with them to create rules, and using effective teacher language are all proactive discipline strategies that lay the groundwork for responsible decision-making among students. These strategies increase the likelihood that students will follow the rules. It would be naive, however, to hope that they will guarantee rule-following completely.

It's not that middle schoolers will break rules because they are middle schoolers. It's that middle schoolers will break rules because they are human beings. Students break rules for the same reasons that adults, including their teachers and the school staff, break rules. Sometimes they don't know the rule or what the rule really means. Sometimes they forget the rule. And sometimes they *choose* not to follow the rule.

At a recent staff meeting at one middle school, the principal reminded the staff to turn in a questionnaire required by the Department of Education. The staff's various explanations and comments about why they hadn't turned in the form sounded remarkably similar to what middle schoolers might say or think when confronted with a school rule.

What staff said	*What students say or think*
"What survey?"	"What rule?"
"I thought it wasn't due until next week."	"I need to do it now?"
"Oh yeah, I forgot. I'll turn it in later."	"I forgot."
"What did that form look like?"	"What am I supposed to do?"
"You were serious about that?"	"That's a real rule?"
"I hate doing DOE surveys."	"I hate that rule!"

Remembering that at times we all break rules helps teachers have empathy for students who break rules. That empathy is crucial. It's what leads us to remain respectful of the child's dignity and choose reasonable, nonpunitive ways of handling the situation. Make no mistake, however: Empathy is not the same as sympathy. Empathy will not stop us from holding students accountable for their actions. Always, we need to let students know that the rules are important and must be taken seriously. Our classes will be in chaos if accountability is absent.

Using logical consequences helps ensure this accountability. And it does something else. It entrusts students with the task of righting a wrong. This trust is deeply important to adolescents. They want to be given the opportunity to show that they can manage their lives in responsible and caring ways. As Chapter 3 of this book makes clear, all three types of logical consequences—time-out, "you break it, you fix it," and loss of privilege—do just that. They show students the effects of their mistakes and provide students a way to correct them. Both the standard of conduct and students' integrity are maintained.

Grades 6–8

Introducing logical consequences to students

Soon after the rules have been created, teachers can introduce the idea of logical consequences to students. As with rule creation, how and during which part of the day they do this depend in part on whether they teach in a team structure. In schools that have teams, one way that works well is for all teachers on a team to agree on dedicating two or three homerooms or advisories in one week to the discussion of logical consequences. The teachers meet on each of these days to share what went well and what points they might need to review or re-emphasize with their students.

Starting the discussion

I start the discussion of logical consequences with students by talking about how it's hard to follow rules sometimes:

"I notice that you've been paying attention to our rules and using them in many situations. I also know that there will be times when we forget the rules or maybe choose not to follow the rules. Which of our team rules is the hardest to follow?"

"Treat others the way you want to be treated," one student says right away.
"Why is that rule hard to follow?"

"Because I don't mind it when kids call me certain names, but they don't like to be treated that way, so I need to remember that, and it's hard."

"Are you talking about street language and neighborhood slang?"

"Yeah, like some kids get mad if I use certain language. I'm not going to give you an example now 'cause I don't want them to get mad all over again. But I like that language."

Back when the students decided to adopt the Golden Rule, we talked about this very issue. I had anticipated that some students might take the rule literally: "If I wouldn't mind being teased about being short, then it's okay for me to tease other people about being short." So I opened a conversation then about what the rule really meant. After a fascinating discussion, the students came to realize that it meant we should treat everyone with respect, just like we all want respect ourselves. But they also learned that part of respecting people is to accept that what feels good to them may be different from what feels good to us.

Chapter Six

Not surprisingly, this idea continues to prove challenging, and I'm glad someone is calling attention to it again.

"So if we're going to follow this rule," I say, "we have to learn what offends other people and what doesn't, rather than using ourselves as the standard, and that's hard to do, right?" Heads nod.

"And do you remember some of the ways we said we can learn this?"

"Listen to what people say," "Just ask them," "Watch them and see what they laugh about and get upset about," the students say.

Not wanting to sidetrack too long from the original focus of this conversation, I say, "So taking other people's perspectives is important but hard to do. What else can make it hard to follow rules?"

The students give a list—from "It's hard to follow them when you're angry" to "You just forget when you're in a hurry."

"One of the ways that a teacher helps students live by the rules is by holding them accountable with logical consequences. How many of you have heard of logical consequences before?" Many hands go up.

Because some parents and other teachers may take a different approach to applying "consequences" for rule breaking, I take out a chart that spells out what I mean by logical consequences so there will be no confusion. The chart looks like this:

Logical Consequences		
How they help us	**What they look like**	**Three kinds**
Teach us the impor- tance of the rules Allow us to fix problems caused by a mistake Allow us to make amends and keep relationships Help us avoid similar problems in the future	Respectful Relevant Realistic	"You break it, you fix it" Loss of privilege Time-out or break time

Grades 6–8

"You can see from this chart that consequences are respectful, relevant, and realistic," I say. "This means that the consequence would somehow be related to the mistake and would be reasonable, and that the discussion about the mistake would be respectful." It's important to assure students of these things early on.

Explaining "you break it, you fix it" and "loss of privilege"

"One of our rules is 'help to create a safe and caring environment.' What's an example of a time when this rule might be broken?"

"The other day, one group didn't put away their trade books and then we had to look for them the next day," Roger says.

"Wasn't that *your* group, Roger?" Brittany teases.

"Well, yeah, but the rule was broken," Roger says, laughing.

"In that case, looking for the books cut into that group's work time so they couldn't finish the assignment. They had to find a time to make up for that," I say. "How about if someone decides to use a ruler to prop open the window and the ruler gets broken? What might happen then?"

"They would need to replace the ruler. Or maybe fix it, if that's possible," one student answers.

"That's what 'you break it, you fix it' means. You find a way to fix a mistake that you made. You can also do this if you've hurt someone's feelings. That's why I've got 'make amends and keep relationships' on the chart. But I'd like to save that for tomorrow's discussion."

For today, I stick to the more tangible example of breaking or misusing materials. "Can anyone think of a time when someone lost the use of a material because they didn't use it properly?"

"Last year, some kid went on the Marilyn Manson website in the computer lab and couldn't use the computer lab for a long time," Jeremiah says.

Veronica volunteers, "My brother took the car out after curfew and my parents won't let him have it back until he can show them that he can be trusted."

"In all of your classes this year, not following the rules for the use of a material may mean that you won't get to use the material for a while. That's what loss of privilege means. When you demonstrate you know how to use the materials responsibly and can make good decisions, you'll be able to use the materials again."

Revisiting time-out

I begin the discussion about time-out by asking how many students have heard of it. Almost every hand goes up. One student groans.

"Time-out can mean a lot of different things to different people. Here's what it means to me and the other teachers on this team," I say. "It's when you leave the scene for a while to collect yourself when you're starting to get frustrated or impulsive, and then you come back to the group when you feel you have your self-control back. What are some times when time-out could be helpful?"

"When kids are interrupting during a meeting," Vong responds.

"Or when someone's just messing around with the science equipment and not doing any work," Rachel says.

"Or when someone's mad and starts yelling at other kids," another student adds.

"Well, by now, you all know that I believe everyone makes mistakes, including teachers, so I expect that at one time or another, everyone might get to use the time-out area. And going to time-out doesn't mean you're a bad person; it just means you need to go away for a while to regain self-control."

Students in middle school generally don't need much more explanation about time-out than this, so I move quickly to enlisting these students' help in setting up the time-out area. "My advisory group last year decided to put up some vacation posters in the time-out area because posters like that have a calming influence. Would you like to keep the same posters or look for your own?" The student who groaned earlier suddenly looks more interested.

After a bit of discussion, the students decide that the following Monday they would bring in posters they think are calming, then vote on which ones to use. We then turn to the question of what to call time-out.

One students says, "Last year we called it 'vacation' and the teacher would tell us that we needed a vacation." The students decide they like that wording. I tell them I'll check with the other teachers on the team to see what other students suggested.

Modeling "vacation"

Grades 6–8   Even with middle school students, it's important to model time-out. Though most will have experienced time-out, it's unlikely they've all experienced the same approach to it. Modeling allows everyone to get on the same page and see afresh what respectful time-out behavior looks like. It also helps remove the stigma of time-out.

For this modeling session, I set up a scenario in which a student is sharing about an assignment, and another begins carrying on a side conversation with a neighbor. Interestingly, most middle school students get into modeling, and this group is no different. One student readily volunteers to play the sharer, another the teacher, and I play the part of the interrupter. Although the time-out, or "vacation," chair is usually near the side door, for this modeling I place it in the center of the circle so that everyone can see it clearly.

The modeling begins. The "sharer" starts, "The reason I chose this book for my report…"

"Psst, psst, psst," I whisper to a neighbor.

"Ms. Brady, take a vacation," the "teacher" says.

Doing my best imitation of a twelve-year-old, I get up, walk with a resigned air to the chair, and plunk myself down. I slouch low. I look at my fingernails, chew them. I check the clock, take a deep breath, and sigh quietly. After another forty-five seconds, I return to the circle.

The students have been watching intently, suppressing giggles. Their amusement, however, hasn't kept them from taking in the important details of my behavior. When I ask them what they noticed, they said "You got up and went to the chair when Alexi asked you to," "You didn't make a face at anybody while you were leaving the circle," "You kept your face, uhm, solemn," "You came back on your own. It wasn't the teacher who told you when to come back," "You were in the vacation chair for less than a minute."

I piggyback on this last observation to make a point about not lingering too long in vacation. "That was all the time that I needed to get my controls back. Some students spend two minutes in the vacation chair, but usually people don't spend more than three. It's important to return to work as soon as possible."

Then I ask, "What about everyone else in the room? How should they act when someone has to go to vacation?" It's important for students to realize they all have a role to play in helping the person regain self-control.

"Everyone should continue what they're doing and let that person do what they need to do," one student responds.

"Exactly. Would anyone else like to practice moving to the vacation chair?" We do one or two more rounds before ending the modeling session.

Apologies in middle school:

The importance of heartfelt verbal apologies

Middle school students, as much as younger children, need to learn ways to make amends for hurting others. So teaching them apology of action, the kind of "you break it, you fix it" used for repairing hurt feelings, is still helpful. However, keep in mind that at the middle school level, sometimes an honest and heartfelt verbal apology can mean as much as, if not more than, a gesture or action.

Tatiana was one of two girls who played regularly on the seventh grade coed softball team. One day on the bus to an away game, Sean began making fun of Tatiana's athletic ability, mimicking her "girly" throw in an exaggerated way. During the game he continued to make snide remarks despite her efforts to ignore him, to tell him to stop, and to make her own jokes about him. The next day Tatiana announced she was quitting the team.

When the teacher asked why, Tatiana explained the incident, venting a range of feelings, from "hurt" to "lonely." The teacher next talked to Sean, who claimed he was just joking and thought Tatiana was "foolin' around too." But when, with the teacher facilitating, Tatiana and Sean sat down to talk to each other and Sean heard Tatiana say how his taunting made her feel, he shifted gears. Yes, she did ask him to stop. Yes, she did look upset. Yes, he could see that he had said some cruel stuff. And he was truly apologetic. "I'm sorry. I shouldn't have said those things," he said in a sincere voice. "They're not true."

"What would you need from Sean so you don't have to quit the team?" the teacher asked Tatiana. Tatiana replied, "I just want him to be nicer to me."

"Can you do that?" the teacher asked Sean. "Yes," Sean replied distinctly.

Sufficiently assured, Tatiana decided to stay on the team. Although Sean took no action to show he was sorry for what he did, Tatiana was okay with the way the incident was resolved because she could see that Sean finally understood how she felt, that he really meant it when he apologized, and that he was serious in promising to be nicer to her from now on.

Apology of action: Also valuable in many cases

The fact that heartfelt words are so important at the middle school level doesn't mean that apologies of action never are. In some cases, action is exactly what's needed.

Grades 6–8

Lee had just gotten a new soccer ball and brought it to school. During an outdoor break time, Robbie, who has a tendency to act before thinking, kicked the ball with all his might straight out into the road. An oncoming truck easily flattened the ball, leaving Lee in tears. At first Robbie insisted that it was an accident, but after a time-out in the classroom, he admitted that he just suddenly felt like kicking the ball as hard as he could. "I didn't mean to get it run over, though," he said. "It just happened that way."

Later, when the two students sat down to talk, Lee, barely holding back sobs, explained that he wasn't supposed to bring the ball to school. "My dad's going to kill me for bringing it after he told me not to." Robbie sighed, "I'm really sorry. It was such a jerko thing to do."

Robbie offered to replace the soccer ball ("I'll have to ask my parents for an advance on my allowance or something"). He also asked if he might write a letter to Lee's dad explaining what happened. "Okay," Lee said. "Maybe he'll only kill me part way."

As with apology of action at the elementary school level, apology of action in middle school helps students see the effects of their mistakes and learn responsibility through righting them, whether the mistakes were honest accidents, intentional acts to harm, or somewhere in between. It also helps students express their feelings when they've been hurt. It helps children repair their relationships and maintain a friendly learning environment.

When teaching students to take action to repair the hurts they've caused, however, middle school teachers often use terms and concepts that especially appeal to adolescents. Ruth Sidney Charney, an experienced teacher and author of *Teaching Children to Care,* has used "restorative justice," a term used in the legal system. The term capitalizes on middle school students' interest in concepts such as justice and their perception of themselves as having the power to repair injustices. Other teachers have used "making amends" or "making reparations," terms that may sound more mature to adolescents than "apology of action," which they may be familiar with from elementary grades.

Whatever term is used, teaching students to use this strategy begins with a careful discussion of the idea of doing something to right a wrong.

Introducing apology of action

I usually introduce apology of action the day after introducing the three main types of logical consequences.

"Yesterday," I begin, "we talked about time-out, loss of privilege, and 'you break it, you fix it' as the three basic kinds of logical consequences we'll use this year to help us correct our mistakes when we don't follow the rules. There's one special kind of 'you break it, you fix it' that I'd like to talk about today. It's used when someone hurts another's feelings. How many of you have ever had your feelings hurt by another student?" Hands go up. "How do people usually show that they're sorry for hurting your feelings?"

"They just say they're sorry," one student says.

"They don't always mean it either," another adds.

"Well, saying sorry helps, and it's important to say it sincerely," I say. "But taking some kind of action to make it up to the person that you hurt is another way to show that you really are sorry. This is called an apology of action or making amends. What are some things people do or say that hurt another's feelings?"

"People call other people names, you know, like racial names and names making fun of the way they look," a student responds.

"People laugh at someone's mistake," another student says.

The students continue with interest on this topic. Before long they've named a long list of hurtful behavior, including spreading rumors and lies, dropping someone as a friend with no explanation, forming cliques and excluding certain people, losing one's temper at someone, taking out one's "bad mood" on others, making fun of someone's test grade, and even failing to show interest when a friend gets a good grade.

Next I ask students to partner up with a neighbor, in what the class calls a "think-pair-share," to come up with scenarios involving some of these hurtful actions and possible ways that a person can make amends to the wronged party in each case. First we quickly review the criteria we established for logical consequences—that they must be respectful of the person who made the mistake, relevant to the mistake, and realistic for the person to do.

Mindful of the importance of teacher language and how a quick pre-activity reminder can prevent so many problems, I say, "Before you start, who can remind everyone what needs to happen in a think-pair-share?"

"We write down one or two ideas on our own and then we share them with someone else, and we listen to our partner when they share," one student responds.

"Okay, go ahead and start. You have ten minutes."

Grades 6–8

The students are completely engaged in this assignment. Their ideas for action apologies are inventive. As I walk around the room listening in on conversations, I see that the students seem to understand the concept of "relevant." Few of them suggest things like making someone carry your books for the day for making fun of your test grade, or asking someone to lend you his CDs for the week for spreading gossip about you.

When the class gathers as a group again to share each pair's ideas, the students are eager to hear what their peers have thought of. Several pairs say that one way to make up for spreading a rumor might be to explain to everyone that the rumor isn't true. Another pair says that if someone makes fun of how you play a sport, s/he could apologize by helping you practice. There are other good ideas. The point isn't to give students a list of actions to apply in rote fashion to certain wrongs, but to get them thinking about how people might feel when certain wrongs are done to them and what might help them feel better.

In addition to introducing apology of action carefully, there are three things I need to do throughout the year if this strategy is to work. First, I need to teach students constructive ways to express their feelings and hold effective conversations about their hurts. One way is to use the "I" voice and name a specific behavior—for example, "I feel angry when you make fun of my. . . " (See the resources on conflict resolution in Appendix A.)

Second, I need to be ready to facilitate such conversations when necessary. Although the goal is for students to be able eventually to hold these conversations themselves, they often need guidance as they practice, especially given how emotionally charged some incidents can be.

Third, I need to let the students involved choose the reparative actions. Though I might help students brainstorm if necessary, I don't decide for them.

Sincere apologies that come from the students and reflect their honest feelings mean much more than gestures assigned by the teacher.

Using Logical Consequences

As at every grade level, using logical consequences in middle school is a matter of thinking about what's appropriate in each situation rather than following some prescription. Deciding on an appropriate logical consequence requires getting clear on what rule was broken, what damage has been done, what needs to be restored, and how best to help this child—with this learning style, this background, this temperament—do the restoring. All this is no different from deciding on logical consequences at the elementary school level.

One thing that is different in middle school, however, is the increased premium that students place on "saving face." Now, more than ever, students need teachers to speak to them privately, to not call attention, to let them do their own talking, to treat them "like adults."

The following are examples of logical consequences in action at the middle school level. They are not meant to be a recipe, but to show the range of possible ways to handle rule breaking and to offer some tips for using logical consequences effectively.

Showing disrespect to a classmate

It's late November, and Mr. Freid's eighth grade class has been addressing the issue of diversity by learning about different cultural traditions, beliefs, and rituals. At today's Circle of Power and Respect, students are sharing whether their families observe Thanksgiving and, if so, how they usually do it.

As Melissa explains her family's Thanksgiving rituals, Sarah tisks loudly from across the circle and rolls her eyes. Everyone notices, and Melissa is obviously flustered. "Sarah, take a vacation," Mr. Freid says. Sarah, looking upset, leaves the area for the vacation chair. Mr. Freid is puzzled by Sarah's behavior because she has never shown disrespect to anyone in the class, and she and Melissa are good friends.

Mr. Freid usually lets students come back from time-out without any discussion. The understanding is that in most cases, students simply need a break from the action and are able to decide on their own when they're ready to come back to the group. No talk is necessary. In this case, however, Mr. Freid senses that he needs to have a conversation with Sarah and possibly with both girls. After a while Sarah returns to the meeting circle.

As the students return to their desks after the meeting, Mr. Freid goes over to Sarah. "Sarah, I need to talk with you about what happened when Melissa was sharing." Sarah crosses her arms and avoids eye contact. "I was surprised by what I saw. I know it's not like you to disrupt meetings." Mr. Freid says. "I hope we can clear this up."

Her eyes filling with tears, Sarah says, "I wasn't trying to cause problems. Melissa and I have just been fighting …"

Grades 6–8

Mr. Freid guides Sarah to a private area of the room and says, "I noticed that you were able to come back to the group and show self-control immediately, so things look good there. The bigger problem seems to be finding a way to apologize to Melissa and to make sure that you both come out of this feeling okay. Will you need help with that?"

"Maybe. It's about her new boyfriend."

Knowing that students generally like and trust Ms. Rice, the school social worker, Mr. Freid suggests asking her to mediate in this situation. Sarah agrees to give it a try, and Mr. Freid picks up the wall phone to call Ms. Rice.

Commentary

It was important that Mr. Freid told Sarah to go on "vacation" even though this was the first time she showed this kind of disrespect. This sends Sarah the message that however understandable her behavior might be, she needs to get herself back in control. Using time-out democratically for anyone who needs it also helps show the class that it's a strategy to help all students, not a punishment for chronic "trouble makers."

Note also that while Mr. Freid is concerned with handling the immediate disruption, he recognizes that the bigger problem here was the strained friendship between Sarah and Melissa. In seventh and eighth grade, school life can be full of challenges related to evolving relationships. Mr. Freid sensed that Sarah and Melissa's problem was bigger than what the girls could handle alone and warranted some adult intervention.

He later found out that when Melissa's new boyfriend came into the picture, she increasingly wanted to spend time with him alone, leaving Sarah feeling shunned. Ms. Rice was able to help Melissa and Sarah sort through their feelings and guide them in redefining their friendship.

Misusing a scalpel

During science class, the students are preparing to dissect owl pellets. They've just had a modeling session on how to use the dissection tools, with an emphasis on the scalpel.

The students are trying to reconstruct the remains of the creatures that the owls ate. Working in pairs at lab tables, they transfer bones and other identifiable matter onto pieces of oak tag. Two partners begin to talk about the scalpels.

"Look at how sharp these things are!" Elise exclaims.

"Yeah, it's hard keeping the scalpel steady with these gloves on, too" her partner Roman replies.

"How sharp do you think these are?"

"Sharp enough. Just go slow, like Ms. Cook said."

"Let's see if they can cut the oak tag."

"I wouldn't do that if I were you," Roman says.

"What's it going to hurt?" Elise says. She picks up the paper and cuts it in a sweeping motion.

Ms. Cook sees her doing this. She walks over to the pair and says quietly, "Elise, you need to stop. Please put the scalpel down."

"Told you," Roman says under his breath.

"Roman, please put your scalpel down, too, for a minute. Elise, we just talked about using these scalpels for one cutting purpose. Do you remember what we said?"

"That we should only cut the pellets with them. I was just trying to see how sharp my scalpel was."

"Yeah, it's pretty sharp. Do you remember why we said we should only cut the pellets with these?"

"'Cause cutting other things will dull the blade."

"That's right," Ms. Cook says. "I'll be putting this scalpel away for the rest of the period. We'll talk again before you finish this lab tomorrow. We'll decide then whether you can give the scalpel another try. Right now, look on with Roman as he does some dissecting. You may want to use the magnifying glass to help you identify any bones that he finds."

Commentary

Ms. Cook understood it was probably just innocent curiosity that made Elise momentarily forget or ignore the fact that the scalpels were to be used to cut only one thing. But she also wondered if Elise somehow missed or misunderstood what was covered in the modeling. If it had been a less dangerous tool, Ms. Cook would have given her a reminder and let her continue to use it. But because it was such a sharp instrument and its specific use and care were so critical, she felt it was appropriate to take the tool away immediately.

However, it was important that Ms. Cook assured Elise that they would talk about her regaining the use of the scalpel after one period. This showed her faith in Elise's ability to show more responsibility.

After taking the scalpel away, Ms. Cook directed Elise to look on with Roman and help identify the bones that he finds. This was a deliberate move. Shifting the focus away from the student's mistake back to the assignment at hand can help the student save face. Not only that, it underscores the importance of academic work and helps reinforce the idea that the reason to take care of classroom equipment is to allow students to do that work well.

Grades 6–8

When Ms. Cook and Elise talked the next day, Ms. Cook saw that the student was indeed unclear on a few of the details of safe and proper scalpel use, so she did some individualized modeling with her before letting her use the tool again. It's not unusual for some students to need such additional modeling.

In this incident, Ms. Cook intervened in time to stop Elise from dulling the scalpel, but if Elise had dulled it enough to make it unusable for this project, Ms. Cook would have talked to her about possible ways to replace the tool or otherwise repair the situation.

Late to class

It's the last week of April in what has been a very warm New England spring. The good weather has added to students' usual restlessness at this time of year, and many are having a hard time making it to class on time. Since school resumed after April break, Ms. Robles has given students extra reminders about their responsibilities. Today, several minutes after she closes the door and begins class, two students walk in.

"Good morning, Derrick and Jackson. Class started eight minutes ago," Ms. Robles says.

Derrick and Jackson look at one another sheepishly. Jackson says, "Yeah, we're late. Sorry. Derrick was showing me something." Ms. Robles notes to herself that this is the second time in three weeks that these two students have been late.

"I'll see you later today to talk about this. Come to this room at 2:30," Ms. Robles says, then continues with class.

At 2:30, the students show up. "Hello, Jackson and Derrick," Ms. Robles says. "We need to talk about your arriving late to class."

Jackson begins immediately to explain. "We left math a couple of minutes late and then lost track of time talking at our lockers. Derrick got a new jacket over April break and was showing it to me."

"That sounds pretty important, but getting to class on time is very important too," Ms. Robles responds.

"We promise it won't happen again."

"Let's make a plan to make sure. What would help you keep track of the time?"

Derrick and Jackson look at each other and shrug. With some prompting from Ms. Robles, however, they soon decide that Derrick could set his watch to beep one minute before class starts. They also decide they could "walk and talk." The two students and the teacher agree to give this plan a try.

Commentary

Ms. Robles understood the students' mood at this time of year, thus the extra reminders about their responsibilities. But she didn't let their restlessness become an excuse for lowering the standards in her classroom. When Derrick and Jackson were late a second time, she realized that reminders alone weren't going to be enough for them, and that a more pointed conversation was needed.

Skillfully, however, she delayed the conversation rather than taking class time to have it. By simply telling the students to come back at 2:30, she minimized the disruption to the class while still letting the boys know that their lateness is something that needs to be dealt with squarely.

When the conversation does take place, it was important that Ms. Robles helped Derrick and Jackson make a practical plan for getting to class on time. This helped prevent the conversation from feeling punitive, giving it instead a positive purpose—to make sure the mistake doesn't happen again in the future. Moreover, Ms. Robles let the students take the lead in making the plan, prompting them as needed but not imposing a plan on them. This is especially important in middle school, when children crave being treated like adults and put such a high premium on taking charge of their own lives. Ms. Robles knew that the more input Derrick and Jackson have in creating the plan, the more invested they'll be in making it work.

Besides having the students come back for a conversation and to make a plan for improvement, Ms. Robles did not impose any other consequence. This was a situation that called for a firm, clear redirection and some practical problem solving rather than one of the three basic types of logical consequences. What needed to be "fixed" in this case was the students' difficulty keeping track of time and the challenge of fitting their socializing into the few minutes between classes. The logical response, therefore, was for them to come up with a plan to address those difficulties.

A clique excludes a classmate

The students in Ms. Smythe's social studies class are beginning a project on land-forms. Ms. Smythe has asked students to form groups of three or four and decide how to divide up the tasks required for this period's assignment. Two friends, Shawna and Nalee, quickly grab Maika to form a group. When a fourth girl, Roslyn, asks to join them, the three say they have enough people in their group already. Roslyn walks back to her desk and sits down. Seeing Roslyn sitting alone, Ms. Smythe goes over and asks if she has found a group to work with yet.

Grades 6–8

"I asked Shawna and Nalee if I could work with them, and they said they have enough," Roslyn says. Ms. Smythe sees right away that Roslyn is having a hard time bouncing back from the rebuff and needs some prodding to find another work group.

Glancing over at the girls, who are looking Roslyn's way, Ms. Smythe says, "I notice that Tony and José have asked Angelica to work with them. Would you like to ask to join their group?"

Roslyn approaches Tony, José, and Angela and is welcomed into their group. Ms. Smythe waits to make sure that Roslyn is set, then walks over to Shawna, Nalee, and Maika. "I understand you turned someone away from working with you. Remember I said each group can have up to four people?" she says to them.

"We knew that, but we didn't want to work with Roslyn," Nalee says. "We don't want to hang around with her. She's not one of our friends."

"This project is not a social event," Ms. Smythe responds. "It's about working together to do our best learning, which is one of our class rules. You can work in a cooperative way with people who aren't your friends. When we change work groups next week, the three of you will need to split up. We'll talk specifically about your choices next Monday. Right now you may take out your rubric and start choosing tasks."

Commentary

Learning can be tricky business at the middle school level, when children's social affairs loom large. Students need to have choices around their learning, but as Ms. Smythe demonstrates, when the social agenda interferes with working and learning together productively, the teacher needs to remind students of the purpose of working together.

Academic learning aside, adolescents need to learn that excluding someone, and clique behavior in general, is hurtful and unacceptable socially. Ms. Smythe made that point when she told the girls to split up the following week. Note that she didn't lecture; she simply told them they'll have to find new workmates. When it comes to logical consequences, the less said in general, the better. It's best to let the consequence do the job.

Note also that Ms. Smythe didn't split up the girls right away or make them take Roslyn into their group. Forcing students to work together when all parties are aware of the rejection can be uncomfortable and can backfire. Instead she gave them the opportunity to form their own inclusive groups the following Monday, when work groups are scheduled to change. That way, it's less likely anyone will feel embarrassed or shamed. And before instructing students to change groups on Monday, Ms. Smythe will talk with the whole class about the importance of being inclusive and working with a variety of classmates.

Chapter Six

A hurtful note

A secret note has been circulating through a sixth grade math class. Near the end of the period, the note, opened, refolded, and passed from desk to desk, makes its way into the open. "Christa puts out," it reads. The note is signed "Darren." There are dour faces and furious glares. A tearful Christa runs into the girls' bathroom and refuses to come out. Any hope of the class focusing on their math exercises is gone.

It takes most of the lunch period for Ms. Sanders and the class to unravel the story, which at times sounds like an endless series of he saids and she saids. It seems the note was part of a tangle of accusations that began with a remark at a teen dance several weeks ago. The rumors had traveled by phone calls, secret tellings, and whispered asides, escalating to involve most members of the class. If students didn't actively contribute to the gossip, they passively helped by not trying to put a stop to it.

As for Christa and Darren, neither had anything to do with the note, which was fabricated by two classmates.

After getting the story straight, Ms. Sanders decides to meet with Christa, Darren, and the two note writers. She sees clearly that what needs to be restored are, among other things, Christa and Darren's "reputation" and their feeling of safety in the class. Christa feels particularly vulnerable, crying, "No matter what, everyone will think I did that stuff!"

At first, none of the four have any ideas for what might help Darren and Christa feel safe again. With some prompting from Ms. Sanders, however, the two note writers offer to write a statement, without using names, about what they did. The statement would include a promise to try their hardest not to start or pass any more rumors. It would also include a list of ideas for what all students could say or do if stories were passed on to them. The two note writers would first bring the statement to Christa and Darren, then to the group. Agreeing that this would begin to help them feel safer, Christa and Darren accept the offer.

Ms. Sanders next turns to helping the whole class repair and learn from the incident. She decides to hold a whole-class problem-solving meeting on what to do if one sees teasing or rumor-spreading. The statement drafted by the two note writers would serve as a springboard for discussion. (See Appendix A for more about whole-class problem-solving meetings.)

Commentary

Grades 6–8

Given the deep emotional damage that rumors can cause, it was appropriate for Ms. Sanders to respond decisively to this incident. And while such a comprehensive response isn't required in every case of rumor spreading or note passing, it was important in this case because so many students were involved and because the rumors and lies were so hurtful in nature.

And although verbal apologies can often be enough or even preferable for making amends, in this case an apology of action was warranted because Christa and Darren's sense of safety in the class was so shaken. They needed some action that would publicly recoup their reputations, and they needed to see evidence that their classmates were taking steps to ensure such rumor spreading wouldn't happen again.

Notice, however, that despite the seriousness of the incident, Ms. Sanders did not dictate what the apology of action should be. She only guided. While it can be tempting to use a heavy hand when we feel outraged, students learn more when they are allowed to decide what kind of reparation would be appropriate. The reparation may also feel more meaningful to the wronged students when they know that it was chosen by those who hurt them rather than the teacher.

It was important that after the two note writers decided to prepare their statement and the list of possible helpful responses to gossiping, Ms. Sanders involved the whole class in dealing with the incident. The critical message to students is that rumors affect the whole class and everyone has a responsibility to help stop them. Not actively passing on rumors isn't good enough. You have to, as the list of ideas generated by the two note writers suggest, actively do or say something to halt rumor spreading when you encounter it.

The Power of Many

When an individual teacher uses the approach to rules described in this book, the classroom can take on a whole different tone. But when a team of teachers or, better yet, a whole school uses the approach, the effect can be even more powerful.

Having a comprehensive school-wide discipline plan is perhaps particularly important in middle school. When teachers see any given group of students for only a period a day, they have to rely more on a larger environment that supports the discipline approach they use during their time with the students.

I've seen again and again what a difference it can make when all teachers and staff at a school use the same approach to discipline. I remember a sixth grade girl at a school I taught in. She struggled with self-esteem, had many social problems, and was constantly in trouble. In fact, she seemed to crave the attention she got from acting out, and her antics were often designed to get herself caught. The more witnesses to the crime and punishment, the better.

Her biggest thrill, however, seemed to come from getting lots of other students to go along with her so they would all get in trouble together. This went well for a while until the adults in the school began moving from an autocratic discipline approach to the approach described in this book. Within a year, the changes in the school climate were noticeable. Students were more invested in following the rules, relationships between adults and students were less adversarial, and communications among students became healthier and more respectful.

By year two, the improvements were even more dramatic. During that year, this child left to attend another school. The following year when she returned, she sensed that something had changed. One day early in the school year, the student was sent to the principal's office alone for cutting class.

When the principal asked her why she was cutting class, she looked at him with complete exasperation, threw up her arms, and asked, "What are you doing to the kids in this school? This school is whacked! A few years ago I could have found ten kids to get in trouble with me. Now I can't even find one!"

Works Cited

Denton, Paula, and Roxann Kriete. 2000. *The First Six Weeks of School.* Greenfield, MA: Northeast Foundation for Children.

Kriete, Roxann, with contributions by Lynn Bechtel. 2002. *The Morning Meeting Book.* Greenfield, MA: Northeast Foundation for Children.

Chapter Seven

TAKING THE RULES BEYOND THE CLASSROOM: STRATEGIES FOR TEACHERS

BY CHIP WOOD

*They're fine when
they're with me. It's just when they come back from art or music
or PE, etc., that I get reports of behavior problems.*

*How is it that kids can be so kind in Morning Meeting
and then so cruel to each other at their lunch tables?*

*He acts fine in class, but the moment he steps onto the playground
he becomes the schoolyard bully.*

*They'd never behave like this on the bus if I were on it.
Why can't they remember the rules for themselves,
or at least listen to the bus driver?*

What classroom teacher hasn't felt this frustration at one point or another? You devote an enormous amount of time and energy to creating a positive climate in your classroom. You work tirelessly to teach students respect and responsibility. You feel a sense of satisfaction when you see students beginning to internalize the rules and develop self-control. And then they leave the four walls of your classroom, and it all falls apart.

It's impossible for the classroom teacher to follow a group of students through every part of every school day—to notice all the small actions, to offer reminders, to redirect children who've gotten off track. But there's a lot the teacher can do to help students themselves apply their rules to settings beyond the classroom. There's also a lot the teacher can do to promote communication and consistency among other adults regarding discipline. Special area teachers, bus and lunch monitors, fellow teachers, administrators, and families can all support what the teacher is trying to achieve with students.

So far, this book has focused on rules in the classroom. In this chapter, I offer teachers strategies for:

- Working with students to apply their rules to settings outside the classroom
- Working with administrators and staff to ensure greater consistency around rules and discipline practices
- Working with families to promote collaboration on discipline practices

Taking the Rules Beyond the Classroom

Working with Students

First, understand how self-control develops

There are two things teachers must keep in mind when teaching children to follow rules even when no adult is around: First, it takes time for children to develop self-control. Second, some children take longer than others.

Remembering these two facts of life will help prevent us from feeling defeated. Just five minutes ago, Cory was working with great cooperation and kindness on a group project. Now he's taunting a classmate and throwing food across the table in the lunchroom. But that doesn't mean Cory hasn't learned a thing about applying the rules beyond the classroom. It just means that how children look when they're learning is often different from how we think they should look when they're learning.

The process of developing self-control is not necessarily linear. There will be many detours along the way that may look to adults like failures. Nor is there only one path to self-control. Different children take different detours. Over a long career in education as a classroom teacher, principal, and teacher educator, I've often observed, as any teacher would, that some children seem to internalize rules more readily, while others struggle to accept even the clearest limits.

We often wonder if parenting is what causes this difference among children. While parenting ability matters, everything I've seen convinces me that it is no more the key variable in this equation than is teaching ability. I've watched exceptionally skillful parents struggle, forced to invent new strategies daily. And I've known many kind, responsible children from families constantly in crisis.

The development of self-control is a gradual cognitive process, like learning to read. In fact, children in this process *are* learning to read—to read the social cues of grownups and peers. Just as in learning academics, in learning social skills there are developmental progressions and limits that exist for all children.

For instance, children's brain growth has a profound impact on their "procedural memory" and their ability to generalize and internalize good habits of social interaction. As respected medical writer Rita Carter notes, we know from brain research that "children find it more difficult to resist their impulses, partly...because the prefrontal lobes are very slow to mature." Meanwhile, the limbic system, the "flight or fight" system that makes one act before one thinks, is quite functional. Carter writes, "Until the frontal lobes are fully working— which may not be until a person is in their twenties—the limbic system is the stronger force." (Carter 1998, 197)

Chapter Seven

Children's development: Things to keep in mind

1. Although children's development generally follows predictable broad patterns, the specific path and pace of each child's development is unique. Physical, environmental, and cultural differences all affect development.

2. Development takes time. We can manipulate standards, but we cannot manipulate development.

3. Modeling matters. Children learn from the actions and expectations of the adults in their lives.

4. We can maximize children's learning by using teaching strategies that respect their developmental needs.

For a fuller description of developmental issues and an extensive professional reading list, see *Yardsticks: Children in the Classroom Ages 4–14.*

Teach students to take the classroom rules outside the classroom

Once the rules for the classroom have been established, teachers can help students learn to take these rules to the lunchroom, the playground, the hallway, and all the other places students go in the school. Teachers need to translate, model, and help students practice the rules in these other settings, just as when teaching students to apply the rules to different settings within the classroom. Below are two examples of what this process might look like.

Taking the rules to the lunchroom

It's the fourth week of school. The fourth grade class has established and begun practicing their classroom rules:

**Taking
the Rules
Beyond the
Classroom**

- Be friendly with everyone.

- Be in control of yourself at all times.

- Take care of materials.

- Do your best work.

The teacher now wants to establish the expectation that these rules should extend beyond the classroom.

She might begin by saying, "We've created some really great rules for how we'll be with each other in this classroom. I know that these rules can also apply to all the areas of our school: the hallways, the playground, the lunchroom, the bathroom. Let's think today about the lunchroom. What do you think we would do to follow our rules during lunch?"

As they do in generating classroom rules, students will often begin by framing their lunchroom rules in terms of what they shouldn't do. The teacher can help them reframe these as what they *should* do. Here, for example, is a partial list generated by this class:

- Talk in soft voices.
  (Began as "no yelling.")

- Stay at your table until the bell rings.
  (Began as "Don't run around.")

- Be nice to the people working in the cafeteria.

- Be friendly and let anyone sit at your table.
  (Began as "Don't tell people they can't sit with you.")

- Remember to eat your lunch.
  (Began as "Don't just goof around the whole time and forget to eat.")
- Be respectful of people's food preferences.
  (Began as "Don't make faces about people's food or tell people you don't like their food.")

Students can then create a poster with these guidelines, which gets hung by the classroom door or even in the lunchroom. If lunchroom rules or general school rules already exist, the class might want to compare them with the list they generated.

After posting their guidelines for lunchroom behaviors, the class begins to model and practice these behaviors, first in their own classroom and then in the lunchroom (see guidelines for modeling in Chapter 2). The best time to practice in the lunchroom is when no one is actually there eating lunch. It can also be helpful to involve a few lunchroom staff. This makes the practice more authentic and lets the lunchroom staff know that you are working on applying classroom rules to the lunchroom.

Finally, before lunch on the next day, the teacher might remind students of the guidelines they've created and let them know that s/he will be checking in with them after lunch to see how things went. These check-in sessions can be short and sweet. Every few days, the teacher can briefly ask students questions such as "How did lunch go today?" "Which rules were easy to follow?" "Which ones were hard?" "Any ideas for making lunch more enjoyable?"

Remember that the goal is to help students get better and better at being responsible outside the classroom, not to achieve instant perfection. Keep the conversation alive. Celebrate the small victories along the way. In time, you'll see a difference in your students' lunchroom behavior. And if all the teachers in a grade-level team or in the whole school do this kind of proactive work, you'll see an improvement in the overall lunchroom climate as well.

Taking the rules to the bus

Behavior on the bus has always challenged children's developing abilities of self-control, not to mention the patience of bus drivers, parents, and principals. The truth of the matter is that nowhere is children's misbehavior and mistreatment of each other more ignored than on the school bus.

This is because the methods to solve the problems are expensive, time consuming, and complicated. If there is agreement to try some solution or other, the implementation is often inconsistent and the follow-up spotty, and the children often become quite savvy about what they can "get away with" on the bus. For the most part, bus monitors, closed circuit TV monitors, bus detentions, and suspensions have not resulted in long-term learning or significant changes in student conduct.

While a classroom teacher can work toward long-term solutions by advocating for a comprehensive school-wide discipline plan (see the next section of this chapter on working with school staff), there are often many factors affecting children's actions on the bus that are beyond the teacher's influence. Still, there are some things a classroom teacher can do to help students live by their classroom rules more closely when they're on the bus.

The first strategy, as illustrated in the lunchroom example above, is to work with your class on translating classroom rules to the bus setting and to check in with the students every few days. The second strategy is to take time at the end of the school day to prepare students for the transition to the bus.

The end of the school day is seldom used proactively enough to help children make the transition to their next learning experience. In most communities this transition now means shifting to an after-school program with another set of adults who may have different expectations. Such programs can be either on-site or a bus ride away.

I know that when I was a teacher, I was often guilty of teaching right up to the last minute, getting in just one more idea or spending a little more time going over the homework assignment, even after the bus calls had started. I didn't pay attention to what the children needed most at that moment.

I now recommend that teachers try to end the school day ten minutes before the buses are called, to have all the cleanup done, the homework explained, and any notices going home already in backpacks. The teachers can then gather the children in a quiet circle on the rug to reflect about the day and rehearse the bus ride home.

This simple check-in can make a big difference in how children are able to handle the bus ride. For example:

- A teacher says, "Are you going to your grandmother's this afternoon, Jeremy? Would you like to take this piece of writing to show her your new words?" This may be just the right amount of rehearsal for Jeremy to make the bus trip without getting into conflicts.

- A teacher announces, "Students on Bus Three, I'd like to see you on the meeting rug for five minutes. The rest of you can read your new library books quietly." This could give the teacher time to model and role play with children on this bus what they need to remember during their ride to the after-school site.

I want to acknowledge that this is the hardest time of day for the teacher to be proactive. S/he is tired and the children are tired. The person on the loud-speaker is tired. Elsewhere I have written extensively about the effects our use of time has on the quality of teaching and on student achievement (see Wood 1999, especially Chapter Nine). How we use the end of the day certainly influences how students conduct themselves on the bus.

Traveling rules: Our rules go with us wherever we go

In many classrooms at Kensington Elementary School in Springfield, Massachusetts, one of the daily jobs is "rule bearer." This child has the responsibility of carrying a laminated poster of the classroom rules wherever the class goes. Whether the group goes to the auditorium for music, the gym for PE, or the library for research, the rule bearer brings the classroom rules along for posting. At the end of the period, the rule bearer carries the rules back to the classroom.

Tina Valentine's fourth grade class was the first to use this idea at Kensington. It has since spread throughout her school and into others. "It's a tangible reminder that no matter where students are or who is teaching them, their classroom rules still apply," says Valentine.

Fellow Kensington teacher Maureen Russell teaches her first graders a ritual for handing off the rules poster, which she attaches to a coat hanger for easier carrying. Upon entering a special area, the rule bearer goes to the special area teacher and announces, "Here are our rules." The teacher responds, "I accept the rules of Room 10," then hangs the rules in a prominent place.

The first time the traveling rules are received, the special area teacher talks with students about what it might look like to follow these rules in the special area. In some cases, the special area teacher might add a rule or two that are specific to that area. To achieve the greatest consistency, the special area teacher also uses the same signals for attention as the classroom teacher and follows the same procedures when a child doesn't follow the rules.

When introducing the idea of traveling rules to students, it's important to involve the special area teachers in the conversation from the start. The more that students can see teachers working together on this, the greater the chances for its success.

Working with School Staff

Seek clarity and consistency in school-wide discipline practices

There's no mistaking a school that has a strong and effective school-wide discipline plan. Students, teachers, and families can immediately sense a positive atmosphere upon their first visit to such a school. The school feels orderly, calm, and safe. In these schools the "welcoming quotient" is typically high. Teachers, students, and families are greeted and spoken to in a friendly manner, and it's easy to gain information about "how things are done around here."

Walk into Reingold Elementary School in Fitchburg, Massachusetts, and you'll see the "Reingold School Rules" displayed in almost every hallway and community gathering spot, from the cafeteria to the bathrooms to the playground. One such display includes the signature of every student in the school. The signatures indicate that the students helped create the rules and agree to them. (See photo.)

Taking the Rules Beyond the Classroom

One elementary school's school-wide rules

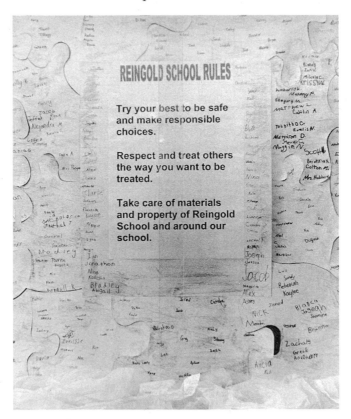

Having an effective school-wide policy means not only having clear rules that govern the entire school community, but having clear policies and procedures for helping students get back on track when rules are broken. There is a clear process for use by all, from lunchroom teachers to bus monitors to classroom teachers.

For Adam, a strong-willed third grader, this means knowing that when he acts out toward a classmate, there is a consistent consequence of going to time-out, in the buddy teacher's room if needed, until gradually he learns more appropriate ways to interact with his peers. For Ms. A., a fourth grade teacher dealing with significant and repetitive misbehavior from one of her students, it means being confident that when she needs administrative backup, the response time will be short and her judgment trusted.

While it's beyond the scope of this book to describe a process for achieving a comprehensive school-wide discipline plan, it's important for teachers to advocate for such a plan if it doesn't already exist.

Creating and implementing such a plan requires care and could take up to two years. However, there are steps that teachers and administrators can take along the way to establish greater consistency around discipline. These include agreeing on school-wide signals for quiet, using a buddy system for times when students need a brief time away from their classroom, and establishing a clear chain of command for times when a child needs a longer break from the classroom.

Clarify adults' roles in creating a climate of trust

While educators have always known the valuable role that trust plays in creating a positive *classroom* learning climate, current research indicates the importance of also paying attention to the trust factor in the *school-wide* community.

According to a report in the *Harvard Education Letter,* "Improvements in such areas as classroom instruction, curriculum, teacher preparation, and professional development have little chance of succeeding without improvements in a school's social climate." Schools with a high degree of "relational trust," the report continues, are "more likely to make changes that help raise student achievement." One study of school reform noted that "schools where poor relationships did not improve had no chance of making academic improvement." (Gordon 2002) (See also Bryk and Schneider 2002, and Palmer 1998.)

All schools have existing codes of conduct that are reviewed occasionally. Most are written with an almost exclusive focus on student behavior. The related and pivotal roles of the adults are seldom well articulated.

Chapter Seven

In talking with administrators about school-wide discipline, it's important to emphasize the need for clear expectations for all adults in a school. This should include both how they are to carry out discipline as individuals and how they are to work together to see that practice is consistent and helpful for all.

Advocate for common school-wide signals for quiet

Over and over, my experience in schools has shown me the importance of the whole school using consistent signals for quiet in common spaces such as the lunchroom, playground, and auditorium. If there's one thing to do to improve the school-wide climate, this would be it.

I have observed that in schools where there is agreement on the signals and how they are used, there is more control and more respect throughout the school. A raised hand or a chime rung once brings an immediate response.

For example, Mr. C. rings the chime at lunch just as three teachers enter the cafeteria. The children stop and give their attention to Mr. C., most of them raising their hands as well to help spread the signal. The three teachers do the same. When the lunchroom is quiet, Mr. C. invites the teachers to continue what they were doing, then begins his message to the students.

It's important in using a school-wide signal that all the adults present show respect for it. When adults continue to talk over the signal, it clearly takes longer to get students' attention, and there is less of an attitude of respect between students and adults.

As mentioned in Chapter 1, not everyone present needs to have copied the signal before the speaker begins talking. The important thing is that everyone gets quiet and attentive. Remember, too, that it's helpful to have an auditory signal, such as a bell rung once, and a visual signal, such as a raised hand, so that teachers can choose the appropriate signal for the situation. (See Chapter 1 for details.)

Initiate and regularly use a buddy teacher system

Earlier chapters of this book talked about the importance of having a buddy teacher for times when a child needs to take a time-out in another classroom to regain control. This system is used when a teacher has asked a child to take a time-out and the child refuses to go or continues to be disruptive either in time-out or immediately upon returning.

Rather than the classroom teacher engaging with the child at this point, which all too often leads to a power struggle, the teacher asks another child to

Taking the Rules Beyond the Classroom

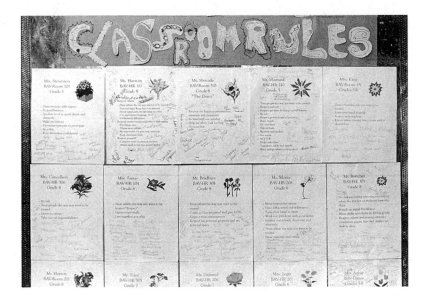

At this middle school, each homeroom makes a copy of its rules for a hallway display.

notify the buddy teacher. The buddy teacher comes to escort the child to the buddy teacher's room while the child's classroom teacher continues to teach. At the end of the class period, the classroom teacher goes to the buddy teacher's room. If the child has regained control and is ready to rejoin the class, the classroom teacher welcomes the child back, and the two return to the classroom together. Later, when the teacher has a moment, the two talk about what led to the need for a time-out and how to avoid a similar problem in the future.

Many teachers worry that this strategy might be embarrassing for students because it means the child must leave his/her classroom and walk into another classroom. This can be embarrassing, which is why it's so important to model and role play the procedure with children before it's ever needed in a real situation. Teachers can help students understand that there is always some embarrassment when you lose control and that no one should make fun of students who need a time-out, whether in the classroom or somewhere else. Teachers can also help students understand that some children will simply need time with a buddy teacher more often than others.

It's important to keep teaching and talking to children about the use of the buddy teacher throughout the year. This will help to minimize the embarrassment and maximize the respect shown to the student in such a situation.

Some teachers also worry that it's an inconvenience for the buddy teacher to have to leave her/his room to get a student. Teachers sometimes ask if they couldn't just have the child go unescorted to the buddy teacher's room. There are a couple of reasons not to do this.

First, for safety's sake, it's important to keep an out-of-control child within adult sight. Second, by continuing with the lesson rather than escorting the child to the buddy teacher's room, the classroom teacher lets the children see that rule breaking isn't going to change their teacher's agenda. With the buddy teacher taking care of the child for the moment, the classroom teacher can continue to teach the rest of the class as planned.

Be clear about procedures beyond the use of the buddy teacher

Taking the Rules Beyond the Classroom

In addition to having a buddy teacher to call on when a student needs to leave the classroom to regain control, a teacher needs to know whom to call on next and what procedure to follow.

If your school has a clear policy, be sure you know it and can communicate it to families. If a policy does not exist, urge the principal to establish one.

Below is an example of such a policy. In looking at it, keep in mind that creating an effective school-wide discipline policy requires the investment and support of all the adults in the school community, including administrators, teachers, and families. It would be unwise for one school simply to adopt another school's policy without discussion. To be effective, a school's discipline plan must be tailored to the specific needs of its community and be supported by its members. Achieving this requires discussion, shared decision-making, and time.

Sample Pathways to Self-Control

We recognize that all children will forget the rules sometimes. This is part of learning to be a good citizen at our school and in life. Teachers and staff will use the following pathways in a consistent manner to handle rule breaking.

Pathway 1: Proactive discipline (creating, modeling, and practicing the rules)

Without proactive discipline, the follow-through measures described below will unlikely have lasting effects on students or on the overall school climate. Instead, these measures will continue to be viewed as punishments for student misbehavior rather than as ways to help students regain self-control and refocus on learning. A key to good proactive discipline is establishing a positive relationship between each child and his/her teacher.

Pathway 2: Reminding and redirecting

When students act inappropriately, teachers and other adults will give them reminders and redirection. Some children will need more than one reminder, but it's generally more effective to limit the number of reminders.

When the misbehavior is flagrant or frequently repeated, it may be appropriate to skip the reminding and redirecting, going directly to time-out or other pathways instead.

Pathway 3: Time-out in the classroom

When reminders are ineffective, teachers will tell students to take a brief time-out to regain self-control. Afterwards, the student will return to the lesson or activity. When the student is productively re-engaged in learning, the teacher may check in briefly to be sure the student understands why the time-out was necessary.

If the student went to time-out without being first given a reminder, the check-in may need to be longer and more detailed.

Pathway 4: Time-out in a buddy teacher's room

Sometimes it's easier for children to regain control when they're away from their class. If the student continues to behave inappropriately in time-out, the classroom teacher will send for a buddy teacher. The buddy teacher will bring the student to her/his room for the rest of the period. At the end of the period, the student's teacher will go to the buddy teacher's room and bring the student back to rejoin the class. Once the student is resettled and the teacher has a moment, the two will talk together about what caused the problem and how it can be prevented in the future.

Pathway 5: Involve the principal or principal-designee

If a student becomes disruptive in the buddy teacher's room or continues to be disruptive upon returning, the principal or designee (see sample chain of command on next page) will be called to take the student to the office or other designated place in the school. The student will stay there until the end of the period or until the principal or designee determines that the student is ready to re-enter the classroom. Before re-entering, the classroom teacher will talk with the child about the incident and welcome the child back to the class.

Parents will be notified that Pathway 5 is being used. This will require the parent to come to school or call at the beginning of the next day to talk with the teacher and re-establish expectations for the child.

Adults are expected to use their best judgment, sometimes skipping earlier pathways and immediately calling for someone higher in the chain of command for extremely serious or dangerous behavior.

**Sample chain of command
for pathway 5 or extreme situations**

1. Use your telephone or send a student to the office with a "red card." This will alert anyone who is in the office that you have a serious situation needing an immediate response.

2. Ms. Gaston, the principal, will respond if possible.

3. Mr. Alston, fourth grade special education inclusion teacher (Room 3), is the second person to be called.

4. Mrs. Spencer, administrative intern (extension 12), is the third person.

5. Ms. McCallister, fifth grade teacher, is the fourth person to be called. In this case, Ms. Ortez next door will take Ms. McCallister's class.

Pathway 6: Involve security/police

In extreme situations, where a student may be physically out of control, a teacher may remove his/her class from the situation and ask for security assistance or request local police or emergency medical services. Such outside assistance needs to be pre-arranged and will be used only in extreme situations that jeopardize health or safety. The school will make every attempt to notify the parent to come get the child before seeking police assistance.

Students will never be sent on their own from a classroom, but will always be escorted by an adult. Adults will not use physical restraint to escort a child unless the physical well-being of a child or adult is threatened. The school will provide several personnel with state-approved training in the use of physical restraint.

**Taking
the Rules
Beyond the
Classroom**

Final notes about pathways to self-control

- These pathways are used for out-of-control behavior and are meant to help children regain their self-control as quickly as possible. For other kinds of mistakes, it may be suitable to use other logical consequences, such as loss of privilege or "you break it, you fix it," to help children develop social skills, solve problems, and learn to make responsible choices.

- These pathways may not be effective in changing all children's out-of-control behavior patterns. In some cases, families, teachers, specialists, and administrators may need to work together to develop an individualized behavior management plan for the child.

Chapter Seven

On sending students to the office

Teachers sometimes ask why they can't have students go to the office on their own, rather than having an adult escort them. I want to emphasize that sending children to the office alone, one of the most often used strategies in education, has also been one of the least successful and most dangerous.

The worst thing we can do with out-of-control children is to send them out of our sight. The children might never make it to the office. They might deface the bathroom. They might go down the street. And if we escort a child to the office ourselves rather than relying on another adult to do it, we take our attention away from our class. We are also likely to engage in and lose a power struggle with the child.

So, when we need to send a child to the office, it's important that an adult come to retrieve the child. It's also important to establish a clear chain of command so that if the principal is not available, the next person in authority can supervise the child.

Each person in the chain of command should know exactly what to do when escorting a child from a classroom. Here are some guidelines:

- Engage in as little dialogue as possible.
- Give the child a cooling down period.

- Inform the child that her/his parents are being notified and will be talking with the teacher before school tomorrow.

- Perhaps engage in some discussion with the child just before the child returns to class.

On welcoming students back into the classroom

Students who have had to leave the classroom require our careful attention when they return. How we welcome them back will make a big difference to how they act afterwards. Students know whether or not "all is forgiven." They can tell it in our facial expression and our tone of voice. There is more than one way to say "welcome back."

"Hello, Doug, we've just started Chapter Seven in math," a teacher might say with a smile. "Take your seat, and I'll be over to help you in a minute." This may be all it takes to relieve the anxiety of a returning student. But think of the difference if this message were conveyed without the last sentence, "I'll be over to help you in a minute," and without a smile. If students are to believe that they have the ability to improve the way they act, they need to sense our conviction about their ability. In addition, seeing how we behave in these moments is one way children learn what it means to forgive and let someone try again.

According to psychological theory, one of three primary mechanisms that support positive goal-directed behavior and a person's sense of self is "adequate feedback with respect to progress." (Averill and More 1993, 624) Thus, it will be important for the teacher to go over to Doug later in the period, not only to help him with his math, but also to tell Doug what's expected of him as he re-enters the classroom. This will also allow Doug to tell the teacher one or two things he will work on to be a more productive student. The teacher will also want to check in with Doug at the end of the week to make sure he knows how he's doing.

Remember that consistency is not the same as linear equality

Consistency around discipline procedures, such as the use of the pathways to self-control, provides the children and adults in the school with a sense of safety and security. Consistency, however, is not the same as linear equality. Not every child will get the same number of reminders or go through the same pathways to self-control. It's wise to remember that "in order to be treated fairly and equally, children have to be treated differently." (Konner 1991, 405)

In more than one school trying to tighten up discipline structures, students asked to leave a group have been heard to say "But you didn't give me my

Applying classroom rules to the lunchroom

reminder!" Self-control is the business of learning to give yourself reminders rather than always relying on a teacher to give them. To cultivate this self-control in children, teachers need to use discipline procedures consistently but flexibly, rather than in a rigid, no-exceptions way.

Students who remember they didn't get a reminder are showing the beginnings of the internalization of control. The teacher might now let them know they are expected to follow rules without reminders most of the time: "I know you don't always need a reminder to follow this rule." This is especially true for students in intermediate grades, although even in intermediate grades, needs may differ from student to student. A child with ADHD, for example, might need more reminders than others about such things as not interrupting.

Working with Families

Communicate often about rules and discipline practices

In working with families on rules and discipline, the more information you provide, the better. In general, the better informed families are of classroom and school-wide practices, the more supportive they'll be, especially when problems arise.

Many teachers send home a letter early in the year explaining the rule-creation process and inviting families to articulate their hopes and dreams for their child (more on this below). Many teachers also send a letter a few weeks later, once the rules have been created, listing the rules and asking families for their support in help-ing students live by these rules in school. This letter might also include information about classroom practices regarding logical consequences. Here's a sample letter:

Taking the Rules Beyond the Classroom

Dear Families,

In these first weeks of school, we've been talking about our hopes and dreams for the year and the rules that we'll need to help us reach them. We want to make our classroom a safe and caring place so that all of our hopes and dreams come true.

To make our classroom safe, we remember:

> **Our Class Rules**
> **Take care of yourself.**
> **Help and respect each other.**
> **Be gentle and take care of all the things in our school.**
> **Be a thinking worker.**

We know that everyone makes mistakes from time to time, and it's how we fix and learn from our mistakes that's most important. When children make mistakes in following our classroom rules, I, as their teacher, will help them see the consequences of their actions and help them fix any problems that their actions caused.

You can help at home. Please keep this letter in a convenient place and review it frequently with your child. We are all working together to create a caring community of learners. Thank you.

Sincerely,

Finally, many principals send home a letter every year articulating school-wide rules and discipline practices and asking families to review these with their child. If this does not happen in your school, you might want to advocate for it.

In communicating with families, keep in mind that it's as important for them to understand the intentions behind discipline practices as it is to understand the practices themselves.

Invite families into the hopes and dreams process

If we really believe the slogan "Parents are partners in their children's education," then we have to make it a top priority to develop relationships with parents.

Earlier chapters addressed inviting families into the process of articulating hopes and dreams for the year. I want to further emphasize the importance of this.

I strongly believe that the first family-teacher conference should take place before school begins each year and should be part of the teacher's contracted responsibilities. Each child's family should meet the teacher face-to-face. This will help the family and teacher build a relationship based on respect and good-will, where the family knows from the beginning of the school year that the teacher has only the best intentions for the child.

This conference might be the time for teachers to ask families the critical question, "What do you want your child to learn in school this year?" Teachers who have held these conferences often report being initially surprised by the answers. Often, half or more of the responses are of a social nature:

- "I want my child to be better behaved."

- "I wish she had more friends. Can you help with that?"

- "I want him to like school."

- "Last year he got into a lot of trouble with his teacher. I want you to be strict with him. I want him to learn."

Of course, there are opinions about academics as well:

- "I want him to learn his math facts. He doesn't know his tables yet."

- "She loves to read. She always has her nose in a book. I don't want her to be bored with what she has to read in school. Will she have any choices?"

- "I want him to have a lot of science. What are you planning?"

- "Her spelling needs improvement. How do you teach spelling?"

By listening, responding, and then writing down the family's top social and academic goals for the child, the teacher sends a clear message: The school cares about what the family thinks. The teacher can then share her/his goals for the class, both academic and social goals, and assure the family that they will talk about the child's progress at the next conference in the fall. The teacher can also indicate that the child, too, will be asked to name goals for the school year and that the child's answers will be used to create classroom rules.

Schools that are unable to immediately institute a before-the-school-year conference often adapt this process by having teachers send letters home with "goal surveys." These are returned at open houses or back-to-school nights.

Back-to-school nights are also a good time to share with families how goal setting is linked to rule creation. At such gatherings, teachers often explain the process the class has just used to develop the classroom rules, which are freshly on display. "These are the rules," the teacher might say, "that will make our hopes and dreams for school this year come true."

Solving problems with families

Every teacher knows it's important for families and school staff to work closely together when children are having difficulties. Every teacher also knows how challenging this can sometimes be. When behavior problems are at play, there's a great temptation for teachers and families to feel angry, cast blame, or become defensive.

Below are some suggestions for working with families, especially in confronting difficult problems. The goal is for teachers and families to get on the same side so that they can focus on helping the child.

Taking the Rules Beyond the Classroom

Make sure families always feel welcome in your classroom

Regularly invite them into the life of the classroom by asking for their help and participation. Keep them well informed through letters or newsletters about happenings in the classroom and school. Make a point of calling families in the early weeks of school to report on the positive things you're noticing about their child.

Always set up an appointment to talk about a problem

Never raise issues or engage in an extended conversation on the spot, even when the family brings up a concern. For example, don't get into a discussion during drop-off or at an open house. Express your concern and make an appointment to talk about it so you can both focus on the issue without distractions.

Take a problem-solving instead of a judgmental stance

Ask questions to avoid jumping to conclusions. Listen actively. Make sure you have some positive things to say about the child. Credit families for their hard work and their love for their child, and show empathy for their situation.

Help families focus on one or two issues for the moment

When there are several issues or problems to solve, find one or two that you both agree are most important to work on for the moment. It's counterproductive to try to tackle everything at once.

Try to include the child in some part of the conversation

For younger students, it might be after the adults have decided on a course of action. For older students, it might be during the problem-solving conversations. This sends the child the important message that parents and teachers are on the same side, working together to solve the problem and help the child.

Occasionally, a teacher and family will need other experts to help resolve a student's discipline problem. Especially when there are no obvious answers, it is the teacher's job to seek others' guidance. Principals, counselors, special education teachers, and colleagues are all important resources and allies. In these situations, it's important to recognize that needing to rely on others' expertise is not a failure on the part of the teacher or the family, but a reality of life. So often in the teaching profession, we feel we need to bravely go it alone. Nothing could be further from the truth. It really does take a village to raise a child.

**Chapter
Seven**

Works Cited

Averill, James R. and Thomas A. More. 1993. "Happiness." *Handbook of Emotions.* Michael Lewis and Jeanette M. Haviland, eds. New York: The Guilford Press.

Bryk, Anthony S., and Barbara Schneider. 2002. *Trust in Schools: A Core Resource for Improvement.* New York: Russell Sage Foundation.

Carter, Rita. 1998. *Mapping the Mind.* Los Angeles: University of California Press.

Gordon, David T. 2002. "Fuel for Reform: The Importance of Trust in Changing Schools." *Harvard Education Letter* (July/August).

Konner, Melvin. 1991. *Childhood: A Multicultural View.* Boston: Little, Brown & Company.

Palmer, Parker J. 1998. *The Courage to Teach.* San Francisco: Jossey-Bass Publishers.

Wood, Chip. 1999. *Time to Teach, Time to Learn: Changing the Pace of School.* Greenfield, MA: Northeast Foundation for Children.

Wood, Chip. 1997. *Yardsticks: Children in the Classroom Ages 4–14.* Greenfield, MA: Northeast Foundation for Children.

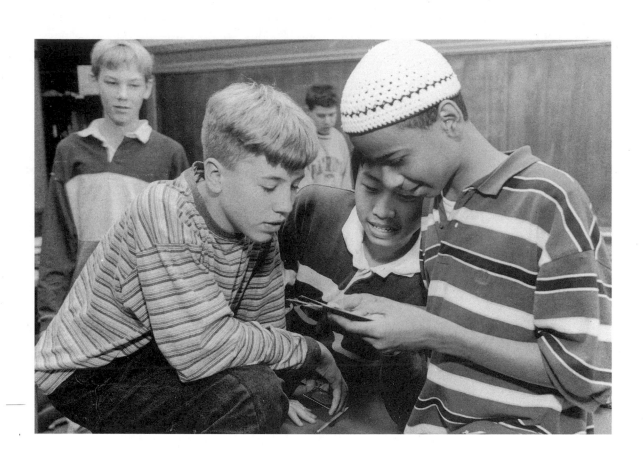

Conclusion

RULES ARE WHAT MAKE
THE GOOD THINGS HAPPEN

BY CHIP WOOD

T oo often we think of rules as necessary evils, restraints which prevent our negative impulses from gaining the upper hand. I believe that rules can lead us in positive directions, serving as guideposts and guardrails as we move toward our goals and ideals.

Ruth Sidney Charney
Teaching Children to Care

Every year educators have the unique opportunity to influence how children view rules. How we set up and use rules in our classrooms and schools—whether we use a collaborative or an autocratic approach, a problem-solving or a blaming approach—will significantly affect whether children grow to see rules as guideposts that help them or restraints that hinder them.

I work with teachers year after year to help them use the discipline approach described in this book. Year after year, I see the impact that this approach has on children's vision of rules and discipline and on their behavior and learning. In classrooms and schools that use this approach, students see rules as positive out-growths of their hopes and dreams. Rules become what make the good things happen rather than just what stop the bad things from happening.

Students in these classrooms and schools recognize that rules help to create a sense of safety and community. They see that rules help create a trustworthy space, a safe climate for taking the risks necessary for learning. As Shelley Harwayne, principal of the Manhattan New School, emphasizes, "It doesn't matter how brilliant our minilessons are or how clever our conferences are if children make fun of each other's handwriting, dialect, or choice of topic … Children will not share significant stories, take risks as spellers, or accept new challenges if the classroom is not secure or supportive." (Harwayne 1999, 104)

When teachers allow children time in the early weeks of school to think about and generate rules for the classroom, children pay more attention to the rules. It sounds almost too simple to be true, but it is true. When children see the context of rules—that rules help us to make our hopes and dreams come true, to accomplish the goals we set for ourselves and our class—they become more invested in living by them. Children have a far greater capacity to internalize and respect rules they helped create than rules that are handed down to them.

Rules Are What Make the Good Things Happen

When children follow the rules they've helped create, more time is available for learning. More books are read, more math problems solved, more spelling words learned, more meaningful relationships created and sustained. However, gaining more time for learning will never occur simply by talking to children about rules or even talking *with* them about rules. To internalize the rules, children must have time to practice the rules, to make mistakes, and to try again.

As you use this approach to discipline, you'll see that practice is as important to social learning as it is to academic learning. Our school environments are ideal "practice fields" for children's social learning. The school is the flight-path destination from the family nest. As a society, we have collectively given clearance for children to practice landing here first, and we should expect plenty of bumps, not all smooth landings right away.

One of our most important tasks as the grownups at school is to protect children from expectations of perfection. We comfort and coach students as they learn, as they make mistakes. Our greatest service is as flight instructors and practice coaches for the business of life. We teach reading and recess. We teach language and lunch. We teach math and manners. We help children build the bridges between self-control and selfhood. And we do this by giving them hundreds of opportunities to practice in a safe and caring environment.

There is no question that the strategies presented in this book take time. It takes time to establish a caring community of learners, to build investment in the rules, to develop children's social skills. But there is also no question that this is time well spent, especially during the first six weeks of school. Teachers who focus on students' social and ethical development along with their cognitive development during these early weeks set students on a positive path for the entire year. It makes sense to establish both ethical and academic expectations.

Will these children need reminders and additional practice throughout the year? Yes. Will they need review and more practice in advanced skills as they move from grade to grade? Talk to any teenage musician, high school athlete, or college student learning a second language and you'll have your answer: Practice, practice, and more practice.

With enough practice, a social skill, too, can become an art, something of grace and beauty, something we would enjoy in our meeting rooms as well as our classrooms, in our supermarket lines as well as our lunch lines, in our movie theaters as well as our school assemblies, in all civil discourse. May we teach our children well.

Conclusion

Work Cited

Harwayne, Shelley. 1999. *Going Public: Priorities & Practice at the Manhattan New School*. Portsmouth, NH: Heinemann.

Appendix A

Problem Solving with Students: Techniques and Recommended Resources

In addition to creating rules together and using the strategies suggested in this book to handle rule breaking, teachers and students need a variety of problem-solving strategies to address the range of conflicts that will inevitably arise throughout the year. While a full presentation of these techniques is beyond the scope of this book, we offer brief summaries of the ones we find most useful. Following each summary is a list of recommended resources for learning more about that technique.

Individual teacher-student conversations

Often a one-on-one conversation with a student is the most effective way to help the student change problematic behavior. The student and teacher discuss problems openly and without judgment and work together to identify possible solutions. This strategy is helpful for all children, but especially for those involved in power struggles and those for whom time-out and other logical consequences are not working. The resources below offer various structures and guidelines for such teacher-student conversations.

Charney, Ruth Sidney. 2002. *Teaching Children to Care: Classroom Management for Ethical and Academic Growth, K–8.* Greenfield, MA: Northeast Foundation for Children. (See Chapter 14, "Teachers as Mirrors: Using Social Conferences.")

Faber, Adele, and Elaine Mazlish. 1995. *How to Talk So Kids Can Learn at Home and in School.* New York: Simon & Schuster.

Gootman, Marilyn E. 1997. *The Caring Teacher's Guide to Discipline: Helping Young Students Learn Self-Control, Responsibility, and Respect.* Thousand Oaks, CA: Corwin Press. (See Chapter 7, "Problem Solving as a Tool for Teachers.")

Strachota, Bob. 1996. *On Their Side: Helping Children Take Charge of Their Learning.* Greenfield, MA: Northeast Foundation for Children.

Student-student conflict resolution protocols

There are many excellent conflict resolution protocols for K–8 students. The goal of teaching children a conflict resolution process is to empower them to solve their own problems. To be effective, the process must be taught carefully and students must have a chance to practice it with the teacher present before using it independently. All the protocols offered in the resources below emphasize the importance of teaching children how to listen actively to one another and work together to resolve conflicts.

Charney, Ruth Sidney. 1991. *Habits of Goodness: Case Studies in the Social Curriculum.* Greenfield, MA: Northeast Foundation for Children. (See Chapter 5, "Letting the Spill Grow: Conflict Resolution in a First Grade" by Linda Mathews.)

Problem Solving with Students

Gootman, Marilyn E. 1997. *The Caring Teacher's Guide to Discipline: Helping Young Students Learn Self-Control, Responsibility, and Respect.* Thousand Oaks, CA: Corwin Press. (See Chapter 8, "Problem Solving as a Tool for Students.")

Kreidler, William J. 1997. *Elementary Perspectives 1: Teaching Concepts of Peace and Conflict.* Cambridge, MA: Educators for Social Responsibility.

Kreidler, William J. 1997. *Conflict Resolution in the Middle School.* Cambridge, MA: Educators for Social Responsibility.

Porro, Barbara. 1996. *Talk It Out: Conflict Resolution in the Elementary Classroom.* Alexandria, VA: Association for Supervision and Curriculum Development.

Problem-solving class meetings

When there is a problem involving the entire class (such as the forming of cliques, inappropriate conduct with a substitute teacher, or carelessness with materials), it can be helpful to have a structure for discussing the problem and working as a group to solve it. There are a number of good protocols for problem-solving class meetings. The ones recommended by the resources below emphasize creating a climate in which students feel safe expressing their feelings and opinions.

Charney, Ruth Sidney. 2002. *Teaching Children to Care: Classroom Management for Ethical and Academic Growth, K–8.* Greenfield, MA: Northeast Foundation for Children. (See Chapter 13, "Problem-Solving Class Meetings.")

Developmental Studies Center. 1996. *Ways We Want Our Class to Be: Class Meetings That Build Commitment to Kindness and Learning.* Oakland, CA: Developmental Studies Center.

Nelsen, Jane, Lynn Lott, and H. Stephen Glenn. 2000. *Positive Discipline in the Classroom: Developing Mutual Respect, Cooperation, and Responsibility in Your Classroom.* Roseville, CA: Prima Publishing.

Sykes, Donna. 2001. *Class Meetings: Building Leadership, Problem-Solving and Decision-Making Skills in the Respectful Classroom.* Markham, ON, Canada: Pembroke Publishers.

Appendix A

Appendix B

Recommended Resources on
Discipline in Classrooms and Schools

Theory

Coles, Robert. 1997. *The Moral Intelligence of Children*. New York: Plume.

Damon, William. 1988. *The Moral Child: Nurturing Children's Natural Moral Growth*. New York: The Free Press.

Dewey, John. 1997. *Democracy and Education*. New York: The Free Press.

Dreikurs, Rudolf, and Pearl Cassel. 1992. *Discipline Without Tears*. New York: Plume Publishing.

Dreikurs, Rudolf, Bernice Grunwald, and Floyd Pepper. 1982. *Maintaining Sanity in the Classroom: Classroom Management Techniques*. Philadelphia: Taylor & Francis, Inc.

Ginott, Haim. 1975. *Teacher and Child*. New York: Avon Books.

Glasser, William. 1998. *The Quality School: Managing Students Without Coercion*. New York: HarperPerennial.

Kohlberg, Lawrence. 1987. *The Philosophy of Moral Development*. New York: Harper & Row.

Noddings, Nel. 1992. *The Challenge to Care in Schools: An Alternative Approach to Education*. New York: Teachers College Press.

Noddings, Nel. 2002. *Educating Moral People: A Caring Alternative to Character Education*. New York: Teachers College Press.

Practice

Charney, Ruth Sidney. 2002. *Teaching Children to Care: Classroom Management for Ethical and Academic Growth, K–8*. Greenfield, MA: Northeast Foundation for Children.

Faber, Adele, and Elaine Mazlish. 1999. *How to Talk so Kids Will Listen and Listen so Kids Will Talk*. New York: Avon Books.

Faber, Adele, and Elaine Mazlish. 1995. *How to Talk so Kids Can Learn at Home and in School*. New York: Simon and Schuster.

Gathercoal, Forrest. 2001. *Judicious Discipline*. San Francisco: Caddo Gap Press.

Gootman, Marilyn E. 1997. *The Caring Teacher's Guide to Discipline: Helping Young Students Learn Self-Control, Responsibility, and Respect*. Thousand Oaks, CA: Corwin Press.

Gossen, Diane Chelsom. 1999. *Restitution: Restructuring School Discipline*. Chapel Hill, NC: New View Publications.

Jones, Fredric H. 1987. *Positive Classroom Discipline*. New York: McGraw Hill, Inc.

Nelsen, Jane. 1996. *Positive Discipline*. New York: Random House.

Nelsen, Jane. 1999. *Positive Time-out: And Over 50 Other Ways to Avoid Power Struggles in Homes and Schools*. Roseville, CA: Prima Publishing.

Nelsen, Jane, Lynn Lott, and H. Stephen Glenn. 2000. *Positive Discipline in the Classroom: Developing Mutual Respect, Cooperation, and Responsibility in Your Classroom*. Roseville, CA: Prima Publishing.

Recommended Resources

Working with More Challenging Behaviors

Greene, Ross W. 2001. *The Explosive Child: A New Approach for Understanding and Parenting Easily Frustrated, Chronically Inflexible Children*. New York: HarperCollins.

Levin, James, and John M. Shanken-Kaye. 1996. *The Self-Control Classroom: Understanding and Managing the Disruptive Behavior of All Students, Including Those with ADHD*. Dubuque, IA: Kendall/Hunt Publishing Company.

MacKenzie, Robert J. 1996. *Setting Limits in the Classroom: How to Move Beyond the Classroom Dance of Discipline*. Roseville, CA: Prima Publishing.

Tobin, L. 1991. *What Do You Do With a Child Like This? Inside the Lives of Troubled Children*. Duluth, MN: Whole Person Associates.

ABOUT THE AUTHORS

Kathryn Brady has been a teacher for twenty-four years, specializing in the education of students with social and emotional difficulties. Currently, Kathryn is the instructional management and behavior specialist for the Fitchburg Public Schools in Fitchburg, Massachusetts.

Mary Beth Forton has taught language arts in elementary and middle schools, specializing in working with students with learning difficulties. She is now director of publications for Northeast Foundation for Children, where she has worked for fourteen years. She is a co-author of *Classroom Spaces That Work*.

Deborah Porter is a primary teacher at Heath Elementary School in Heath, Massachusetts. Her twenty-eight years in education include teaching at Greenfield Center School and co-founding and teaching at the Heath Preschool. She has been a *Responsive Classroom*® workshop leader for the past sixteen years.

Robert A. (Chip) Wood is a co-founder of Northeast Foundation for Children and has over thirty years of experience as a classroom teacher, elementary school principal, and teacher educator. His books include *Yardsticks: Children in the Classroom, Ages 4–14* and *Time to Teach, Time to Learn: Changing the Pace of School*.

ABOUT THE
RESPONSIVE CLASSROOM® APPROACH

This book grew out of the work of Northeast Foundation for Children, Inc. (NEFC) and an approach to teaching known as the *Responsive Classroom* approach. Developed by classroom teachers, this approach consists of highly practical strategies for integrating social and academic learning throughout the school day.

Seven beliefs underlie this approach:

1. The social curriculum is as important as the academic curriculum.

2. How children learn is as important as what they learn: Process and content go hand in hand.

3. The greatest cognitive growth occurs through social interaction.

4. To be successful academically and socially, children need to learn and practice cooperation, assertion, responsibility, empathy, and self-control.

5. Knowing the children we teach—individually, culturally, and developmentally—is as important as knowing the content we teach.

6. Knowing the families of the children we teach and encouraging their participation is as important as knowing the children we teach.

7. How we, the adults at school, work together to accomplish our shared mission is as important as our individual competence: Lasting change begins with the adult community.

**More information and guidance on the
Responsive Classroom approach are available through:**

Publications and Resources

- Books, videos, and audios for elementary educators
- Website with articles and other information:
  www.responsiveclassroom.org
- Free quarterly newsletter for educators

Professional Development Opportunities

- One-day and week-long workshops for teachers
- Classroom consultations and other services at individual schools and
  school districts
- Multi-faceted professional development for administrators and all staff
  at schools wishing to implement the *Responsive Classroom* approach
  school-wide

For details, contact:

RESPONSIVE CLASSROOM
NORTHEAST FOUNDATION FOR CHILDREN, INC.
85 Avenue A, Suite 204   P. O. Box 718
Turners Falls, MA 01376-0718
Phone 800-360-6332 or 413-863-8288
Fax 877-206-3952
www.responsiveclassroom.org

Rules in School
By Kathryn Brady, Mary Beth Forton,
Deborah Porter, and Chip Wood
For K–8 teachers (2003) 272 pages ISBN 978-1-892989-10-9

Establish a calm, safe learning environment and teach children self-discipline with this approach to classroom rules.

- *Guidelines for creating rules with students based on their hopes and dreams for school*
- *Steps in modeling and role playing the rules* ■ *How to reinforce the rules through language*
- *Using logical consequences when rules are broken* ■ *Suggestions for teaching children to live by the rules outside the classroom*

Learning Through Academic Choice
By Paula Denton, EdD
For K–6 teachers (2005) 224 pages ISBN 978-1-892989-14-7

Enhance students' learning with this powerful tool for structuring lessons and activities.

- *Information on building a strong foundation for Academic Choice* ■ *Step-by-step look at Academic Choice in action* ■ *Practical advice for creating an Academic Choice lesson plan*
- *Many ideas for Academic Choice activities*

Parents and Teachers Working Together
By Carol Davis and Alice Yang
For K–6 teachers (2005) 232 pages ISBN 978-1-892989-15-4

Build school–home cooperation and involve parents in ways that support their children's learning.

- *Working with diverse family cultures* ■ *Building positive relationships in the early weeks of school* ■ *Keeping in touch all year long* ■ *Involving parents in classroom life, including parents who can't physically come to school* ■ *Problem-solving with parents*